D1569435

Minorities in Revolt

Minorities in Revolt

POLITICAL VIOLENCE IN IRELAND, ITALY, AND CYPRUS

Dominick J. Coyle

Special research and collaboration: **Francesca Serafini**

RUTHERFORD ● MADISON ● TEANECK
FAIRLEIGH DICKINSON UNIVERSITY PRESS
LONDON AND TORONTO: ASSOCIATED UNIVERSITY PRESSES

Associated University Presses, Inc.
4 Cornwall Drive
East Brunswick, N.J. 08816

Associated University Presses Ltd
27 Chancery Lane
London WC2A 1NF, England

Associated University Presses
Toronto M5E 1A7, Canada

Library of Congress Cataloging in Publication Data

Coyle, Dominick J., 1933]
   Minorities in revolt.

   Bibliography: p.
   Includes index.
   1. Northern Ireland—Politics and government.
2. Italy—Politics and government—1945–1976.
3. Italy—Politics and government—1976–
4. Cyprus—Politics and government. 5. Government,
Resistance to—Case studies. 6. Minorities—Europe—
Political activity—Case studies. 7. Terrorism—Europe—
Case studies. I. Title.
DA990.U46C69   323.1′1   81-65866
ISBN 0-8386-3120-7   AACR2

PRINTED IN THE UNITED STATES OF AMERICA

Contents

Acknowledgments

A work associated with terrorism—however seriously assembled—cannot reasonably contain many public acknowledgments, and no doubt some people who have helped with the preparation of this study will accept my general gratitude in preference to my naming names. There are others who will not endorse without reservation some of my proposals for easing intercommunal tensions in the countries under review, and hence it is probably in their best interests that I should not name them here. I would, however, like to record my appreciation to a number of distinguished constitutional authorities in Ireland (North and South), in Italy, and in both parts of divided Cyprus for their assistance and useful guidance as the work progressed, and for their comments on parts of the final manuscript touching on their immediate areas of competence.

There are those who should be named. Dick Dickinson provided some research funds through Fairleigh Dickinson University, Rutherford, New Jersey, and the university's Dr. Nasrollah S. Fatemi helped by providing encouragement and liaison. Francesca Serafini in Rome not only undertook much of the research touching on Italy but provided a great deal of intellectual argument that made for a sharper focus. Sally Keane in Dublin augmented research regarding Ireland with a cheerful efficiency, and Nicoletta Rosati assisted with some translations. Brana Radovic prepared the maps and Barbara Gibbons put together the final typescript. All of them gave much to the end product, while others suffered—not least my wife, Anna, and our children, who endured the inevitable dislocation involved, but not without some valuable criticisms from the sidelines. My appreciation and thanks to them all, including a number of colleagues on the *Financial Times* who helped in numerous small ways, and some not so small. I should only add the usual cautionary note that I am ultimately accountable for this book, its defects and virtues.

London
February, 1982

Introduction

Most of the worse catastrophes of History have been caused by the obstinate resistance to change when resistance was no longer possible.

Brooks Adams

An Opposition which can never become a Government tends to lose a sense of responsibility, and a party in power which can never (in foreseeable circumstances) be turned out tends to be complacent and insensitive to criticism or acceptance of any need for change or reform.

Cameron Report

The thesis underlying this study can be stated simply. It is that there exists a relationship, perhaps even a correlation, between the exclusion, whether actual or felt, of an identifiable group of people—hereafter somewhat loosely characterized as "minorities"—from the normal governing process and politically motivated violence. The sequence may be causal or indirect or, more likely, it is argued here, a combination of the two. To support the thesis I have taken three national case histories; the choice is subjective, and obviously there are others, some of which may be even more relevant. The wise shoemaker stays with his last, however, and events in Ireland, Italy, and Cyprus have engaged me professionally over more than two decades. From this experience, supplemented by special research for this particular work, I have drawn the parallels and conclusions presented here. The reader, finally, must determine whether the circumstances, the facts, and the analysis combine to support the general thesis. For this reason I have chosen deliberately the somewhat unconventional methodology of three separate case studies, even at the risk of appearing to write three books in one. This methodology is a convenient manner of presenting historical and contemporary facts and developments, interspersed with commentary and analysis, to equip those lacking intimate and detailed knowledge of the countries under review—and

9

in particular of the terrible violence of the past decade and more—
to make reasoned judgment.

I append an early word of caution. This book is not wholly an
empirical study, for even the casual reader will readily appreciate
that some components examined here do not, unfortunately, lend
themselves to such analysis. Mention need only be made of the
Italian Communist party (PCI) and its largely private relations with
the Soviet Union, ignoring for the moment its own ultimate political objectives within Italy itself, to highlight this reservation.
Whatever their claims, few outside observers really can know precisely and for certain, and can study in detail, the true extent of this
relationship; the same, incidentally, goes for the party's own rank-
and-file membership. Yet, for all the rigors of "democratic centralism,"[1] the Communist party in Italy today is more open than,
for example, Communist parties in Eastern Europe, and the experienced observer is not reduced wholly to metaphorical tea leaves
for his analysis and conclusions.

To this caveat I want also to add early on a general observation,
not so much in the sense of anticipating criticism but in order to lay
some stress on the fairly obvious fact that no two political, economic, cultural, and social systems are identical. Hence, when
parallels, or, more importantly, comparisons are made throughout
this work between elements and events in the countries under
review, they are not intended to be absolute. However, it is because parallels exist, often bilaterally and sometimes in all three
cases, that this examination seems justified. It is also a contribution
toward a better and wider understanding of the modern phenomenon of politically motivated violence and outright terrorism. This
development, I will argue and, more significantly, illustrate by
events, has been facilitated in large part by the failure of the established political and bureaucratic processes to understand and to
accommodate, in particular, the reasonable fears, the demands,
and the aspirations of minorities and, in general, to be aware of,
and to respond to, changing values, desires, and expectations, especially those of a better educated and usually more socially aware
younger generation. Finally, in these introductory notes, I would
like to draw from a well-known theory of social movement and
behavior a blanket assertion, which, I believe, is more or less
applicable by way of an overall understanding of the pattern of
violence in Italy, Ireland, and Cyprus, although clearly not the
whole explanation. In this context, incidentally, sight should not
be lost of the fact that subversive and antidemocratic forces almost

invariably move in to exploit—either for their own ideological ends or as surrogates for alien totalitarian powers—intercommunal unrest and community divisions in democratic states.

Nonetheless, as the national case studies presented here illustrate, Bernard's sociological dictum applies:

> Mobs develop with special ease under social conditions in which conflicting interests, ideals and controls are prevalent. The presence in close proximity of two or more races with fairly distinct customs, traditions and standards; of distinct social classes, such as capitalist and labour, rich and poor; of radically distinct religious alignments, each sect or religion holding firmly to its own tenets; of two rival gangs, each intent upon dominating the situation; or of two or more political parties, each with its patronage and graft to protect and candidates to elect, is especially conducive to the appearance of the mob spirit and mob action. Such conditions easily evoke race, class, religious or partisan animosities and hatreds which become chronic prejudices.[2]

The fit of the Bernard formula to Ireland and Cyprus is almost perfect; its application to Italy, although not complete, is nevertheless extensive. Further, in all three cases, political hegemony has long been in the hands of the same elite: the Christian Democrats[3] uninterruptedly in Italy for more than three decades; the Protestant Unionists in Northern Ireland for half a century after the creation of the British substate in 1920[4] and the Greek-Cypriots, effectively, in Cyprus since the island obtained its independence from Britain in 1960.[5] There is a racial and cultural mix in Cyprus between Greek- and Turkish-Cypriots. There is perhaps less of a cultural mix in Northern Ireland today, although, as I shall show later, the Protestant[6] people were mostly planted into the province from Britain (many of Scottish stock) early in the seventeenth century as a deliberate act of colonial policy, thus laying the seeds of the cultural and religious divide in Ireland. The religious divide, too, is clear-cut in Cyprus, given that the majority, which is Greek-Cypriot, are Christians (Greek Orthodox), whereas the Turkish-Cypriot minority are Muslims, as in mainland Turkey. In Italy the country is at least nominally 98 percent Roman Catholic, yet today approximately one in three of the Italian electorate supports the Communist party and, officially and frequently, the Vatican has insisted that one cannot be a good Catholic and also a Communist, a view which, not surprisingly, the PCI leadership challenges. In all countries the political influence of the various religions is still considerable, to state it mildly. Again, Bernard's "conflicting interests, ideals and controls" resulting from major cleavages between differing traditions are only too apparent. After adding what sociologists call the *strain* dimension, the mix can become highly explosive, as events have tragically demonstrated.

Strain in this context is an essential, if not always precisely quantifiable, component that ordinarily is necessary to spark off collective behavior, and, reasonably, the greater the felt strain, the more explosive the outcome. Smelser[7] has argued that one of the most frequent causes of strain is deprivation,[8] relative or absolute, real or imagined. It can stem, as it did in Northern Ireland, from administrative discrimination and the passage and largely partisan implementation of unpopular legislative measures. Equally, a failure of the executive to enact reformist programs in support of which there is broad, if minority, backing, can set the stage for hostile actions, or some related form of collective behavior. In truth, any deep-seated frustration may constitute a strain that engenders hostility, for in essence strain reflects a situation in which significant numbers of people come to believe that something is wrong in their political, economic, or social environment, whether separately or in combination, leading to an impairment of, or an inadequate functioning of, the components of social action.

In Northern Ireland (described widely in the British media as Great Britain's "last colony") in 1968–69 such strain gave birth to a concerted campaign to secure ordinary civil rights for the Roman Catholic minority there. In Italy, at about the same time, it contributed to the start of the student protest movement, which, following many turns and gyrations, produced eventually the main strands of many of today's terrorist factions, including the notorious Red Brigades. In Cyprus in the early 1960s, strain resulted from the Turkish-Cypriots feeling that they were being treated by the Greek-Cypriot majority as second-class citizens, being offered limited minority rights and protections but, essentially, being excluded from the real governing process, and all in a largely patronizing fashion quite different from the copartnership concept seen by the island's minority to be intended by, and reflected in, the original 1959–60 independence settlement and constitution.

Because a consistent common thread in this work is violence, I will make an early interruption here to relate generally its extent, if only as a necessary backdrop for objective study and appreciation of the causes. The extent and continuation (in Italy and Ireland principally today) of violent death is such, tragically, that numbers are often out of date before they are released officially. Additionally, one of the more depressing aspects of violence in both countries in recent years has been not just its sheer extent but the fact that the mounting numbers of its victims have tended to inure the popular mind to it. A public sympathy of sort lingers, sometimes in relation to the status of the latest victim, but nowadays seldom for very long. The Italian case is particularly interesting in this regard, for, increasingly, calls by the leadership of the established trade unions for work stoppages or more formal strikes in protest against violence go largely unheeded and unsupported. Each successive death there, and in Northern Ireland, too, brings a general, albeit rather brief, wringing of hands, but little else besides. In truth, violence has become commonplace, and there is a terrible complacency that brings with it almost an acceptance that the respective political processes under terrorist attack have no longer either the will or the ways to fight back effectively. The media headlines occasionally loom large, and so often do the funerals, but only the numbers seem real, and it is as well to state them starkly.

Early in 1980, three members of the Ulster[9] Defence Regiment, a part-time and almost exclusively Protestant security force, were shot dead while on patrol close to the Northern Ireland border with the Irish Republic. These killings brought the total of deaths in more than a decade of Irish violence past the two thousand mark.[10] (Another seventy were to die violently before that year was out.) The local newspapers saw these particular murders largely as a headline benchmark along the barometer of death, and they marked the event with extensive reportage; ordinarily, the killings might have merited an "inside, down-page" reference, for the media, too, have become inured to violence. In Italy, 1980 opened with an average of ten recorded terrorist acts each day over the first three months. In the same quarter, nineteen people died in political violence, including three judges. During the year as a whole approximately 120 terrorist killings occurred—including, arguably, the most terrible single act of terrorism in so-called peacetime, an explosion in the Bologna railway station in August in which 85 people were killed. The scorecard for such deaths showed 44 in 1979, 37 the previous year, and 31 in 1977.

Statistics are less reliable for Cyprus, where in any event there is a tendency to bemoan, and quickly to bury, the dead rather than count them. An exception, however, is the political leadership of both communities, which has often exaggerated the incidence of violent deaths for propaganda reasons. The Turkish-Cypriot leadership[11] has claimed that "we lost thousands of dead and wounded in 103 villages" during inter-communal violence between 1963 and 1967, whereas a Council of Europe commission, which investigated complaints by the government of Cyprus[12] of alleged violations of human rights by occupying Turkish mainland forces in 1974, suggested that about two thousand Greek-Cypriots were either killed or remained missing as a result of events immediately prior to the invasion and the fighting that resulted from it.[13]

I shall return to this crude category of violence and death, in some chronological detail, later. For the moment, I shall concentrate on the why, to seek to isolate some at least of the general circumstances that brought it about; other contributory elements will emerge in the respective national case studies. What is immediately relevant here is to attempt to highlight together, as it were, some common strands, and also to take note of the separate circumstances that led ultimately to the violent explosions. In a sense it is also important to pose early on the fundamental question of whether the violence could have been avoided, or in any event reduced greatly, had the ruling elites acted differently. In this regard I should state clearly my own belief that the answer is almost certainly yes, an answer that is not just qualified by the hindsight of events. What I am arguing, largely, is that the failure on the part of the ruling establishments to look beyond their narrow, if understandable, commitment to preserving the status quo, to protecting their own political power and hegemony, irrespective of the legitimate aspirations, felt needs, and demands of others, encouraged a climate of violence and contributed substantially to its escalation. As Adams observed, and as quoted at the outset, it became essentially "an obstinate resistance to change when resistance was no longer possible," coupled with a refusal to see, or at the very least a failure to appreciate, that rising demands in support of reasonable reforms were not tantamount to imminent revolution. Frustrated by political conservatism, discrimination, and often administrative indifference or, worse, plain corruption, closed off from any political avenues seen to be capable of influencing orderly change, the activists took to the streets in protest. As ever, their ranks were infiltrated by others of more revolutionary intent who would be satisfied with nothing short of pulling down the entire established order, although they were seldom clear on what to erect in its stead. There was nothing greatly new in the phenomenon; the ruling elites merely demonstrated, yet again, a failure to learn from the experiences of the past, and today we continue to live with the inheritance of that failure.

How did it happen? A common link has been the protracted political and administrative hegemony of one faction in all the three countries under review, a faction intent quite deliberately on maintaining its traditional dominance over all those seen to be its enemies, sometimes simply out of fear as to what might happen if ever roles were reversed. Thus, the Protestant Unionists—in support of the continuing union of Northern Ireland with Britain— traditionally viewed the Catholic nationalists there as essentially a fifth column in their midst, intent finally not on securing civil rights but on planning to destroy the substate in favor of bringing about an All-Ireland Republic. In Italy most Christian Democrats have long feared, as they continue to do today, the Communists' electoral strength, in part because they do not want to let go of their own political hegemony, but also because very many moderate DC voters remain concerned, reasonably, over the long-term aims and objectives of the PCI. Whatever the Communists say to the contrary, and in recent years they have said a great deal designed to assure Italians and others of their commitment to democracy and political pluralism, there persists a huge reluctance by most non-Communists to believe them, or to accept that the party has turned its back on revolution. There is also in Italy a widespread feeling that the PCI would not willingly surrender power if ever it secured it, whatever the electorate might decide subsequently. This, of course, is a feeling in the true sense of the word, for the underlying concern cannot be subjected to any advance test, but only to the real thing, and by then it could be too late. Successive U.S. governments have highlighted this concern, although latterly conceding that the decision must rest finally with the Italian electorate.[14] Former Secretary of State Henry A. Kissinger has both spoken and written on what he has determined are parallels between expressed commitments by contemporary Italian Communist party leaders to democratic pluralism and remarks much earlier by other Communists in a similar vein, which have been disproved by events. In particular, he has noted pluralist commitments by Communists in Hungary (1944), Poland and Bulgaria (1946), and Czechoslovakia (1947). Concluding from these experiences, Kissinger observed:

Certainly Communist parties are willing to come to power [in

Western Europe today] by democratic means. But could they permit the democratic process to reverse what they see as the inevitable path of "historical progress?" Would they maintain the institutions—press, parties, unions, enterprises—that would represent the principal threat to their power? Would they safeguard the freedoms that could turn into instruments of their future defeat? No Communist party that governed alone has ever done so, and the vast majority of those democratic parties which entered coalitions with European Communists are now in the indexes of history books rather than ministries or parliaments.[15]

Again, there are genuinely held fears in Cyprus, and I draw quite deliberately the distinction between fears that are genuinely based and those genuinely held. From the Independence agreement with Britain until the Turkish invasion in 1974, many Turkish Cypriots, especially those remaining in mixed villages, believed that they risked being murdered in their beds. The Greek-Cypriot majority lived largely with memories of more than three centuries (1571–1878) of "colonial" rule by Turkey, purported to believe that it could happen again, with Turkey moving to virtually annex the small island, or at very least to partition it. In that sense, as in Northern Ireland, the majority viewed the minority as a fifth column to advance Turkey's interests, while that minority in its turn, suspected, and with good cause, that the Independence settlement with Britain had not ended Greek-Cypriot aspirations for *Enosis*,[16] especially on the part of Greek Orthodox church leaders.

In capsule, therefore, there have been actual or alleged fifth columnists[17] at work in all three countries, and they remain seen by many as continuing with their efforts today: Ulster's Catholics to advance a united Ireland, Italy's Communists as surrogates for the Soviet Union,[18] and, in Cyprus, the Greek- and Turkish-Cypriots motivated primarily by the seen best interests of Greece and Turkey, respectively. To any who would regard the parallel as being unnecessarily pejorative, I would emphasize not only that this parallel does exist but, more importantly, that it is necessary to understand the fear arising from the belief. For this fear in turn, and perhaps not always consciously, is what has substantially shaped relations between the opposed communities and factions in the countries with which this study deals. Additionally, this fear is not limited only to those who have held the reins of real power. It exists, too, among the partisan masses, where it has been crudely exploited for electoral reasons by their political leaders. The ruling

Unionist party in Northern Ireland has for more than fifty years been a monolith of Protestantism, a party not of class but of religion, for in Ulster religion largely dictated then, and does still today, one's voting allegiances.[19] When, belatedly, Unionist governments moved to respond to some of the reasonable demands of the Catholic minority, they were either eroded from within or brought down by their own electorate. The story has been rather similar in Italy, where the DC is more a mass anti-Communist party than a party of class. It is a party torn constantly by internal friction, by the power aspirations of its own *currenti*, and what has kept it together has been little more than its opposition to the Communists. I agree substantially with the notion that for the DC to agree in present circumstances to share directly in government with the Communists would be to risk losing the delicate adhesive that has kept it together, however disparate its many groupings. Such a coalition might not be a government of equals, but rather an administration dominated quickly by the Communists, with their greater internal cohesion, more effective organizational structure, and a proven ability to deliver their mass support behind even abrupt changes in policy.[20] As I have argued, the anti-Communist stance of the DC, supported strongly by successive U.S. administrations in Washington and also by the Vatican, has enabled the party to retain, with remarkably little variation,[21] its electoral backing over more than three decades and to keep the Communists as a permanent "political minority." The Italian ruling party enjoys support mainly for what it is seen to stand against, rather than for what it actually achieves for its supporters. As such, it has an essentially negative following, which, in one sense, explains why the DC has demonstrated little real need to respond to the expectations of its mass supporters, particularly those lower down on the socioeconomic scale. This also explains why its supporters have a felt need to vote DC at election time and then largely to ignore the whole process of government between elections, seeing in the same governing process something that is indifferent to their needs or else impervious to them.

To turn again to the Ulster experience, it is a not widely known fact outside of Ireland itself that, despite fifty years of exclusive Protestant rule, many working-class Protestants live in conditions of poverty that are equal only to those endured by many Ulster Catholics, and yet they still insist on supporting electorally the Protestant monolith (cracked badly into many factions as the 1970s closed), so deeply planted are the seeds of their fears.

In Cyprus, intercommunal fears and mistrust were perceived to be such that the very concept of community cross-voting was never seriously considered by those who framed the original independence[22] settlement. It provided, in effect, for the president and vice-president to come, respectively, from the majority and minority communities, each of whom elected separately a specified number of its own political representatives to a central legislature.

In all three cases under examination, the underlying motivations of the mass electorate have seldom been conventional in the usual pattern of developed democracies. They did not reflect class or nonextremist ideological differences. The concept of moderate center-right and center-left has not generally applied, nor, strictly speaking, have there been divisions, devoid of ideological extremes, between free enterprise and socialist philosophies, between outright capitalism and progressive socialism. Instead, the main divide has been either racial or religious, and usually both in combination, or, as in Italy, between seen political extremes, Christian Democracy and Communism. At practically all points along the political spectrum voters knew, and they continue to know today, to what it was they were opposed, not what they favored positively. This pattern of electoral polarization has, inevitably, done nothing to erode existing community divides, but much to reinforce them. A result is the lack of a truly secular ideology in all three countries.

Community divisions and electoral polarization coupled with an ambiguity by the ruling authorities toward violence—and sometimes even their apparent condoning of it, if not directly or explicitly—can combine in a dangerous recipe for disturbances and, in more extreme manifestations, for generating counterviolence. Again, we must look to the respective case studies for the specifics, for the essential and detailed historical and contemporary narrative, but in general what emerges are some more parallels. The independence of twenty-six counties of Ireland from British rule[23] was won finally by the use of violence; the creation of the substate that is Northern Ireland came from the threat by Ulster Protestant leaders to use violence[24] in order to prevent the granting of home rule by Britain to the whole of Ireland. In the other troubled island under study, Cyprus, the violence of the "freedom-fighters" or the "terrorists" of EOKA[25], supported directly by Greek-Cypriot religious leaders, forced Britain to move finally in 1959 toward granting a qualified form of independence, despite repeated official assertions that Cyprus was one of a number of unique, strategically vital locations under British rule that could never hope to achieve full freedom. Again, violence has been an integral part of much of Italy's long history; it was used by Cavour and Garibaldi to bring about, at least notionally, national unification in the second half of the nineteenth century. Later, mob violence helped to install the Fascist dictator Mussolini, and, in considerable measure, it was the violence of the Italian Resistance—prominent in the leadership of which were the Communists—which brought him down in 1943.

This widespread use of violence has left a legacy, and we have the residue today, principally for two reasons. Firstly, its effectiveness in bringing about revolutionary change has been demonstrated positively, and, secondly in the cases under examination, the original objective of its advocates have not been fully achieved: The Irish-Nationalist ideal of an All-Ireland republic has been frustrated by the imposition of partition. The island of Cyprus was de facto partitioned following the Turkish invasion, thus infuriating the Greek-Cypriot majority there and apparently closing off the road to Enosis. The original Marxist concept of a Communist revolution in Italy has failed to materialize. Substantially in all three cases, although again not without some lingering ambiguity, the remaining old revolutionaries, and most of their successors, have chosen to forsake violence in favor of democratic change, but remnants persist, and other activists have emerged, who are committed to the use of violence for political ends, claiming in justification that nothing less will bring about their revolutionary objectives or, for that matter, even those relatively modest reforms sought by a much wider, albeit still a minority, constituency.

To the extent that ruling authorities have appeared unresponsive to reformist demands, whether out of inflexibility, ignorance, or indifference, this larger constituency has often perceived itself, although not always without intellectual torment, as being more on the side of the revolutionaries than of ruling governments, even when opposed to their use of violence, particularly in its more extreme manifestations of terrorism. This relative ambiguity toward violence on the part of many seeking reforms has allowed governments to represent legitimate protest as revolutionary intent and, as a result, to assume exceptional administrative or legislative powers, or both together, which themselves are generally discriminatory in their application. Such powers can have a wide range, including derogations from accepted civil rights conventions, wider police powers, detention, and internment without due legal process. The discriminatory application of these powers, for

example the extensive use of internment without trial almost exclusively against the Catholic population of Ulster,[26] inevitably had
the effect of driving the mainly moderate Catholic minority there
demanding civil rights into the hands of a relatively few activists
intent on wholesale revolution, on bringing down the entire constitutional order. Equally inevitable perhaps, opposing forces
quickly surfaced to answer in the same violent language, or in
preemptive moves to sustain the established order, or simply to
prevent legislative reforms that were represented partisanly as
dangerous concessions to those advancing revolution.

There are some further parallels from the perspective of this
study. The gunmen of the Provisional Irish Republican Army
(IRA)[27] retain today as their declared objective not only driving
Britain's armed forces and the overall British presence from Northern Ireland but also bringing down the existing constitutional order
in the adjoining Irish Republic. Their intentions thereafter are less
precise[28], but they involve the establishment of a thirty-two-
county All-Ireland republic of unclearly defined ideological hue,
but seemingly with a strong streak of nationalism and socialism.
Their underlying brand of republicanism is that reflected by the
leaders of an abortive and badly planned uprising against British
rule in the whole of Ireland in 1916.[29] To the extent that the
Provisional IRA had during most of the violent decade of the 1970s
professed to be "defending" the Catholic population of Ulster
against the British military presence and discriminatory Unionist
administration, it commanded ambiguous support and a curious
loyalty from many Catholics in the substate, although most of them
abhorred the terrible violence. However, because the IRA is also
committed to bringing down the Dublin government, and the terrorist movement is illegal in the Irish Republic where its members
have, periodically, also been interned without trial, successive administrations there have stood opposed to their terrorist actions,
but again not always unambiguously. The popular feeling persists
in the Irish Republic that somehow the IRA gunmen are fighting
alongside Ulster Catholics against British oppression and Protestant Unionist domination, an Ulster minority that, traditionally,
has been assumed by successive Dublin governments to be Irish
nationalists desiring, ultimately, the creation of an All-Ireland republic, although one realized through negotiations with Britain
and with Northern Ireland Protestant leaders, and not born out of
the gun.

The element of doublethink has been obvious; many Dublin

politicians, and a lot of their constituents, have endeavored to rationalize their ambiguity toward violence and its perpetrators with such semantical niceties as being "in favour of the aims of the IRA, but disagreeing totally with their terrorist methods." This distinction remains, and it is not always seen or appreciated by the Protestant people of Ulster. They already fear deep down that someday a British government in London may grow tired of the whole Northern Ireland imbroglio, fears which are not helped by Britain's acceptance, sometimes officially but largely from developing convention, that the Irish Republic does have a legitimate interest in, and concern over, the Ulster crisis. Britain has already[30] accepted that the Irish Republic wishes to bring about All-Ireland unity by consent, and it has said that it would not stand in the way of such a development, provided that unity was acceptable to *a* (not the) majority of the Ulster people. Indeed, the fear of an eventual British withdrawal from Northern Ireland has prompted some Ulster Protestant leaders to advocate the total reintegration of the province into Britain, whereas others have argued in favor of a wholly independent Ulster, if necessary taken unilaterally as the white leadership under Ian Smith did in the 1960s in Rhodesia (now Zimbabwe).

And what of Italy? There, too, a pattern of ambiguity toward violence has been evidenced on the part of the establishment, or that of its immediate agencies, although it may be well to distinguish between what could—however erroneously—be termed the essential "nobility" of violence in Ireland and Cyprus to advance broad nationalist objectives, however misguided its perpetrators, and much of that in Italy, which has a different motivation and clearly a different ultimate intent. Specifically, extreme elements of the neo-fascist Movimento Sociale Italiano (MSI)[31] have been involved frequently in acts of so-called black terrorism, often with the connivance, and sometimes the actual participation, of elements of the Italian secret services, and, it has been alleged, with the knowledge of their political masters in high places. One such notorious incident is now well documented. On December 12, 1969, a massive bomb explosion occurred at the offices in Milan of the Banca Nazionale dell'Agricoltura in Piazza Fontana, killing immediately sixteen people and adding greatly to the so-called strategy of tension of the period. The Italian security forces initially placed the responsibility on left-wing extremists—which was precisely what the perpetrators had intended—and numerous arrests followed. Almost ten years later, on February 23, 1979, after the longest criminal trial in Italian history, a court sitting at Catanzaro gave judgment on the Piazza Fontana affair. It had no doubt that elements in the security forces, acting in collusion with right-wing extremists, had been responsible for the Milan bombing. Their aim was to induce a climate in which a rightist government could introduce tough measures against the political and the extraparliamentary left, while at the same time associating further in the public mind the notion that the Communist party had not lost its revolutionary zeal, that whatever about the PCI's leaders, not all party activists eschewed the use of violence for political ends. A distinguished panel of witnesses at Catanzaro, including the then prime minister, Giulio Andreotti, said that they could throw no new light on the Piazza Fontana affair; others professed to an inability to remember in any significant detail what had happened so long ago. In general, the public was inclined to believe the worst of their politicians, a not uncommon response in Italy.

The Catanzaro verdict pointed clearly in the direction of black terrorism, but there is little firm evidence that this and similar incidents have done much to reduce the credibility gap that exists between the Communist party and a large section of the Italian electorate on the PCI's attitude toward political violence.[32] In a sense, this is hardly surprising for a party with revolutionary origins trying to represent itself today as a party of constitutional radicals, a party advancing radical socioeconomic policies to be achieved through constitutional means and, at least initially, in alliance with other political forces that are perceived to have strong democratic credentials. As the PCI was seen in the late 1960s and throughout the 1970s to be moving closer toward the center of constitutional power, extremist forces have emerged as a new minority on the party's left.[33] This has presented the PCI with a real dilemma, namely, how to broaden its electoral base toward the political center without losing support on the left. A throwaway line in 1974 by Giancarlo Pajetta, one of the party's top strategists, to the effect that "Left of the PCI is the PCI" has come back to haunt the Communist party, given that myriads of left-wing factions (some incorporating the name Communist) have admitted to their involvement in large-scale political terrorism and have charged the PCI with having sold out on its revolutionary birthright. Inevitably, the acknowledged association of these leftist factions with political terrorism has spread some contamination to the PCI itself.

Many of these same factions have capitalized on the widespread disaffection in Italian society with the established political, economic, and social order, and they have provided a vehicle for this dissent. Intermittently now for well over a decade, that dissent has been given voice in protest actions and mass demonstrations and, at the more extreme end, in outright violence. Again, as in Ireland, by no means all of those who have given up hope of securing relatively modest administrative reforms from the existing political order have a real commitment to violence, but they do frequently demonstrate an ambiguity toward its use by more extreme elements preaching revolution rather than reform. Further, at least some of these dissidents perceive that the state of their deprivation, whether actual or imagined, is such that they have nothing to lose. In short, as is the case with many Ulster Catholics, they simply do not trust the state.

In Cyprus, the dominant Greek-Cypriot leadership following independence showed little real concern for, and appreciation of, the legitimate demands (mainly economic) and aspirations (overwhelmingly political, social, and cultural) of the Turkish-Cypriot minority, while also demonstrating an ambiguous attitude to violence, both against the Turks and in support of Enosis. The Independence settlement for the island, creating an "independent and sovereign"[34] republic, was for all practical purposes imposed on the people without consultations, and the detailed provisions of a complex constitution did nothing to integrate the two peoples but, on the contrary, was designed to try and ensure in an overrigid framework their respective rights and freedoms. Archbishop Makarios, the Greek-Cypriot leader and first president of Cyprus (1960–77), claimed[35] subsequently and quite openly to have signed the settlement package in London under duress, and he made it clear that Enosis remained the ultimate aspiration of Greek-Cypriots. This action did little, of course, to reassure the Turkish-Cypriot minority. Not surprisingly they used the letter of the constitutional law more to secure their own rights and defined privileges than to participate in a genuine intercommunal partnership in the new Republic of Cyprus.

The many conflicts between the two Cypriot communities are documented later, but two aspects are worth noting here. One was the failure to agree on the composition of a new national army. As a result, paramilitary forces on both sides emerged backing their respective community leaders, Makarios and Dr. Fazil Kütchük, and before long the two men were in large measure prisoners of their own illegal armies. In addition, the small Greek and Turkish

military contingents[36] on the island were augmented surreptiti-
ously by the governments in Athens and Ankara. On the majority
side remnants of EOKA emerged with the declared aim of advancing the cause of Enosis; in response there resurfaced on the minority side the pre-Independence resistance group, TMT.[37] As a
further affront to the minority, the man with direct ministerial
responsibility for internal security island-wide was a top EOKA
leader, Polycarpos Georgadjis, and other old EOKA hands were
distributed liberally in police ranks and in the civil service.

Frustrated by the constitution's blocking mechanisms to unfettered Greek-Cypriot hegemony, and incensed by the minority's
insistence of sticking rigidly to the constitution's provisions, even
when it meant that ordinary government was largely unworkable,
Makarios proposed unilaterally a number of constitutional amendments, a move viewed, not unreasonably, by the Turkish-Cypriots
as a deliberate assault on their rights and protections. To concede
such amendments would, the Turkish-Cypriots argued, leave them
at the mercy of the Greek-Cypriot majority, which, through the
archbishop, was seeking unrestricted majority rule. The Turkish-
Cypriots and the government in Ankara gave Makarios a firm no,
and five days later, on December 21, 1963, violence erupted in
Nicosia. The intercommunal tensions then and in the first half of
the following year set off forces, including a virtual economic block-
age against the minority maintained by a central government,
which by then was exclusively in Greek-Cypriot hands, and this
action led to the near-partitioning of the island.[38] The Turkish
military invasion of the island when it came, following a number of
earlier threats from Ankara, merely resulted in making this partition complete, although enlarging greatly the Turkish-Cypriot enclave.

In summary, then, and by way of concluding this introductory
exposition to the three national studies, I have indicated that
among the significant elements of society in Ireland, Italy, and
Cyprus, aspirations, deprivations, and demands created strain
components, which developed eventually into what sociologists
refer to as "value-oriented movements."[39] Such movements can
best be diffused when the agencies of social control—preeminently
the responsible government and the political parties, but also the
security forces, the courts, community leaders (including religious), and the media—behave intelligently, and with flexibility.
Ideally, these agencies would function so as to prevent the emergence of hostile collective behavior by moving in good time to

minimize, if not wholly to eliminate, the underlying causes. When they fail in this ideal, and democratic authority tends to as a normal rule, it is important that there is an effective and impartial response in meeting any hostile challenge. Specifically, there need to be avenues available to accommodate the expression of grievances, including, importantly, the possibility of in time changing the existing governing majority. There should also be channels, whether established or specially created, to permit peaceful agitation for changes in society. The reaction to any violence must be firm, impartial, and unambiguous if it is to be effective. Smelser[40] argues that "when authorities are hesitant, biased or even actively supportive of one side in a conflict, they give a green light to those bent on hostile expression. When authorities issue firm, unyielding and unbiased decisions in short order, the hostile outburst is dampened."

The evidence shows, and much of it can be seen or reasonably deduced from the case histories following, that the agencies of social control in all three of the countries under review here failed on most, if indeed not all, of these counts. For a number of reasons, some similar, others different, they reacted to protest, legitimate aspirations, and justifiable concerns firstly with indifference and then inflexibly, in part because they tended to misread social protest as a front for threatened revolution. The response, too, when it came in any positive manner, was often ungenerous, politically partisan, permeated with vacillation, and sometimes imbued with condescension. It suffered overwhelmingly because the ruling elites, whether the Italian Christian Democrats, the Ulster Unionists, or the Greek-Cypriots, were not seen by those in protest as being either unbiased or potentially responsive, and because their supporting majorities were inclined to view any concessions to "dissidents" as representing, ultimately, a loss to themselves— economically as well as politically—and of the established hegemony of their class.

NOTES

1. In theory, at least, this allows for free debate in reaching decisions, but no toleration of dissent once decisions have been made.

2. N. J. Smelser, *Theory of Collective Behaviour* (London: Routledge and Kegan Paul, 1962), p. 48.

3. All abbreviated reference will appear as DC, reflecting the party's Italian name, Democrazia Cristiana.

4. The British government assumed "full and direct responsibility" for the administration of the province on March 24, 1972, at the height of intercommunal violence, thus ending the devolution of extensive authority to the Northern Ireland Parliament at Stormont, Belfast, begun in 1920.

5. The 1974 invasion of the island by Turkish mainland forces resulted in the effective partition of Cyprus and the physical separation of the two communities, but this action merely completed a trend that had started ten years earlier.

6. The word *Protestant* is used here collectively, as it is widely in Ireland, to embrace a number of differing Protestant denominations, and no slight or offense is intended.

7. Smelser, *Theory of Collective Behaviour*, chap. 5.

8. Deprivation can, of course, take many forms, political, economic, social, cultural or environmental, and it need not result from discrimination. In fact, however, it usually does.

9. The terms *Ulster* and *Northern Ireland* are used interchangeably here, as they are widely in Ireland itself, although the traditional province of Ulster contains nine counties, only six of which go to form Northern Ireland, the other three (Cavan, Donegal, and Monaghan) being part of the Republic of Ireland.

10. Relating terrorist killings and associating deaths to population and equating the result relative to the United States is a crude and unsatisfactory process, but it does demonstrate starkly the extent of the killings. In the Irish case, it is as though one quarter of a million Americans had died from violence in less than twelve years.

11. See Rauf R. Denkthas, "A Short Discourse on Cyprus," published by the Turkish-Cypriot Public Information Office, Nicosia.

12. The government of the Republic of Cyprus, now exclusively under the control of the Greek-Cypriots, remains recognized internationally, but the minority has set up its own "Turkish Federated State of Cyprus."

13. An unknown number died in a coup mounted (unsuccessfully) against the government of Archbishop Makarios in 1974 by the then ruling military junta in Greece. Five days later Turkish forces landed on the island on July 20. Greek-Cypriots have tended to play down the numbers killed in the coup and to attribute wrongly almost all the deaths to the Turkish invasion.

14. The official text of a U.S. State Department statement, issued in Washington on January 12, 1978, noted in part: "As the President and other members of the Administration have publicly stated on a number of occasions, our Western European allies are sovereign countries and rightly and properly the decision on how they are governed rests with their citizens alone. At the same time, we believe we have an obligation to our friends and allies to express our views clearly. . . .

"Our position is clear: We do not favour [Communist participation in Western governments] and would like to see Communist influence in any Western European country reduced. . . . The United States and Italy share profound democratic values and interests. As the President said in Paris last week: 'It is precisely when democracy is up against difficult challenges that its leaders must show firmness in resisting the temptation of finding solutions in non-democratic forces.' "

Ironically, it was the new government in Paris of President François Mitterrand which contained Communist ministers after the 1981 National Assembly elections.

15. In an address to a Washington conference on Italy and Eurocommunism, June 7–9, 1977, and printed with other contributions in *Eurocommunism: The Italian Case*, eds. Austin Ranney and Giovanni Sartori (Washington, D.C.: The American Enterprise Institute for Public Policy Research, 1978).

16. The union of Cyprus with Greece, the political campaign to secure which is detailed later in the section on Cyprus.

17. Defined in the *Oxford English Dictionary* as "(loosely) traitors, spies" in times of war, a definition from which many Ulster Protestants, Italian DC leaders, and the Greek-Cypriot leadership would not, at heart, dissent.

18. Despite many PCI moves to distance the party from Moscow on a number of individual cases, including the 1968 Soviet invasion of Czechoslovakia and the Russian move into Afghanistan at the end of 1979, Italy's anti-Communists view the party's moves as being either tactical or strategic, whichever can best advance its ultimate aims.

19. In April 1970, a nondenominational group formed the Alliance Party in Ulster, claiming in a launching statement to have "succeeded in creating a province-wide political organisation of the moderate people which is firm on the constitutional issue," in other words, in support of the union with Britain. It was a gallant attempt to cross the religious divide, but Alliance by 1973 had managed to secure less than 10 percent of the popular vote and only eight of the seventy-eight seats in the since-defunct Northern Ireland Assembly.

20. In 1956, despite some opposition and a heavy cost in domestic political terms, the then PCI leader Palmiro Togliatti was able to insist on his party's public backing of the Soviet intervention in Hungary. Equally, the party was able to switch tactics, and its stance, and also to overcome some internal opposition, by criticizing the Russian moves into Czechoslovakia and Afghanistan and martial law in Poland.

21. Since 1953, the DC popular vote in successive general elections averaged 39.4 percent, varying plus or minus respectively by a maximum of 3 percent (1958) and a minimum of 1.1 percent (1963). In the same period, the PCI vote increased from 22.6 percent to a high of 34.4 percent in 1976, mainly at the expense of the socialist groupings. The PCI's first real electoral decline came in 1979 when the percentage vote dropped back to 30.4 percent.

22. The constitutional settlement was put together by the British, Greek, and Turkish governments, and without any meaningful consultations with representatives of the people of Cyprus. As such, both island communities, but particularly the island's Greek-Cypriot majority, are essentially right in their insistence that the independence agreement was imposed on them.

23. The 1920-21 settlement followed an intensive guerilla campaign waged by the outlawed Irish Republican Army (IRA), and, in turn, sparked off a bloody Irish civil war essentially between those prepared to accept a partition settlement and those wanting to fight on against Britain for an All-Ireland Republic.

24. Supporting Ulster's Protestants then was the British Conservative party, and Lord Randolph Churchill, who in an anti-home-rule and arguably treasonable speech in Belfast, declared: "Ulster will fight; Ulster will be right."

25. EOKA is an acronym for Ethniki Organosis Kyprion Agoniston, or National Organisation of Cypriot Fighters.

26. Internment without trial was introduced by the prime minister, Brian Faulkner, who also held the cabinet portfolio covering internal security, in August 1971. He said then in a statement: "I have taken this serious step solely for the protection of life and the security of property. . . . We are, quite simply, at war with the terrorists, and in a state of war many sacrifices have to be made, and made in a cooperative and understanding spirit."

27. A latter-day reflection of the original IRA, which itself evolved from the Irish National Volunteers early in the century as the military wing of the political campaign for Ireland's independence from British rule.

28. See below (p. 63) the reflections of a leading republican militant of the 1950s as to the differing attitudes and objectives within republican ranks.

29. The Easter Monday Proclamation of "The Provisional Government of the Irish Republic to the People of Ireland".

30. See British and Irish declarations at the tripartite Sunningdale Conference, 1973 (Appendixes).

31. It is illegal in Italy to represent a political party as being the legitimate successor of Mussolini's Fascists. The MSI has withstood such charges, but the distinction is in many respects more legal than real. In electoral terms the MSI commands the support of about two million Italians, based on the 1979 general election when the party captured 5.3 percent of the national vote.

32. Perceived notions of the Italian electorate were demonstrated in a study of mass-level response to party strategy reported in *Communism in Italy and France*, ed. Donald L. M. Blackmer and Sidney Tarrow (Princeton, N.J.: Princeton University Press, 1975, table 14, p. 485. In answer to a question designed to elicit respondents' opinion of whether political groups were involved in political violence, 86 percent of Italians linked the neo-fascists with violence, and almost three-fifths (58.3 percent) said the Communists.

33. Including at various times, or currently, the Manifesto dissident Communists, the Communist party of Italy (Marxist-Leninist), Democrazia Proletaria, and Avanguardia Operaio, among a host of others.

34. Article I of the Constitution states that "the State of Cyprus is an independent and sovereign Republic. . . ." In fact, the settlement package worked out between the British, Greek, and Turkish governments—all three members of NATO—impinged on both concepts. *Enosis* and partition were excluded specifically, thus undermining the conventional concept of majority rule; Britain retained absolute control over two military base areas, itself a direct conflict with the concept of full sovereignty.

35. In many statements and interviews, including a number with the author.

36. The Treaty of Alliance between Cyprus, Greece, and Turkey, imposed on the island as part of the settlement package, provided for the establishment of a Tripartite Headquarters to include 950 Greek and 650 Turkish military personnel. Ironically, in view of the subsequent invasion by Turkey, the Tripartite Headquarters was to be a manifestation of the commitment of the contracting parties "to resist any attack or aggression, direct or indirect, directed against the independence or the territorial integrity of the Republic of Cyprus."

37. Turk Mudafaa Teskilati, or Turkish Defense Organization.

38. The United Nations Security Council authorized the dispatch of a UN peacekeeping force (UNIFICYP) to Cyprus in 1964, and it remains there at this writing. In numerous reports by the secretary-general to the Security Council, particularly his quarterly commentaries covering the first two year's of the force's presence on the island, there is independent documentation of wide-ranging restrictions imposed against the minority. In a comment on the Makarios proposals and the subsequent fighting, Mr. Galo Plaza, appointed by the secretary-general as UN mediator on Cyprus, reported in part on March 26, 1965: "Whatever possibility may have existed at that time—and by all accounts it was slight—of calm and rational discussion of these proposals between the two communities disappeared indefinitely with the outbreak of violent disturbances between them."

39. Smelser, *Theory of Collective Behaviour*, p. 313.

40. Ibid., p. 265.

Minorities in Revolt

Part I
Irish Nationalists

1 Early Irish History

I appeal to all Irishmen to pause, to stretch out the hand of forbearance and conciliation, to forgive and forget, and to join in making for the land they love, a new era of peace, contentment and goodwill. . . . May this historic gathering be the prelude to the day in which the Irish people, North and South, under one Parliament or two . . . shall work together in common love for Ireland.

King George V

The year was 1921; the occasion, the formal opening of the new Parliament of Northern Ireland at Stormont in Belfast by the British monarch. His conciliatory speech was intended to open up a new era in Anglo-Irish relations, and, within Ireland itself, to bring to an end almost one thousand years of intermittent and, at times, terrible violence and human suffering. It did not bring peace; instead, it marked the formal division of Ireland, the partitioning of a small island country. The enforced political settlement institutionalized not one but two minorities. The Catholic population of roughly half a million in six northeastern counties of the island became a minority under an undisguised "Protestant Parliament and a Protestant State,"[1] although in the country as a whole, Ulster's one million Protestants knew themselves to be less than one in four of Ireland's total population, which is overwhelmingly Roman Catholic—a realization prompting a siege mentality that has persisted until today. Whatever King George's aspirations for eventual Irish unity, or at least for harmonious relations between the two parts of Ireland, the intentions of Ulster Protestants were already clear. They had secured their own Parliament, their own power, albeit subject to the ultimate sanction of the British Parliament at Westminster, and they intended to keep both— Parliament and Protestant (Unionist) hegemony—by whatever means circumstances dictated, whether fair or foul. There was more than a mere hint that foul measures might even run to violence against the British Crown in the last resort if London should

33

ever move to abandon them into an independent All-Ireland republic.

For more than half a century since then, unfettered Protestant ascendancy held sway, exercised through the Ulster Unionist party. Coinciding almost exactly with the fiftieth anniversary of devolved self-government in Ulster, a British home secretary, Reginald Maudling, got close to the underlying cause of the problem that had produced sporadic violence in the province and then the final explosion that has pushed the intercommunal horror and bloodshed of Ulster into the world's headlines for more than a decade now. He said in 1971: "The normal process of the elective democracy worked well in Britain so long as the party in opposition had a reasonable chance to become the government . . . but one must recognize that there are different circumstances in a country where the majority does not change."[2] He added, with some understatement, given that successive British governments had tolerated, without much interference, the discriminatory policies of Stormont regimes against the Catholic minority for half a century, that "it is reasonable and desirable to see how it is possible to broaden the basis of government in Northern Ireland, and certainly to avoid a situation where a man of talent who can serve his country is debarred from doing so solely by religious beliefs."

A militant Ulster Unionist, William Craig, a former cabinet minister with, ironically, responsibility for the maintenance of law and order in the province, responded to this overdue expression of official British government concern by encouraging openly the formation of a Protestant paramilitary force, telling its first members: "We are determined to preserve our British traditions and way of life. God help those who get in our way, for we mean business."[3] In this context, "British traditions" amounted to a euphemism for continuing Protestant hegemony in Ulster, the maintenance of the union with Britain, and no concessions to those aspiring, however generally, to Irish unity.

What, however, quickly got in the way of Ulster's Protestants was not just the substate's Catholic population or their so-called protectors in the illegal Irish Republican Army (IRA), but the Stormont regime's resistance to reasonable civil rights demands. Britain intervened. The British prime minister of the day, Edward Heath, announced[4] that all legislative and executive powers exercised by Stormont were being withdrawn, transferred to the United Kingdom government, which would, henceforth, pending new political arrangements, be directly responsible for the govern-

ing of Northern Ireland. The phraseology was formal and constitutionally proper; the implication was, in many ways, more meaningful, for it represented a final acceptance by Britain that the
constitutional settlement of fifty years earlier in Ireland had failed.
London would have to devise a new formula, to quote Mr. Heath,
which would "ensure for the minority as well as the majority community, an active, permanent and guaranteed role in the life and
public affairs of the province."

The peace for which King George had hoped for had never taken
root, for the stony ground of Ulster sectarianism had proved itself
to be too hostile a soil to nurture intercommunal rapprochement.
Few of the Irish themselves wish to believe it, and those who do
are reluctant to acknowledge it openly, but the fact is that periodically, since the 1920 settlement, and more or less permanently
after 1969, Ulster has been a battleground for something akin to a
holy war, for, in this confessional substate, politics is largely religion under another guise. To Protestant Unionists, the Catholic
minority is determined to bring down the substate, ultimately to
coerce a million Protestants into an All-Ireland Catholic state. A
basic fear of most Protestants, and it is genuinely held, goes
further; it is that, in such circumstances, the island-wide national
majority might take its revenge, might repay Protestants in discriminatory kind, or even worse, for their years of domination over
Catholics, for keeping them as second-class citizens not just for half
a century but for centuries past. The jackboot could be on the other
foot!

These Protestant fears are not altogether without support in
Irish history, and, to too many of the Irish, history remains all-
important—worse still, their own often distorted version of it.
Much of this history can be glanced over rather quickly here, but it
cannot be ignored, for it is a necessary backdrop to a proper understanding of the Ireland of today, and also for a better appreciation
of the tragic events in Northern Ireland, particularly since 1969. I
shall also try, in the process, to explode some widely held notions—held by many Irish and non-Irish alike—including the myth
that all of Ireland's problems, both today and down through much
of its history, have come from neighboring Britain. This, at best, is
only partly true, but it is more true than the nonsense preached by
the militant republicans in the IRA that nothing but Britain and
her stubbornness, the old "John Bull" stance, stands in the way of
achieving Irish unity, of real peace and harmony throughout the
island, between Catholics and Protestants. Irish history tells a

somewhat different story, and not just with a different emphasis.
Myths do, of course, grow, sometimes through half-truths, into
historical "facts" through a process of endless repetition. When this
process is introduced selectively to the young, as in Ireland, for
example through the partisan teaching of history at school, history
is often "rewritten" and with potentially dangerous consequences,
not the least by providing a doubtful inspiration for the use of
violence for political ends. Ulster has suffered directly from more
than its fair share of this in the past decade.

The conventional Irish nationalist myth follows this line: Irish
separatism has been a potent force for centuries, but the widespread aspiration for national independence from Britain was put
down with a savage ferocity. The country's Catholic population
make up the only true Irish; the Protestants, who have long been
dominant in Ulster, are not really Irish, but British, and they,
supported by successive London governments, stand in the way of
realizing the Irish dream of centuries past of achieving total and
island-wide independence. On the basis of this distorted view of
history, young Irish people have been persuaded to take up the
gun illegally against the structure of the Northern Ireland substate
and its majority Protestant population, finding ample justification
for their actions in historical parallels, in the glorious deeds of their
forebears. Death, whether to themselves or to others, will ultimately bring its reward by advancing the cause to its eventual and
inevitable fulfillment, national unity.

There is certainly much in Irish history, and in the history of
relations between Ireland and England over the centuries, to produce such a distorted perspective, but it is not the whole story.
The undiluted facts of Irish history show that, for the first millennium a.d. and more, authority in Ireland was divided unequally
among various tribes of Celts and their constantly warring kings
and chieftains, one of whom, Diarmaid MacMurchada, the Leins-
ter king, in 1166 actually approached the English monarch, Henry
II, for armed assistance to help him in his battles with other Irish
chiefs. What he got were not the English, but Norman land-
seeking adventurers speaking Norman French who, like previous
uninvited raiding Norsemen, became integrated with the "native
Irish" through intermarriage and the adoption of the native language and customs. Apart from the perspective of time, it is arguable whether these later arrivals became, in due course, any "less
Irish"[5] than the earlier Celts, or Gaels, from the European mainland. One particularly useful study by an Englishman of Irish his-

tory since the arrival of the Normans has this perceptive observation:

> For centuries afterwards, men who owed a nominal feudal loyalty to the English king, continued to settle in Ireland and become, in the medieval phrase, *hiberniores hibernis ipsos*— "more Irish than the Irish." Many became indistinguishably Gaelic. The term "Old English" was later applied to them if their identity had remained in some ways distinct from Gaelic tribal society. But the distinction between the Old English and the other Catholic Irish was, as far as the royal authority was concerned, often only one between the king's rebels and the king's enemies."[6]

Indeed, it was the growing independence demonstrated by these same Normans, their questioning of feudal obligations to the monarch, that prompted King Henry himself to visit Ireland in 1172 in an effort to reinforce his writ, the authority of which (ironically, in view of the Catholic-Protestant divide in Ulster today) was reinforced when the English pope, Adrian IV, in some obscure mandate, endorsed Henry's suzerainty over Ireland. He quickly obtained allegiance from the Irish chieftains and sought to establish a government in the annexed Norse kingdom of Dublin, although English authority was limited generally, and eventually by the fifteenth century, to a small area around what is now the capital city of the Irish Republic, Dublin. Elsewhere, this Anglo-Norman colony was largely in the hands of its Norman settlers, and it was not until the Tudor monarchs—Henry VIII, Mary, and Elizabeth—that a concerted and successful attempt was made to establish the authority of the British Crown throughout Ireland. This action led to the final defeat of the Gaelic-Irish leaders, Hugh O'Neill and Hugh O'Donnell, who had held sway in much of traditional Ulster,[7] which, for reasons of physical geography and ancient Celtic alliances, had a political identity largely separate from the rest of the country.

This was a decisive period in Irish history, and in Anglo-Irish relations, for two principal reasons. It resulted in a direct confrontation between Gaelic tribal traditions and administration and the norms and traditions of British authority and, after the Reformation, it introduced Protestant settlers into Catholic Ireland. As such, it contained the seeds of today's Ulster problem, but it was not then an Irish-British political confrontation—an unwillingness by the Irish to accept the authority of the British crown[8]—but a clash of traditions and religion.

It is worth going back in history a little at this point, on both these counts, in order better to understand the confrontation. Early Celtic Ireland was divided into about 150 local kingdoms (*tuatha*) subject to overkings who were, in turn, under a loose suzerainty of five provincial monarchs. Despite the lack of a central political authority, the country had a remarkable cultural unity expressed in a standard literary language, free of dialect variations (unlike the situation in Ireland today), in the hands of a professional body of poets, historians, and lawgivers, heirs of the pre-Christian druids. This society was based on the extended family (*fine*) in which laws were enforced through an elaborate system of sureties and fines. By Gaelic, or Breton, law, the ownership of all land was held by the tribe or family, and the chief, who was elected, held title to it for his lifetime only.

Christianity was introduced into Ireland in the fifth century. The missionary work of St. Patrick in the latter half of the century, in his case limited mainly to the area of Ulster, contributed greatly to its rapid acceptance, and it brought the Irish into contact[9] with the world of classical learning. The organization of the early church in Ireland was based on monasteries rather than the conventional diocesan structure elsewhere, and many of the monasteries became famous centers of learning. Monks first committed to writing the oral Gaelic literature of the Irish Celts, produced lyric poetry, and developed the La Tène artistic tradition in the illumination of manuscripts.[10] After the fall of the Roman Empire to the barbarians, Irish monks undertook missionary activities throughout much of Europe, and also in Britain. Columcille founded the famous monastery at Iona in the West of Scotland; Columbanus established numerous monasteries throughout France and at Bobbio in northern Italy, where he died. The sixth to the ninth centuries were, in truth, Ireland's golden age.

Since those earliest times, the desire for land and a firm commitment to Catholicism were strong motivations in the Irish character, and they remain so today, albeit with some waning of religious fervor. Hence, moves by the Tudor monarchs to establish British hegemony throughout Ireland in the sixteenth century and later brought these concepts into sharp conflict. The Gaelic chieftains were offered an ostensibly peaceful compromise of surrendering their land to the English king and immediately having it regranted to them, but, in the process, acknowledging that the only valid title rested with the monarch. This compromise was resisted and, following the final defeat of the Gaelic leaders, O'Neill and O'Donnell, at Kinsale in 1601, British policy in Ireland switched from offering compromise to outright land confiscation and oppression. In particular, sizable parts of Ulster were "planted" deliberately with settlers, mainly from Scotland[11] and England, who were Protestant. This was not just a major social revolution in Ulster but also a religious revolution throughout Ireland as part of the Tudor policy of anglicization. The Protestant church was established by law, although most of the Irish, despite the proscription of their own church, remained staunchly Catholic. Hence, the cause of the Gaelic tradition became linked with the Catholic tradition, and it remains so today. Despite ecumenist trends of recent years, this linking is the reason why many Ulster Protestants, and some of their established religious leaders, believe that the Catholic church in Ireland (and certainly many of its priests) has an ambivalent attitude toward the use of violence in support of a united Ireland.

The "Flight of the Earls" after Kinsale,[12] as the seventeenth century opened, was followed in 1641 by an eleven-year bloody civil war in Ireland. Ostensibly a campaign by Ulster's Gaelic-Irish to reconquer their lands from the "planters," it was in fact an Ireland-wide campaign by Catholics for a redressing of their, by then, acute economic, social, and religious grievances, and it opened with the sectarian massacre of Protestants. The Puritan Parliament in England had, in the same year, suppressed the Catholic religion in Ireland, and the republican, Oliver Cromwell, proceeded to beat down the Catholic rebels with appalling ferocity, and all in the name of God and England. About one-third of all Irish Catholics of whatever origin died in the war; most of the rest were reduced to the status of landless and starving peasants. The restoration of the monarchy in England in 1660 gave some hopes that Catholic grievances might be alleviated, as indeed some were, and Catholic hopes rose higher still when James II, brother of Charles II and himself a Catholic, succeeded him twenty-five years later. James, as King of England and Ireland, restored many Catholic rights, including (importantly) legislation—which was never, in fact, implemented—to repeal Cromwellian land settlements to Protestants, many of them his own troops. The memory of this measure haunts many Ulster Protestants today—a fear that what has been settled can be repealed, that Ulster in an All-Ireland Republic could undergo a reversal of land ownership and the reimposition of the Gaelic-Irish and Catholic tradition throughout the province. Their politicians do much to foster this fear, and it lies at the bottom of their siege mentality, and behind the traditional Ulster Loyalist cry of "not an inch," in response to republican overtures from Dublin, however reasonably voiced.

In the event, James II was, before long, to lose out to his Protestant son-in-law, William of Orange, who defeated him in a number of clashes in Ireland, notably in the famous Battle of the Boyne (1690). To this day, the emotive Protestant cry of "Remember 1690" is directed against Ulster Catholics and intended to underline the Protestant ascendancy then established, which was to endure in the whole of Ireland for more than two centuries and, until quite recently, in Ulster. The Williamite victory was followed by the so-called Penal Laws directed exclusively against Irish Catholics, who, thereafter, were to be excluded from all aspects of political life, from the army, from civil and municipal affairs, from any control over education, and from the open worship of their religion. Land, the key to political power, could not be acquired by Catholics in ordinary circumstances; land owned by a Catholic could not be willed to an eldest son but had to go equally to all sons; if one son was Protestant he was entitled to all the holding; if a Protestant woman, owning land, married a Catholic, title went immediately to the Protestant next of kin. By the start of the eighteenth century, 15 percent of the land of Ireland was owned by Catholics; by 1750 the percentage was only 7. The rape of Catholic Ireland was complete.

Yet it was only toward the end of that century something akin to a genuine Irish nationalist sentiment began to emerge, a demand, however tentative, for an independent existence separate from England. For many centuries the argument had been about the nature and quality of the English role in Ireland, not the principle of it. When this embryo concept of separatism surfaced, it had quite limited support within Ireland, and this support came mainly from Protestant[13] liberals. The long-established Irish Parliament in Dublin had been nothing more than an appendage of its British counterpart in London, merely an Irish instrument of the royal prerogative. Seats in Parliament were literally bought through the corrupt pattern of royal patronage, and liberal Irish Protestants campaigned—with some eventual, if rather limited, success—to have the Dublin Parliament sovereign over the affairs of Ireland, albeit always under the ultimate authority of the British Crown. In turn, this relative autonomy, and the seen best intersts of England, resulted in some improvements in the lot of Irish Catholics, including the repeal of many of the more extreme provisions of the Penal Laws. In time, some Irish Catholic leaders were to emerge, notably Daniel O'Connell, to demand full Catholic emancipation—not only the right to vote, but also to enter Parliament.

Meanwhile, events elsewhere were moving apace and were to have important implications for Ireland, although not immediately with the mass of the Catholic population. These were, firstly, the American campaign against the British colonists, resulting finally in American independence and, within a decade, the French Revolution. The latter had, of course, repercussions far outside French territory and provided an important inspiration for populist movements toward independence. In Ireland these events did not go unnoticed. The demonstration that a deadlocked society need not remain deadlocked coincided with the first stirrings of Irish nationalism. The French connection, too, had a historical basis, not least because of the influence of the "Wild Geese"—those Catholic followers of James II who, after their defeat by the Williamite forces, had been allowed to leave Ireland for France, where many of them, and their descendants, rose to ranks of importance in the French military forces and indeed in the governments and armed forces of other European countries. With France eventually at war with England (1793), a mutuality of interests developed between the French and the Irish to act against England and, in the background, the nucleus of a separatist republican movement also emerged in the United Irishmen under the nominal leadership of Theobald Wolfe Tone, a Dublin-born Protestant.

NOTES

1. Lord Craigavon, first prime minister of Northern Ireland. See John Magee, *Northern Ireland: Crisis and Conflict*, (London: Routledge and Kegan Paul, 1974), p. 4.

2. Ibid., p. 137.

3. Meeting at Lisburn of the new Ulster Vanguard Movement, February 12, 1972. Ibid., p. 141.

4. At Westminister, March 24, 1972. Ibid., p. 150.

5. Some of Ireland's most illustrious sons have Norman names, including the noted author of *Ulysses* and other works, James Joyce.

6. Robert Kee, *The Green Flag: A History of Irish Nationalism* (London: Weidenfeld and Nicolson, 1972), p. 10.

7. The name derives from that of the ancient ruling aristocracy, the Ulaid, whose center of power was near Armagh, today the headquarters of both the Roman Catholic and Church of Ireland (Protestant) churches.

8. The Dublin ceremony in 1541, in which Henry VIII had himself proclaimed "King of

this land of Ireland as united, annexed and knit forever to the Imperial Crown of the Realm of England," was attended by so many Irish chiefs that the bill was read to them in Irish and they expressed their consent in that language too.

9. The Roman Empire never did extend into Ireland, its expansion northward having stopped in Britain.

10. The most noted example is the Book of Kells, which is kept in Trinity College, Dublin.

11. A people mostly of Celtic stock, some of whose ancestors had actually come from Ireland and thus were hardly less "Irish" than the Irish whose land they acquired.

12. O'Neill and O'Donnell, respectively earls of Tyrone and Tyrconnell.

13. Used in its widest sense, including in this context, Presbyterian "dissenters," nonconformist Protestants whose church structure and concept of equality reflected more of a republican ideal than the hierarchical establishment of the Protestant church under the monarchy. As nonconformists, Presbyterians suffered many discriminatory British laws—the reason why many of them emigrated to the American colonies.

2 Emerging Irish Nationalism

To subvert the tyranny of our execrable government, to break the connection with England, and to assert the independence of my country—these were my objects. To unite the whole of Ireland . . . to substitute the common name of Irishmen, in place of the denominations of Protestant, Catholic and Dissenter—these were my means.

Wolfe Tone

Tone's United Irishmen, founded in 1791, had three guiding principles: (1) that English influence in Ireland was the great grievance of the country; (2) that the most effective way to reform it was to reform the Irish Parliament; and (3) that no reform could be any use unless it included the Catholics. The third of Tone's objectives was to set even moderate Protestants against Catholics, thus reinforcing the basis of the present debacle in Ulster. What Protestant Ireland of that time sought was its own sovereign Parliament, the right to determine finally its own affairs but, positively, not a corresponding right to be enjoyed by Catholics. Tone, however, was essentially a republican; his United Irishmen constituted the first real organized Irish nationalist movement. The movement was important for two principal reasons. Firstly, its nationalist philosophy remains to this day the basic credo behind the Irish Republican ideal as advanced by the IRA and, secondly, because its attempt at revolution, with committed but ill-planned French naval support as the eighteenth century came to a close, was seen by an England then at war with France as the final treason of the "rebellious Irish." The result was the Act of Union, the complete merging of Ireland with England on January 1, 1801, a union intended to end Irish Catholic resistance forever, but also a move to give assurance to Irish Protestants by incorporating them in the overwhelming Protestant majority in the two countries. The Union, in institutionalizing formally the link between Ireland and England, provided an essential focus for emerging Irish nationalism, altering

the traditional debate about the quality of English rule in Ireland
into a more tangible objective of breaking the link with England.
As such, it did nothing to defuse emerging Irish separatist ambitions, and eventually it did much to actively encourage them. It
injected the "Irish question" into British politics, where it remained to plague and frustrate English politicians of all parties for
more than a century to follow. As the campaign grew eventually for
Irish independence, Protestant Ulster responded with equal determination to maintain the union with England, if not for the whole
of Ireland, then at least for that province. It sealed the community
divide in Ireland that remains today.

Events within Ireland, and in Anglo-Irish relations, in the
nineteenth century were of great importance in the context of the
Irish struggle for freedom, but they are less relevant here in the
direct context of this work, and they can be passed over quickly.
The Irish leader Daniel O'Connell led and won finally in the British Parliament the drive for Catholic emancipation, and he next
turned his considerable personal energies and political skills to
trying to secure the repeal of the Act of Union. The progressive
evolution of democracy in Britain throughout the century led to a
series of reform measures, which substantially enlarged the electorate there and, to a lesser degree, also in Ireland. This increased
the influence of the rising Irish Home Rule party under Charles
Stewart Parnell, and the concerns of Ulster Protestants were
sharpened when, eventually, the Irish party was to hold the balance of power in the British Parliament.

Earlier (in 1886), the British Liberal leader, William Ewart
Gladstone, had introduced the first of a number of Irish Home
Rule bills. They were opposed strongly by Ulster Protestants and
by their supporters in the British Conservative party. The former
were determined to keep the whole of Ireland within the Union,
but some of their leaders had begun to think that ultimately it
might be necessary to change tactics and to settle instead on the
establishment of a Protestant Unionist enclave in the northern
counties of Ireland, as indeed was to emerge. Parnell, for his part,
had aligned himself with the militant Irish nationalist Fenian
movement, a secret society founded in Dublin but nurtured and
funded mostly in the United States by Irish-Americans. In doing
so, he had provided, uniquely in Irish politics, a constitutional
front for a revolutionary nationalist movement. One writer on the
period had this capsule comment:

The support that Fenianism had hitherto received from the Irish in Britain and America was largely transferred to Parnell and his party. The progress of parliamentary democracy in the United Kingdom favoured the Home Rulers, as the weight of Catholic numbers in Ireland began to be reflected in Irish parliamentary representation. Before 1880, the majority of Irish Members of Parliament (MPs) were Protestant and, before 1885, landowning. But, in the General Election of 1885, the first to be fought on a really popular franchise, this situation was transformed. Home Rulers won 85 of the 103 Irish seats at Westminister . . . and they fairly represented the solid mass of Catholic opinion, lay and clerical, which was basically moderate[1] and distinctively lower middle-class. It was this result which persuaded Gladstone, at the head of a large Liberal majority, to commit his party to the home rule cause and to make his epic attempt in 1886 to place home rule on the statute book.

At this point, 1886, Ulster once again moved into the forefront of Irish and British politics. In the general election of 1885, Home Rulers won 17 and Unionists 16 of the 33 Ulster seats . . . the "verdict of democracy", for the first time fully expressed in Ulster, pinpointed divisions that had their origins in the British colonization of the 17th. century, and set a pattern that continued until the end of the Union and, in a sense, still remains.[2]

Political polarization in Ireland was now virtually complete, but this time under a largely democratic order. The confrontation was clearly between Protestant Unionists and Irish Catholic Nationalists. It remains so today. Ulster then, however, was the traditional northern province of nine counties where, on the basis of the 1911 census, as the home-rule campaign neared its climax, Protestants of all sects outnumbered Catholics by the relatively narrow margin of 890,000 to 690,000, a margin that many Ulster Unionists viewed as being too close for sectarian comfort and long-term survival. A two-to-one edge in favor of the Protestants was thought to provide a more secure and defendable bastion, and the idea took root of surrendering the predominantly Catholic Ulster counties of Donegal, Monaghan, and Cavan.

Meanwhile, the Parnellite party had fallen into some disgrace in Ireland after its leader had taken a mistress, the wife of a Liberal MP, William O'Shea, an association that did not endear him either in Catholic Ireland or in the England of the day, and John Redmond was subsequently to reunite and reorganize the Irish party. Two abortive attempts to pass a Home Rule Bill were followed in

1914 by success—but its implementation was delayed by the outbreak of World War I. More significantly, in the context of the
Irish nationalist movement, there was an abortive rebellion against
British rule on Easter Monday, 1916, in Dublin, and the subsequent execution of its main leaders, who had proclaimed an Irish
Republic. Ulster Protestants under Dublin-born Sir Edward Carson had earlier threatened rebellion if Britain sought to extend
home rule to the whole of Ireland, and some British army officers
garrisoned at the Curragh, near Dublin, made it clear that they
would resign rather than act on instructions to enforce the Westminster writ in Ulster.

Asquith, the new British prime minister (1908) had retained
(reluctantly) Gladstone's commitment to Irish home rule, and he
was forced to deliver on it when, after two inconclusive general
elections in 1910, his Liberal government depended for its survival
on the voting support at Westminster of the Irish party. On the
other hand, he had no will to face the challenge of Ulster protestants. The result, perhaps inevitably, was a compromise, which,
ultimately, resulted in the partition of Ireland under the 1920
Government of Ireland Act, providing, essentially, for two Parliaments, one in Dublin and the second in Belfast. It is generally
accepted that most British legislators did not consider then that
this partitionist solution in Ireland would be permanent,[3] nor indeed is there any evidence that the majority among them wished it
to be so. In any event, it was, despite a bloody Irish civil war
launched by those opposed to the partitionist settlement.

By 1918 and the end of the World War I, the relative moderation
of the Redmonite party had been swamped by the much more
nationalist Sinn Fein (Ourselves Alone) party of Eamon De Valera,[4] and the Irish break with England was, for all practical purposes, final. However, Protestant Unionists had secured their own
enclave in Northern Ireland, and De Valera himself, who had
resisted this settlement, was obliged finally to acknowledge it. In
1932 he led his Fianna Fail (Soldiers of Destiny) party to victory in
an Irish general election and, some five years later, drafted a new
Irish Constitution, asserting a claim to the whole territory of Ireland, in effect putting Ulster Unionists on notice that their tenure
should not necessarily be considered as permanent.[5]

The Northern Ireland constitutional entity was created from a
siege mentality by those who saw a potential or actual Catholic fifth
column in their midst. It is hardly surprising, however deplorable
and undemocratic, that Belfast governments—always as noted ear-

lier, Unionist—sought to protect their citadel, and the armory maintained at their disposal was considerable. Early on (1922), the Parliament of Northern Ireland enacted the Civil Authorities (Special Powers) Act to deal with IRA terrorism, but it was maintained and used predominantly against Catholics who did little more than mere blink in the direction of Irish nationalism. Its Section 2 (4) had little relevance to civil liberties, stating:

"If any person does any act of such a nature as to be calculated to be prejudicial to the preservation of the peace or maintenance of order in Northern Ireland and not specifically provided for in the regulations, he shall be deemed to be guilty of an offence against the regulations . . ."

This particular piece of legislation has been the most controversial in the province since its inception, but there were other laws, and some conventions, that were used extensively to discriminate against the Catholic minority. Job discrimination abounded, constituency boundaries were gerrymandered,[6] local authority housing was allocated largely on a sectarian basis and in such a manner as not to disturb Protestant-Catholic voting patterns in giving areas. An openly Protestant armed auxiliary police force, the "B" Specials, was established. Finally the London government intervened, after the worst discrimination was well documented. Given their siege mentality and the periodic assaults by the IRA, one must understand the motivation of Ulster Protestant legislators, but their discriminatory zeal went too far, their condescension even farther. Thus, Lord Brookeborough, the province's third prime minister, in an interview[7], branded most Catholics as disloyal subjects, while also commenting: "Catholics have less to complain about than the U.S. negroes, and their lot is a very pleasant one compared with that of the nationalists in, say, the Ukraine." A fragmented Catholic political leadership, at least until the formation in 1970 of the Social Democratic and Labour party (SDLP), was less interested in matters touching on the Ukraine than in securing basic civil rights for Ulster's Catholics. The British Parliament, under a developed convention, had sought to isolate itself from Northern Ireland, where there was clearly government, but not government by consensus. Finally, and abruptly, two circumstances combined to change the system. One was the development of the civil rights campaign; the second, and perhaps even more persuasive in moving the British government and changing the face of Ulster Protestant majority rule, was televison. Scenes of police officers battering civil rights marchers became an almost nightly dose for British television viewers. Could this be happening not, for example, in South Africa or in Lord Brookeborough's Ukraine, but rather in an integral part of the territory of the United Kingdom of Great Britain and Northern Ireland? The Mother of Parliament at Westminster awoke from its apathy toward Ulster and its developing cancer. The Catholic minority had had enough.

NOTES

1. [Parnell's party was moderate in the sense that it was essentially constitutionalist, and its links with the Finians were more a matter of tactics than from any determined personal commitment to violence. His objective, which reflected the majority sentiment in Catholic Ireland, was for Irish autonomy, not a total break with Britain. Many European observers of the day viewed Irish patriotism in a similar way, notably the doctrinaire Italian Republican Mazzini, who argued (see Bolton King's *Mazzini* [London, 1902]) that the Irish demand was essentially one for better government only. Although he professed sympathy with Ireland's "just consciousness of human dignity, claiming its long violated rights" and the country's "wish to have rulers, educators, not masters," he maintained that the Irish claim was not a national claim. He argued, wrongly, that the nationalist movement would not be permanent, and he refused to see in it any elements of true nationality because the Irish "did not plead for any distinct principle of life or system of legislation derived from native peculiarities, and contrasting radically with English wants and wishes," nor claimed for their country any "high special function" to discharge in the interests of humanity. Karl Marx, on the other hand, detected a more genuine base to Irish nationalism (see *A Handbook of Marxism*, ed. Emile Burns [London: Victor Gollancz, 1935]), but he was interested in it mainly in the expectation that "the revolutionary fire of the Celtic workers" might merge with the "restrained force but slowness of the Anglo-Saxons" to advance the cause of socialist revolution, although he acknowledged that these two people were not in harmony.]

2. T. W. Moody, *The Ulster Question, 1603–1973*, (Cork: The Mercier Press, 1974), p. 22.

3. The Act provided for, in part: With a view to the eventual establishment of a parliament for the whole of Ireland, and to bring about harmonization between the parliaments and governments of Southern Ireland and Northern Ireland, and to the promotion of mutual intercourse and uniformity in relation to matters affecting the whole of Ireland, and to providing for the administration of services which the two parliaments mutually agreed should be administered uniformly throughout the whole of Ireland, or which, by virtue of this Act, are to be so administered, there shall be constituted as soon as may be after the appointed day, a council to be called the Council of Ireland. (It never came into force).

4. The Sinn Fein electoral victory in 1918 included the first woman ever elected to the British parliament, Countess Constance Markievicz, who, like all the successful Sinn Fein candidates, refused to take their seats and, instead, established their own representative assembly, Dail Eireann, which met in the Mansion House, Dublin. Most of the initial debates were conducted in the Gaelic, or Irish language. (The first woman who was elected in Britain and who actually took her seat at Westminster was an American, Nancy, Lady Astor, one of the early constitutional advocates of women's rights there.)

5. The new Constitution was approved in a national referendum on July 1, 1937, by 685,105 votes to 526,945, hardly a massive endorsement of its Article 2, which declares:

"The national territory consists of the whole island of Ireland, its islands and the territorial seas." This, admittedly, is modified somewhat by Article 3: "Pending the re-integration of the national territory, and without prejudice to the rights of the Parliament and Government established by this Constitution to exercise jurisdiction over the whole of that territory, the laws enacted by that parliament shall have the like area and extent of application as the laws of Saorstat Eireann [Irish Free State, in fact, the partitionist settlement giving independence to twenty-six of Ireland's thirty-two counties, the area now making up the Irish Republic] and the like extraterritorial effect."

6. Set artificially in order to endure Unionist electoral victories.

7. Dublin: *Irish Times*, October 30, 1968.

3 Marching for Civil Rights

The Northern Ireland Civil Rights Association (NICRA) was formed in Belfast in February 1967, with a constitution modeled generally on that of the National Council for Civil Liberties in Britain. It had seven main, and generally moderate, objectives:

1. Universal franchise in local government elections in line with the voting pattern in the rest of the United Kingdom;
2. The redrawing of electoral boundaries by an independent commission to ensure fair representation;
3. Legislation against discrimination in employment at the local government level and the provision of machinery to remedy local government grievances;
4. A compulsory points system for housing that would ensure fair allocation on a nonsectarian basis;
5. The repeal of the "Special Powers" Act;
6. The disbanding of the Ulster Special Constabulary, the "B" Specials;
7. The withdrawal of the Public Order (Amendment) Bill, which, among its other provisions, made nonviolent sit-down demonstrations an offense.

Not surprisingly, given the situation in Northern Ireland, NICRA's membership was predominantly Catholic, although the political parties, trade unions, and cultural bodies of all kinds in Ulster were invited in a representative capacity to attend the inaugural meeting and assist in the formation of the association. The membership of the first governing council was politically varied in range and, according to the Cameron Report,[1] "included persons of known extreme republican views and activities," as well as members of the Northern Ireland Liberal and Labour parties. One of its better-known members, and a subsequent chairperson, was Betty Sinclair, a professed Communist. Miss Sinclair, it is right to add, was

50

to be a voice of moderation whenever civil rights marches came into confrontation with the police. [She died in December, 1981.]

NICRA's first protest march was from Coalisland to Dungannon in August 1968, a demonstration organized formally by the Campaign for Social Justice. Its inspiration was the allocation of a new local authority-built house in the mainly Protestant village of Caledon where, under prevailing conditions, the local Unionist councillor had effective control over the allocating of council houses. No. 9 Kinnard Park, Caledon, where a Catholic family had been squatting for some months, was allocated to a nineteen-year-old unmarried Protestant girl, the secretary to the Unionist councillor's personal lawyer, himself a Unionist candidate for the Stormont Parliament. The house next door was occupied by a Catholic family facing eviction. The merits of the respective claimants could hardly be disputed; Emily Beattie's primary qualification, and it was sufficient, was her religion. The Coalisland to Dungannon march was initially cleared by the police (all public marches required advance approval) but, following the intervention of local Unionists, who threatened to stage a countermarch, the NICRA march route was changed under police directive. The march itself involved initially about 2,500 people and was headed by two Catholic members of the Northern Ireland Parliament. It was efficiently marshaled—some of the stewards were later identified by the police as known Irish republican activists, and ten of them were said to be members of the IRA—and accompanied by a large force of police. Behind the police a crowd of Protestants followed, estimated to number 1,500, "some of whom were potential counterdemonstrators," according to Cameron. In any event it was a peaceful demonstration, although some of the speeches could, on any reasonable interpretation, be termed inflammatory, notably that by one of the MPs, Gerry Fitt, who also held a seat in the British Parliament.

Of itself, this Coalisland-to-Dungannon march was not of any great importance. It is detailed here, however, because it represented the first major and organized public demonstration by Ulster Catholics demanding their civil rights, and it ignited a flame of protest that has not yet gone out, although the torch is now controlled largely by the gunmen. It started a wave of protest and counterprotest that brought the province to the verge of civil war, pitting paramilitary forces on both sides of the political divide in a bloody confrontation of murder, assassination, bombings, bank robberies, and explosions, which, in the following twelve years,

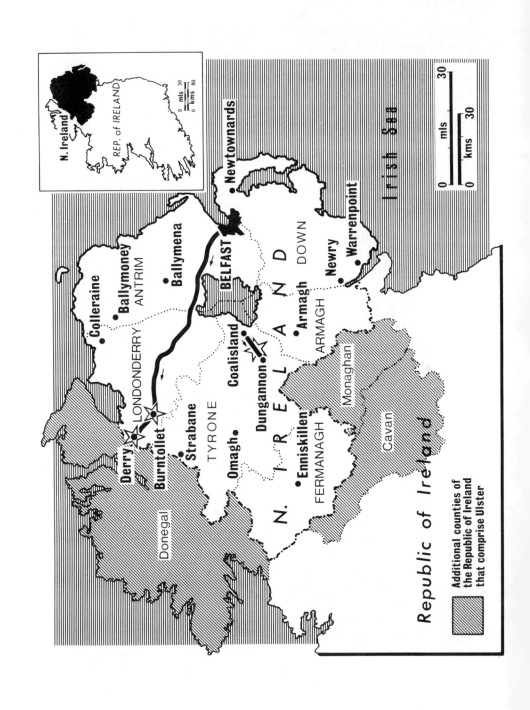

N. Ireland

REP. of IRELAND

0 mls 50
0 kms 80

Irish Sea

Newtownards

Coleraine
Ballymoney
ANTRIM
Ballymena

BELFAST

DOWN

Armagh
ARMAGH
Newry
Warrenpoint

LONDONDERRY

Coalisland

Dungannon

Derry
Burntollet
Strabane

TYRONE

Omagh

N. I R E L A N D

Enniskillen

FERMANAGH

Monaghan

Cavan

Donegal

Republic of Ireland

0   mls   30
0   kms   30

Additional counties of
the Republic of Ireland
that comprise Ulster

cost more than 2,000 lives, well over half of them civilians. The death toll included about 335 members of the British army, approximately one hundred part-time Ulster defense auxiliaries, and more than 125 police officers. The Ulster crisis brought about directly the resignation of three Unionist prime ministers, cost the province its own Parliament, led to violence on the streets in both London and Dublin—where the British embassy was burned to the ground (see below)—and, later, to the assassination there of Christopher Ewart-Biggs, the British ambassador. It has not at this writing brought peace to Ireland, North or South.

The Coalisland-to-Dungannon march was just the start. Six weeks later came the next major demonstration, this time a protest march within the City of Derry along a route traversing some wholly Protestant districts and terminating inside the city's ancient walls, where Protestant defenders had held out against the Catholic King James in the famous Siege of Derry about 270 years earlier. It was thus seen as being a direct affront to the city's Protestants, and it was clearly intended to be such by at least some of the organizers,[2] a loose ad hoc committee representing the Londonderry Labour party, the Londonderry Labour party Young Socialists, the Derry Housing Action Committee, the Derry City Republican Club (little more than a front for the IRA), and the James Connolly Society, named after one of the executed leaders of the 1916 Easter Rising in Dublin. In its report of the event the Cameron Commission concluded, among other findings:

1. We have no doubt that both Mr. Fitt and Mr. [Eddie] McAteer, then the Catholic-nationalist leader of the opposition at Stormont, were batoned by the police, at a time when no order to draw batons had been given and in circumstances in which the use of batons on these gentlemen was wholly without justification or excuse;[3]
2. We have good reason to believe [also] that during the six weeks since the Coalisland-Dungannon march, certain left-wing activists had decided that their campaign would benefit from violent conflict with the authorities. The decision [by the police] to prohibit the march on October 5 from part of its proposed route gave them the opportunity to prove their point.[4]

Equally accurately, the Cameron inquiry team wrote: "One of the consequences of the break-up of the demonstration was that press and television reports ensured that some very damaging pic-

tures of police violence were seen throughout the United Kingdom
and abroad. This produced a violent reaction of feeling in many
places and led directly to the formation at Queen's University,
Belfast, of a protest movement which subsequently became the
People's Democracy."[5]

People's Democracy had been formed just four days after the
Derry march. It was intended to be a permanent protest group. It
had no formal constitution as such, and, significantly for the future,
its membership was not limited to university students. Anyone
attending meetings was free to speak and to vote on decisions at
such meetings, and the movement quickly became a vehicle not
just for the advancement of civil rights but also for promoting the
mainly Trotskyist ideologies of its leading activists. Their objective,
it soon became apparent from speeches and interviews, went far
beyond the aims of NICRA and similar bodies and, in essence, was
the destruction of the existing political and social order in both
parts of Ireland with the intention of bringing about an All-Ireland
socialist republic. As such, its long-term aim did not differ from
that which was also developing within a faction of the IRA.

The People's Democracy organized its first big march—from
Belfast to Derry—early in January 1969. It was interrupted along
the route by Protestant demonstrators, and a full-scale and bloody
ambush took place at Burntollet Bridge, where, on well-chosen
high ground, a mob of Protestants, including some identified members of the "B" Specials, attacked the marchers. Parallel rioting
broke out in Derry City, and both incidents, taken together, almost buried the concept of nonviolent protest in Ulster. Again to
quote Cameron, the Belfast-Derry march "had disastrous effects"
for moderates. "It polarised the extreme elements in the communities in each place it entered. It lost sympathy for the civil
rights movement. . . . We are driven to think that the leaders must
have intended that their venture would weaken the moderate re-
forming forces in Northern Ireland. We think that their object was
to increase tension, so that, in the process, a more radical programme could be realised. They saw the march as a calculated
martyrdom. . . . Having said that, we would add that we consider
the protection afforded them by the police was not always adequate."[6]

However, People's Democracy was not alone in moving to increase the tension. Into the fray in the defense of Ulster and its
constitutional link with Britain, and in furtherance of his own
brand of evangelical fundamentalist Protestantism, which he saw

threatened, not only by Catholic agitation but by the ecumenical spirit released from the Second Vatican Council, came the Reverend Ian Paisley. A Free Presbyterian minister, Paisley was chairman of the Ulster Constitution Defence Committee, which avowedly controlled the Ulster Protestant Volunteers, whose precise objectives were never clearly established but, in the context of Ireland's bloody history, whose very name denoted an ultimate military purpose.[7] The UCDC's constitution sets out its objective, thus:

"The Ulster Constitution Defence Committee and the Ulster Protestant Volunteers which it governs, is one united society of Protestant patriots pledged by all lawful methods to uphold and maintain the Constitution of Northern Ireland as an integral part of the United Kingdom as long as the United Kingdom maintains a Protestant Monarchy."[8]

The Reverend Paisley is a formidable figure. Well over a decade after Derry and Burntollet, when the People's Democracy had lost its way to the gunmen, Paisley was still very much on the active scene, having been elected, in turn, to the Northern Ireland Parliament, the Parliament at Westminster, and, in June 1979, to the European Parliament. He and his followers—and they have grown enormously as successive established Unionist politicians failed to respond to his extremist demands—harassed the civil rights marchers from the beginning and then harassed out of office any Protestant politician who would not do their sectarian bidding. When the platform and the pulpit proved inadequate to answer the seen challenge of republican nationalism and of "Popery," Paisley went political, winning a by-election on April 17, 1970. He marked the day by telling Harold Wilson, the then British prime minister, whose government had, in the final analysis, full control over, and responsibility for, Northern Ireland, that "he should keep his nose out of Northern Ireland."[9] About five weeks earlier, speaking on American television, Dr. Michael Ramsay, the then Protestant archbishop of Canterbury, said of Paisley: "I wouldn't call Ian Paisley a man of God. He is a religious and political partisan. He doesn't help us believe in God exactly."[10]

By then, however, sectarian Ulster was fast getting out of the control of either the politicians or the churchleaders; the shadow of the gunman was moving quickly across the land.

NOTES

1. *The Cameron Reports: Disturbances in Northern Ireland* (HMSO, Belfast, Cmnd 534, 1969), p. 77.

2. The organizers claimed that the route was chosen deliberately simply to demonstrate the nonsectarian nature of the protest.

3. *Cameron Report*, p. 28.

4. *Cameron Report*, p. 44.

5. Ibid., p. 31.

6. Ibid., p. 47.

7. Its Rule 4, quoted in the Cameron Report, says that "no one who has ever been a Roman Catholic is eligible for membership."

8. *Cameron Report*, (appendix IX).

9. Richard Deutsch and Vivien Magowan, *Northern Ireland: A Chronology of Events* (Belfast: Blackstaff Press, 1968–71), vol. 1, p. 63.

10. David Frost TV program, March 10, 1970.

4 The Irish Republican Movement

We declare the right of the people of Ireland to the ownership of Ireland and to the unfettered control of Irish destinies, to be sovereign and indefeasible. The long usurpation of that right by a foreign people and Government has not exting- uished the right, nor can it ever be extinguished except by the destruction of the Irish people. . . .We hereby proclaim the Irish Republic as a Sovereign Indepen- den State.

Dublin: Easter Rising Proclamation, April 24, 1916

Within three weeks of the Easter Monday rebellion, the seven signatories of the proclamation had all been executed,[1] but a fire of militant republican nationalism had been rekindled and, for some Irish, it has not yet gone out, even after the eventual establishment of the independent twenty-six-county Irish state. The proclamation has become, and remains today, something of a Magna Carta of the Irish Republican movement, and the ideals of Wolfe Tone and of the executed leaders remain the professed beliefs of the Provi- sional Irish Republican Army. At this convenient point then, it is useful to chart the origins of the IRA, initially devoid of that "Provi- sional" label, for the split in IRA ranks came later, at a time when the eruption in Ulster had already begun. Curiously though, and not generally reflected in Irish history as represented by North or South, the formation of the Irish Volunteers, the forerunner of the present day IRA, indirectly had its inspiration in Northern Ireland, where an "Ulster Covenant" had been signed in 1912 by almost half a million Ulster men and women who pledged—some in their own blood—to use "all means which may be found necessary to defeat the present conspiracy to set up a home rule parliament in Ire- land.[2] Among the "means" decided on was the creation of an Ulster Volunteer Force, and this force inspired the establishment of a similar paramilitary body in the South.

The Irish Volunteers were formed at a meeting in Dublin on November 25, 1913, following a suggestion in a newspaper article

by Eoin MacNeill, then vice-president of the Gaelic League,[3] that
a force similar to the new Ulster Volunteers should be established.
MacNeill and his followers believed that the Irish Volunteers
would be committed to fight only in the event of an alliance of
British Conservative politicians and Ulster Unionists combining to
block home-rule legislation for Ireland in the British Parliament.
Others had different ideas, and that inaugural Dublin meeting was
infiltrated by leading elements in the Irish Republican Brother-
hood (IRB), a revolutionary movement formed in 1858 and linked
with the Clann na Gael in America under the general title of the
Fenians.

Bungling, bad planning, splits, and last-minute changes in
plans—the last because MacNeill was personally opposed to initiat-
ing violence—marked the 1916 Easter rebellion, with the result
that the British military forces in the city were taken on by no more
that 1,200 Irish Volunteers and members of the so-called Citizen
Army of trade unionist James Connolly. The Irish public largely
ignored the event, and some in Dublin that Monday even scoffed
as Pearse read out the proclamation. Yet the "provisional government" he proclaimed is, to this day, the only one to which the IRA,
and certainly the present Provisionals (Provos), acknowledge allegiance. The provisional government was extended to the First
Dail in 1919 after Sinn Fein, under De Valera, had swamped the
old Redmondite party in the general election and set up its own
assembly (unrecognized, of course, by Britain). That government is
also seen as being legitimate, and no other parliament in Dublin
since has gained IRA approval. For much of the past sixty years the
IRA has been declared illegal in both parts of Ireland, and its
members have been interned for periods on both sides, yet its
remnants survive and are revived by periodic outbreaks of republican "idealism." Measured by its own criteria, its record has been
one of almost total failure, a record that prompted one of the more
serious students of its origins and history to observe:

> The movement for an Irish Ireland, Free and Gaelic, at times
> seems to stretch back over a thousand years into the Celtic
> twilight. The specific struggle for an Irish republic had a history
> of nearly two centuries and even the organisational structure of
> the IRA is over fifty years old. A long and living revolutionary
> tradition is not unique; but what is peculiar to the IRA, by
> contrast with most revolutionary groups, is persistence in the
> face of failure. With few exceptions, revolutionary movements

succeed or fail within a relatively brief space of time; they are transformed by power, or wither away in isolation, evolve into new forms or are swallowed by old ones. . . . Some revolutionary parties, of course, live on in exile, but seldom for more than a generation; some accept, albeit reluctantly, the dialogue of democracy; some eschew violence, or in some manner deny their original means if not their goals; some are extirpated or betrayed. The militant Irish Republican Movement, however, has continued almost unchanged; the goal is the same, an Ireland both Free and Gaelic without cant or compromise, and the means is the same, physical force. And time after time, with deadly regularity, as the means of the movement have proven inadequate, and the strength of the opponent or the entrenched institution and prejudices too great, the IRA has failed. But the movement epitomised in the IRA has nonetheless persisted and endured.[4]

In the civil rights campaign in Northern Ireland of 1968–69, the IRA was caught very wrong-footed. The last "physical force" period, the 1956–62 campaign, had ended with a formally proclaimed termination "of resistance to British occupation" approved by the IRA's Army Council on February 3, 1962, and made public two days later. The proclamation concealed a degree of disunity within the republican movement as great as any in its history, and its "success rate" in terms of "incidents" had declined from the relative high of the 1956–57 period. Arms and ammunition were both in short supply, new recruits to the ranks even fewer. In the Irish Republic the police continued to harass republican activists; in the North life continued substantially unaltered. The IRA threat to bring down the Stormont government had gone the way of many similar IRA promises—nowhere. Rory Brady, a country schoolteacher, gave up the leadership of the Army Council and was replaced by a Dublin house painter, Cathal Goulding. Eight years later, the movement split, leaving on one side a Marxist-oriented Official Sinn Fein and its military wing, the Official IRA (Officials), and, on the other, Provisional Sinn Fein and its associated Provisional IRA (Provisionals, or Provos). The two men emerged again, but on differing sides. Goulding was still chief of staff of the Official IRA;[5] Brady became head of Provisional Sinn Fein.

The actual split had built up gradually against the background of the Northern civil rights campaign and its overspill into intercommunal violence. Official IRA policy prior to the breach had been to infiltrate the civil rights campaign, to put less emphasis on gun-

power and more on ideology, to claim that the real struggle in
Ireland was between the establishment and the working class, the
real objective, the bringing about eventually of an All-Ireland
socialist republic. The IRA was still controlled largely from Dublin,
but in Northern Ireland itself sectarian rioting had becoming commonplace, and most Catholics there had little interest in a Republican Movement that appeared to be contaminated with Communist and associated principles, which preached something
bordering on heroic virtue, such as turning the other cheek when
you were hit by a Protestant extremist. In the Catholic ghettos of
Belfast a new wall poster appeared, declaring: "IRA—I Ran Away."
What the Catholics wanted was defense against Protestant mobs,
not sermons in extreme socialist ideology.

The split was coming nearer; the crunch point—or at very least
the excuse—became the traditional "abstentionist policy" of the
IRA providing that no republican elected to parliaments in Belfast,
Dublin, or London, would ever take up the seat. It was all in the
best republican tradition, because De Valera and his Sinn Fein
colleagues had refused in 1919 to go to Westminster. To many,
however, times had changed. A by-election had been called for an
Ulster constituency following the death of its Unionist MP. In the
mid-1950s, the seat had been won by a republican, on an abstentionist ticket, but he was deprived of it, in any event, as a convicted
felon. He was renominated for the subsequent by-election, increased his winning margin, and was again declared unqualified. In
the second by-election, a third candidate was induced to enter the
contest, thus splitting the ordinarily solid republican nationalist
vote in Mid-Ulster, and a Unionist won.

By early 1969, things had changed greatly in the province. The
civil rights movement was gathering strength all the time, and
NICRA wanted a political voice at Westminster to further its
cause, not an abstentionist republican. A young university student,
Bernadette Devlin, won the seat with the backing of NICRA, that
of the constituency's nationalist population, but also, if reluctantly,
that of the Republican Movement. In a sense it was a small crack in
the abstentionist policy. In her maiden speech before the ordinarily sedate British House of Commons, the new MP, alluding to a
particular street demonstration, roared across the chamber: "I am
not speaking about one night of broken glass, but of fifty years of
human misery." The following Monday, Terence O'Neill resigned
as prime minister of Northern Ireland, the first major political
victim of the developing crisis. He had earlier fired his hard-line

minister for home affairs, William Craig, who, four days prior to O'Neill's resignation, made a speech, which, on any reasonable interpretation, was bordering on the seditious and was certainly an open incitement to violence. Craig said, in part: "There is too much loose and reckless talk about [British] intervention. The people of Ulster will not surrender their parliament without a fight. What we see to-day on the streets of our province—the disorders—will look like a Sunday school picnic if Westminster tries to take our parliament away."[6]

The following day an explosion wrecked the main water pipeline serving Belfast. This act was initially attributed to the IRA, but subsequent indications suggested that it was the work of Protestant extremists and was intended to add to the developing strategy of tension and to drive the relatively moderate O'Neill from office. That same evening five hundred British troops were flown into Northern Ireland as a "precautionary act," according to the London government. O'Neill was replaced by James Chichester-Clark, who had earlier resigned as agriculture minister on the rather odd principle that he was not opposed to the introduction of the British franchise pattern in the province—NICRA's "one man, one vote" demand—but was against the timing of its introduction. The resignation had been enough to distance himself from the unpopular O'Neill, unpopular not so much in the province but within his own Unionist party, which considered him "soft" on Catholic dissidents and also too subservient to the British government, which had begun to wake up to what was happening on the streets of Ulster.

Chichester-Clark had a short political honeymoon. Violent clashes continued throughout the province, Protestant vigilante groups began to appear on Belfast streets, and the July 12 Battle of the Boyne commemoration ceremonies produced its usual crop of violent speeches and some minor rioting, but it was exactly a month later, on August 12, 1969, when the balloon went up. A Protestant parade in Derry, celebrating the famous victory over James II, was stoned by Catholic youths from the Bogside area, a nationalist stronghold. The Protestants retaliated, following the Catholics back towards the Bogside. Police charged the area and, later, used CS gas in what fast became a full-scale riot situation. The Catholics barricaded their stronghold, labelling the area "Free Derry"! Chichester-Clark announced the immediate recall of Parliament from vacation and, in a move that infuriated Ulster Protestants, the Irish prime minister in Dublin, Jack Lynch, announced that he had instructed the Irish army to establish field hospitals along the southern side of the border with Northern Ireland. His government, he said, had also asked Britain to request a United Nations peacekeeping force for Ulster because, in his view, Stormont was no longer able to control events.

In the prevailing climate many Ulster Protestants feared, deep down, an invasion by the army of the South, not the IRA this time but the official defense forces of the Irish Republic. Not a few old Catholic nationalists secretly hoped for just that. Two days later, the first British troops appeared on the streets of Derry to try and restore order, Chichester-Clark having, in effect, acknowledged directly to the government in London that Stormont could no longer keep the peace. In Dublin, Lynch ordered the calling up of the country's first-line reserve troops. The British prime minister, Harold Wilson, interrupted his holiday and hurried back to London. The pope issued a statement in Rome saying that war, especially civil war, should no longer have a place in the modern world. A statement from the IRA said that its "active service units" in Northern Ireland were defending Catholic areas that were being "attacked by deliberately fomented sectarian forces backed by the "B" Specials with the aim of destroying the natural solidarity and unity of working-class people."

However, Northern Catholics had not seen much of this claimed IRA defense, and working-class solidarity in Ulster was a myth. What the Catholics wanted was protection; what the republican militants in Ulster wanted were guns. They were soon to have them. That year 13 fatal casualties resulted from the violence; in the three successive years the numbers killed rose, respectively, to 25, 173, and 468. The Provisional IRA had come on the Ulster scene with a real vengeance. By the end of 1969 the IRA had split. The hard-liners, holding to the Magna Carta of Tone and the 1916 Rising, and clinging to the abstentionist policy, formed the Provisionals and said: "We declare our allegiance to the 32-county republic proclaimed at Easter, 1916, established by the first Dail Eireann in 1919, overthrown by force of arms in 1922, and suppressed to this day by the existing British-imposed six-county and 26-county partition states."[7]

The gunmen had left the ideologists—the Provos taking to the streets and the Officials to their socialist tracts and the platforms, becoming a kind of umbrella organization of an embryo Irish National Liberation Army. Goulding, speaking for the Official IRA, was to say later that its policy in Northern Ireland "is to see that there is mass involvement, that street committees and all kinds of civil resistance committees become kinds of people's soviets, actually administering the areas."[8]

Yet the split was important for another reason, whose full implications were only to emerge over succeeding years. It marked, in great measure, an important geographical shift within IRA ranks away from Dublin and the Irish Republic and more toward Belfast, Derry, and Armagh in Northern Ireland. The axis of the republican leadership, centered traditionally in the South of Ireland, but with much more sympathetic popular support in the North, was to change. It was a significant shift, and it deserves noting here also because, ever since the 1920s, the media, Irish and foreign alike, had tended to lump the IRA together without much, if indeed any, distinction between its activists from the two parts of Ireland, thus cloaking a marked difference in motivation and psychology, and indeed objectives. There were, in fact, two quite distinct streams of political consciousness, and an appreciation of them is important to an understanding of the episodic militant campaigns, and also for the understanding of the differing responses—at least initially—to the Ulster civil rights movement. This distinction is best drawn by reference, respectively, to "Southern" and "Northern" republicans.[9]

The Southern Republican of the Fifties: The typical Southern activist of the 1956–62 campaign period was in his early twenties. He was Catholic and, most probably, came from a stable home background that was working-class or petit bourgeois. He was a tradesman, clerk, or a semiskilled operative and had attended the Christian Brothers[10] school, like so many of the children in this class grouping, at least to Primary certificate level, and often up to Intermediate and Leaving Certificate (second-level education). He had grown up during the World War II years in a society that had peasant populism for politics, fundamental faith for religion, and emigration and low growth for economics. His background was usually urban. Like all children who attended school at the time, he had been taught the Gaelic language, a policy favored by the majority of the Catholic politicians of Dail Eireann and, indeed, by the mainly peasant-background teachers who taught in the schools. The Gaelic language as a lingua franca had, for all practical purposes, been abandoned by the Irish people for more than one hundred years. Although the Southern republican generally favored the notion of the use of the language, he seldom spoke it in normal conversation, but he nodded emotionally toward an ideal, propagated by one of the leaders of the 1916 Easter Rising, Patrick Pearse, of an Ireland that was "Free and Gaelic, Gaelic and Free." He was a devout practicing Catholic in most instances; when the Irish Catholic hierarchy publicly refused the sacraments to members of the IRA in the mid-fifties, it came as a severe shock and trauma to the member to find that he was, in essence, disowned and rejected by a church to which he felt himself firmly attached. His religious faith and his nationalism were emotionally entwined.

He was involved in a physical force movement because he believed that the only way that change had occurred in Ireland over the years was from violence, or the threat of its use. At a simple level, he believed that it was his duty to finish off the task started in the 1916–21 period, when twenty-six of Ireland's thirty-two counties had been shaken from the political domination of Britain. The remaining six counties had to be recaptured. Again at a basic level, he would argue that the forces of occupation in the Northern counties, that is, the British army units that were stationed there, had to be removed by force of arms and, indeed, most of the IRA's early actions in the mid-fifties campaign were directed against British army bases in the North. The Dublin politicians had been preaching for many years about the "evils of partition," but they had done little except talk about it. By confronting British army forces, the republican would, in time, get backing from the ordinary Irish people, just as it had happened before from the inspiration of the 1916 leaders. At the second level of thinking, the Southern republican believed that the politicians had betrayed the revolution of the twenties. They had not attempted to put into life the promises of the new dawn drawn up in the 1916 Easter Proclamation. Instead, they had produced and helped to develop an inward-looking Catholic-dominated Parliament for the Catholic people of the South, just as surely as their Northern counterparts had produced a Protestant Parliament for the majority of Protestants of that part of the country. The economy in the South was then stagnant, job opportunities were minimal, and emigration was the normal way the country dealt with its problem of nongrowth. Living conditions were generally poor.

Our "rebel" would most probably have been reared in one of the several drab council (local authority-owned) estates, which were a feature of both Dublin and Belfast at that time, and which still stand as a monument to the poverty of thinking of the times. Without knowing precisely what the reasons were, he would have nurtured a subconscious desire for social change and a better and more colorful way of life. He certainly did not see the theater for change to be purely in Northern Ireland. Tactically, he believed that this was the best ground on which to make a demonstration, and on which to gain support. He wanted "the Republic of the thirty-two counties which would embrace all of the people of the island, irrespective of class or creed." He wanted an end to clerical dogmatism and influence in politics, both North and South. He wanted to end economic dependence on Britain and to break the final connection between the two islands. He desired a more thoughtful, even liberal, society; he wanted an end to the "sham," or largely artificial, republicanism of Dublin politicians, and he wanted growth and change from the economic stagnation that characterized that particular era.

Exactly how all this was to be accomplished, he did not know. His contribution, like that of an earlier nineteenth century Irish radical, John Mitchell,[11] was simply to smash the prevailing order so as to allow for a new order to take place. The only group that offered a possibility of pursuing this line of political dogmatism was the IRA, a group renowned for its tradition of physical force and with a less deserved reputation for political achievement. For the idealist/radical/social malcontent of the 1950s, joining the IRA was the most logical of steps.

The Northern Activist: The Northern republican was moved by a different set of forces and fantasies. He was of a similar age and background as his Southern counterpart, but with the difference that he was as likely to have come from a rural background as from a city. Again like his Southern compatriot, he would probably have had no previous involvement with any other part of the Republican Movement prior to joining the IRA; for instance, he would not have been a member of the Fianna, the boy-scout Republican Movement. His parents would probably not have been associated with the Republican Movement, although it is possible that perhaps one of his relatives might have been at some level in the 1920s. He had been brought up as a Northern Catholic, which meant segregation from Protestants at school, at social life, and games, and, if he was from the city, even segregation by locality. He had a ghetto mentality. He saw himself firstly as a Northern Catholic nationalist, then as a member of the Six Counties, and lastly as someone having affinity with the Southern majority Catholic population. His primary motivation was to destroy the Stormont Parliament. The immediate enemy, as far as he was concerned, was not the British army but the "B" Specials, the auxiliary police of mainly Protestant near-neighbors.

His political motivation was directed less to the development of a thirty-two county republic of free individuals. Rather, he was concerned with the removal of perceived grievances in relation to discrimination in terms of housing allocation, electoral divisions, job allocations, and opportunities for advancement in a province where, to be Catholic, was to be second-class. Essentially, his demands were for civil rights. He viewed his Southern compatriot's dreams of the thirty-two county republic with a certain amount of suspicion, even cynicism. Had not Southern Catholics abandoned Northern Catholics by accepting finally the partitionist settlement in the twenties? When, in fact, had the Dublin Parliament taken the needs of the Northern Catholics even moderately seriously? When he spoke the Gaelic tongue, he used the Donegal dialect, again not so subtly emphasizing the difference between Northerners and Southerners. This tension showed itself in the Republican Movement and in the IRA, centering on disagreements between the Belfast and Dublin commands. The Northern republican saw much more vividly than his Southern counterpart the prison as a battlefield, a tradition going back to the 1920s. This tradition demanded that the incarcerated republican would refuse to wear prison clothes and would fight the prison system in every way he could for the duration of his stay. He would seek, as a prisoner, a unique and particular form of "political" status.

When disappointment faced him, and when hopes of success of the campaign appeared low, he used, as did his Southern counterpart, the necessary emotional justification of tradition. The fight he was engaged in had been going on for generations; merely carrying out a protest in arms in any one generation was itself an achievement. Everything he had learned from the cradle, in a deeply introverted society, supported him in the belief that the Catholic/Nationalist ethos was worth fighting for and, if necessary, dying for. His faith in the essential goodness and value of the Catholic/Nationalist tradition sustained him over long years of deprivation in penal institutions, North and South, largely ignored by the populace for whom he believed he was making his sacrifice. The tradition would be safe and the torch would be handed on to the next generation to resume the fight for ultimate victory. Terence McSweeney,[12] one of the great heroes of the 1920s era, had summed it up for him in his famous words: "It is not those who inflict the most but those who endure the most who will ultimately prevail." Ultimately, the IRA tradition would prevail. This was his prayer and battle hymn."

NOTES

1. Thomas J. Clarke, Sean Mac Diarmade, P. H. Pearse, James Connolly, Thomas McDonagh, Eamonn Ceannt, and Joseph Plunkett.

2. John Magee, *Northern Ireland: Crisis and Conflict* (London: Routledge and Kegan Paul, 1974), p. 48.

3. Founded in 1893 with the declared aim of preserving the language and culture of Gaelic Ireland.

4. J. Bowyer Bell, *The Secret Army* (London: Sphere Books, 1972), pp. 437–38.

5. The "Officials" committed to physical force merged effectively in the early 1980s into the new Irish National Liberation Army.

6. Richard Deutsch and Vivien Magowan, *Northern Ireland: A Chronology of Events*, (Belfast: Blackstaff Press, 1968–71), vol. 1, p. 25.

7. Bell, *The Secret Army*, p. 431.

8. Quoted by Rosita Sweetman, *On Our Knees* (London: Pan Books, 1972).

9. The present author acknowledges the assistance with this analysis of an IRA activist involved personally in the violence campaign of the late 1950s who, for obvious reasons, must remain unidentified. The language of his directly incorporated "reflections" has been altered only where necessary for clarification for a wider audience, in order to allow for a better understanding of the reasoning—if often confused—which has prompted successive generations of young Irish, North and South, to take up arms to advance an ideal.

10. A teaching community of religious brothers involved extensively in first- and second-level education in Ireland.

11. An Ulster Protestant lawyer (solicitor) and publicist who supported O'Connell's repeal (of the union with Britain) campaign, but differed on means, Mitchell arguing that fine words, unsupported by force, would never persuade the British government.

12. Lord Mayor of Cork arrested by British forces in the city in 1920, and who died in Wormwood Scrubs jail in England after a hunger strike lasting seventy-three days.

The Provisional IRA in 1981 launched a major hunger-strike campaign in support of demands for "political status" for its men held in The Maze prison near Belfast. The first IRA man to die—after going without food for sixty-six days—was Bobby Sands, who during his hunger strike had been elected to the British Parliament by a narrow victory in a by-election in the Northern Ireland constituency of Fermanagh/South Tyrone. Sands was not allowed to take his seat. The IRA hunger-strike campaign was joined by a number of jailed members of the Irish National Liberation Army leading to a mounting toll of deaths and increasing pressure on the British government of Mrs. Margaret Thatcher—including visits to The Maze by a team from the International Red Cross and by a personal emissary of Pope John Paul II—to make concessions to the prisoners. Mrs. Thatcher's immediate reply was that some concessions in prison conditions were possible, but she was not prepared to act under the duress of the hunger-strike campaign. The campaign was called off after 10 prisoners had died—and for marginal improvements in prison routine.

The campaign also spilled over into the Irish Republic where Dr. Garret FitzGerald became prime minister of a Fine Gael/Labour coalition administration following an inconclusive general election in June 1981. Two successful independent candidates in the election were republican activists, one of them, Kevin Doherty, who was then on hunger strike. He died within a few weeks of his election—to a Parliament whose legitimacy he had never accepted.

5 The Community Divide

There is no military means of preventing people, determined on destruction, from living out their disaster. This is not a job for soldiers. . . . It is for political leaders to govern wisely and justly. I accept the guarantees of the British Government that they will do so in Northern Ireland. . . . My Government is the second guarantor.

Jack Lynch, Irish prime minister*

This intervention from Dublin, in what became known as the "second guarantor" speech, infuriated Ulster Protestants. How, they asked, was the Lynch government in Dublin going to enforce its writ, if necessary, as second guarantor? Northern Ireland, to its Protestants, was an integral part of the United Kingdom, and thus of no concern to Dublin. Events in Ulster were moving fast, however; even the initial objectives of the civil rights movement were no longer the real issue. The Catholics in the province, supported by Dublin, now wanted a share in real administrative power. The gunmen continued on their way, the Provos in particular intent on creating maximum chaos and eventually driving the British and their forces out of Ireland. Parts of Belfast joined "Free Derry" as "no-go" areas to the security forces, as Catholics lived behind their barricades and the gunmen denied entry to the police. Protestant extremists adopted similar tactics. In March 1971 Prime Minister Chichester-Clark flew to London for talks with the British government. He was under pressure from his own Unionist hard-liners to end the Catholic "no-go" areas, and he asked London for more troops and tougher action. If not, he said, he would resign. Four days later he did, having been in office for exactly twenty two months. His successor, Brian Faulkner, lasted precisely one year.

It was a dramatic and terrible year for Ulster during which the emerging polarization of the two communities became virtually

*July 11, 1970: In a radio appeal asking Ulster Catholics not to interfere in the following day's Protestant annual march.

complete, but there was also some political progress. The six so-called civil rights MPs in the Stormont Parliament had come together to form the Social Democratic and Labour party in 1970, and, by August the following year, the Faulkner government was able to publish and present to Parliament a booklet[1] setting out a number of legislative and administrative changes, which, on paper at least, met almost all the original demands of the civil rights movement, including the concession of "one man, one vote" in local elections. The enactment of these measures, under pressure from the civil rights campaign and the increasing concern of the British government, did not bring about instant change, but it did represent an end to the most blatant forms of discrimination in Ulster. Yet by then the militants were not interested in civil rights demands. The Provisional IRA was growing strong and better armed almost by the day. Money to buy weapons was coming into Provo hands from sympathetic Irish-Americans in particular, who could not, or did not wish to, distinguish the Provisionals from the earlier IRA of De Valera and the War of Independence era. To them it was sufficient that the headlines in America spoke of British troops killing "innocent Irish Catholics" even if the Provisionals themselves had brought on most of the killing. These same headlines were helped enormously when, on Sunday, January 30, 1972, British paratroopers opened fire on Catholics demonstrating in Derry, thirteen of whom were killed. The army insisted that the paratroopers had come under attack from snipers and implied initially that the thirteen killed had been armed. Four of the dead men, according to the army, were on the "wanted list," a charge subsequently withdrawn during an inquiry headed by Lord Chief Justice Widgery.[2] In Dublin, the government condemned the action by British troops as "unbelievably savage and inhuman." John Hume, for the SDLP, in a radio interview, said that the settlement to the problems was "a united Ireland or nothing." Kurt Waldheim, secretary-general of the United Nations, offered to assist in trying to resolve the crisis, but the British government rejected the overture. The British embassy in Dublin was burned down by a protesting mob. A new commemorative event went into the annals of Irish history, known simply as "Bloody Sunday." Less than two months later, Faulkner was no longer prime minister, Ulster's Protestants had lost their own Parliament after fifty years, and the British government had taken over direct responsibility for the running of the province. That responsibility remains squarely with London and the Westminster Parliament after almost a decade.

Following "Bloody Sunday," Faulkner was summoned to London, where the prime minister, Edward Heath, told him that his government wished full control for security in the province to rest with London. The Unionist cabinet resisted and threatened to resign. On March 24, 1972, Heath faced the Unionist challenge, telling the British Parliament that the transfer of responsibility for law and order was an indispensible condition for progress in finding a political solution for Northern Ireland. The proposals that he had put to Faulkner and the Belfast cabinet were:

A. Periodic plebiscites on the border (Irish Partition) issue as a reassurance that there would be no change without the consent of the majority of the people of Northern Ireland;[3]
B. A start to be made on phasing out internment in Ulster;
C. Transfer of responsibility for law and order to Westminster.

Items (A) and (B) were acceptable to the Faulkner government, but not (C). Direct British rule produced a predictable response. The Unionist party promised a policy of noncooperation, militant Protestant leaders called for industrial stoppages, the mainly Catholic SDLP appealed for an end to violence, and, in Dublin, Lynch saw the British initiative "as a step forward in seeking a lasting solution to the remaining problem in Anglo-Irish relations." The undertaking to start phasing out internment in Ulster was seen by Protestant militants as British pussyfooting in the face of continuing IRA violence. It had been introduced the previous August in a bid to stem the rising tide of killings, but all it succeeded in doing was to further alienate the Catholic population, which, earlier, had generally welcomed the arrival in the province of British troops. The British army had been prepared for a "Catholic backlash" over internment, but its extent took senior officers by surprise. There had been immediate protest demonstrations, bombings, burnings, and rioting throughout the province, and no single event in Ulster in the previous decade had done so much to increase Catholic support for, or at very least acceptance of, the Provisional IRA as did the introduction of internment. More than 300 people had been rounded up in a predawn swoop by soldiers and police on August 9, 1971—all of them Catholics. Charges of brutalities in the interrogation of detainees quickly followed, charges that were well exploited by the Provisionals and found to be essentially true by a Committee of Inquiry.[4] It found "ill-treatment" rather than "physical brutality," a distinction that Ulster Catholics considered to be more semantic than significant.

Internment followed by "Bloody Sunday" made the community divide complete. Government had totally broken down in Ulster. The British army could not keep the paramilitary Catholic and Protestant forces apart; bombings and sectarian assassination became a daily event. Into this caldron of hate and violence came the new British administrator, William Whitelaw, as secretary of state for Northern Ireland. It was Saturday, March 25, 1972. Britain's settlement package for Ireland of half a century earlier had finally collapsed. The gunmen and Ulster's Catholic minority, sometimes acting in unspoken collusion, and always with a degree of ambiguity one toward the other, had made government impossible. Politically motivated violence had brought down Stormont. The collective sigh of relief of Northern Catholics and of the Dublin government was audible; the threats of the hard-line Ulster Protestants got tougher. William Craig told a group of British parliamentarians that he and his followers would make direct British rule in Northern Ireland unworkable. In Belfast thousands of members of the Ulster Defence Association marched through the streets wearing military-style uniforms and dark glasses. Even more extreme Protestant voices talked of rebellion against the British government—the taking up of arms, if necessary, against the British army. Official statistics issued on May 29 showed that 348 people had died in the violence since 1969. The next day one more died—a twelve-year-old girl caught in cross fire.

Whitelaw was an ideal choice as Britain's administrative chief in Ulster. A North-of-England landowner with an impeccable Conservative party background, Whitelaw brought to his task a penetrating political mind concealed behind an infectious joviality. He had another considerable talent, a seemingly infinite patience for talk and persuasion, even between elements known to be bitter opponents. Within six months he had learned much about Northern Ireland, and in October he published a discussion paper that included the following:

A Northern Ireland assembly or authority must be capable of involving all its members constructively in ways which satisfy them and those they represent that the whole community has a part to play in the government of the province. As a minimum, this would involve assuring minority groups of an effective voice and a real influence; but there are strong arguments that the objective of real participation should be achieved by giving minority interests a share in the exercize of executive power if

this can be achieved by means which are not unduly complex or
artificial, and which do not represent an obstacle to effective
government.[5]

This carefully worded observation concealed an important decision
that Whitelaw had already reached: the best if not indeed the only
solution to the Ulster problem would be a system of power sharing
between the two Irish traditions. The minister hoped to persuade
their respective political leaders to accept this principle voluntarily, but he was prepared to enforce it if necessary by insisting that
it was the price they would have to pay if Britain was to agree to
again devolve regional government to Ulster. By March the following year (1973), Whitelaw had put considerable constitutional
shape on his discussion proposals, providing for elections to a new
Northern Ireland Assembly, which, having determined its own
procedural rules, would have to reach agreement with him on the
formation of an executive. Such a new Northern Ireland executive
would, in effect, have to include representatives of both the Prot-
estant/Unionist and Catholic/Nationalist communities. In a paper
presented to the British Parliament, Whitelaw touched on the core
of the Ulster question:

> A fundamental problem since the earliest days of Northern
> Ireland's existence has been the disagreement, not just about
> how Northern Ireland should be governed, but as to whether it
> should continue to exist at all. Those in Northern Ireland who
> have supported its continued membership of the United King-
> dom have seen themselves as faced by an unremitting campaign
> to discredit and dismantle the constitutional system. Their oppo-
> nents, on the other hand, have claimed that valid political oppo-
> sition has been treated as subversion, and used as a pretext to
> exclude them from any share of real power or influence in North-
> ern Ireland's affairs.[6]

For Whitelaw, his first full year in Ulster had been an instructive
period. Conceptually, at least, he had identified the heart of the
problem and had proposed some unique (for Ulster) solutions.
However, he still had some difficult problems to solve. The sectarian violence was growing daily, with illegal paramilitaries fronting
both communities, getting better organized, better armed, and
more ruthless. The old Unionist party monolith had already broken
into three more or less distinct groups. The relative moderates still
supported Faulkner; the hard-liners suspected Whitelaw's political

line and accused him of tolerating the Catholic "no-go" areas and preventing the British army from using its military might to smash the Provisional IRA; the Unionist/Loyalist alliance under the Reverend Paisley, with fast-growing Protestant grass-roots support, could rightly be labeled the "no surrender" lobby, with its "not an inch"mentality.

Yet Whitelaw could claim some small successes, too. Shortly after his appointment, Dublin had tightened its surveillance over IRA activities in the South. The Lynch government had introduced special courts to permit nonjury trials on the accurate grounds that intimidation by the IRA often made it difficult to secure jury convictions. The long-standing Offences Against the State Act, introduced originally to combat IRA terrorism, was amended to facilitate the prosecution of terrorists. Indeed, despite residual suspicions of Dublin's ultimate political intentions, some moderate Ulster Protestants considered that Lynch had, at last, moved realistically to help in suppressing terrorism, to try to prevent the IRA from using bases in the Republic from which to mount their murderous attacks against Northern Ireland. This seen change of heart by Dublin did something to ease Protestant memories of an incident a few years earlier, when Lynch dismissed two of his senior cabinet ministers, Charles Haughey[7] and Niall Blaney, on suspicions of their involvement in the use of official funds to buy arms and ammunition for the IRA—charges which the courts did not subsequently establish. In Unionist nostrils, the smell of official Dublin collusion with the IRA had remained, and it was grist to the mill of Protestant extremists, such as Paisley, who insisted that Dublin's real long-term objective was to undermine the Northern Ireland substate and, finally, to absorb it. Further, an increasing willingness by London to listen to diplomatic representations by Dublin over events in, and British policies for, Ulster, appeared to confirm for many Protestants that Britain had conceded an "Irish dimension" to the Northern problem. The 1972 Whitelaw Discussion Paper had acknowledged as "an evident fact" the existence of such a dimension and went on to observe, to the intense irritation of Ulster Unionists, the following:

Whatever arrangements are made for the future administration of Northern Ireland must take account of the province's relationship with the Republic of Ireland: and to the extent that this is done, there is an obligation upon the Republic to reciprocate. Both the economy and the security of the two areas are, to

some considerable extent, inter-dependent, and the same is true
of both their relationships with Great Britain. It is, therefore,
clearly desirable that any new arrangements for Northern Ireland should, whilst meeting the wishes of Northern Ireland and
Great Britain, be so far as possible acceptable to and accepted by
the Republic of Ireland which, from January 1, 1973, will share
with Britain the rights and obligations of membership of the
European Communities. It remains the view of the United
Kingdom Government that it is for the people of Northern Ireland to decide what should be their relationship to the United
Kingdom and to the Republic of Ireland; and that it should not
be impossible to devise measures which will meet the best interests of all three. Such measures would seek to secure the acceptance, in both Northern Ireland and in the Republic, of the present status of Northern Ireland, and of the possibility—which
would have to be compatible with the principle of consent—of
subsequent change in that status; to make possible effective consultation and co-operation in Ireland for the benefit of North and
South alike; and to provide a firm basis for concerted governmental and community action against those terrorist organizations which represent a threat to free democratic institutions in
Ireland as a whole.[8]

In the highly sensitive question of relations between the two parts
of Ireland, Whitelaw's cautious prescription had a touch of Solo-
mon about it, but it further alarmed Ulster Unionists. It also
tended to reinforce IRA arguments that Britain, under the threat of
continuous terrorism, might be willing not only to concede the
possibility of some change in the constitutional status of Northern
Ireland but to encourage it actively. The previous July the Provisional IRA had secured an immediately more tangible gain, and
Ulster Protestant leaders had a new stick with which to beat the
British government. The incident was, in many ways, quite
bizarre. About 20,000 members of the British security forces, army
and police, were by then working around the clock to try to establish an uneasy peace and to apprehend top IRA leaders, while the
London politicians and the media there regularly abused Dublin
for its alleged failure to crack down hard on the Provisionals, to
prevent their access to either weapons, explosives, or safe havens.
Violence was mounting throughout Ulster; in 1972 as a whole there
were more than 10,000 shootings, 1,400 explosions, almost 2,000
armed robberies, 468 deaths, and 3,813 civilian injuries.[9] Yet in
this climate of violence six top IRA leaders were flown secretly to
London for private talks with Whitelaw.[10] Disclosing this meeting

in the House of Commons three days later, the secretary of state said that the demands put to him by the Provisionals were, in his view, unacceptable to any British Government. Basically, the IRA wanted:

A. The British government's public recognition of the right of the Irish people, as a whole, to decide the future of Ireland.
B. A declaration of intent to withdraw British forces from Irish soil by 1975 and an immediate withdrawal from certain areas of Northern Ireland.
C. An amnesty for all political prisoners in Britsh and Irish prisons and for all internees, detainees, and wanted persons.

Whitelaw's dramatic peace overture failed, and the six IRA leaders were returned to Ireland by courtesy of the British Air Force. Like Ulster Protestants, the Dublin government was furious because it had come under consistent attack in Britain for not acting resolutely to detain IRA leaders. The British army, both officers and other ranks, harbored a feeling of betrayal by their political masters. Matters were not helped when Harold Wilson who, as prime minister, had first ordered the British army into Ulster, disclosed that, on a visit to Dublin, he had met privately with Republican activists. In any event, two[11] of the six IRA men who had traveled to meet Whitelaw in London were arrested shortly thereafter by security forces of the Irish Republic. For his part, and in an attempt to rehabilitate himself with Protestant/Unionist leaders, Whitelaw moved with "Operation Motorman" and used the British army to break down the Catholic barricades, to bring to an end the multiplying "no-go" areas in the province.

It was a short-lived rehabilitation because Whitelaw's dialogue with political representatives, following publication of his constitutional proposals, indicated that what Britain had in mind, in the context of relations between the two parts of Ireland, was a formal Council of Ireland,[12] a cross-border institution representing the existing Dublin Parliament and the new Assembly proposed for Belfast. This, to many Ulster Protestants, was simply a Trojan horse on the way to eventual Irish unity. Twenty-four hours after publication of Whitelaw's formal proposals, a new Loyalist grouping was convened[13] in Belfast: it included Craig and Paisley and Lawrence Orr, a hard-line Unionist MP at Westminister, together with representatives of the Ulster Defence Association and the Loyalist Association of Workers. A statement said that the new group was agreed on four central points: (A) the defeat of the IRA; (B) the rejection of the Council of Ireland; (C) full parliamentary representation, in effect, a rejection of Whitelaw's plan for Protestant-Catholic power sharing; and (D) control of the Ulster police by elected representatives of the Ulster people. In effect, it was a clear demonstration that the main body of Protestant/Unionist opinion, including the illegal supporting paramilitary forces, had decided to confront Britain's peace package for Ulster directly.

The elections for the new Northern Ireland Assembly demonstrated just how the traditional Ulster Unionist monolith had collapsed. Faulkner's Official Unionists were able to muster only 29 percent of the popular vote and a mere twenty-two seats in the seventy-eight-member Assembly. However, when joined with the Catholic SDLP and the nonsectarian Alliance party, the forces committed publicly in advance to working a political formula within Whitelaw's power-sharing framework had a 50 to 28 majority in the Assembly and could claim to represent about 60 percent of the Northern Ireland electorate. However, Unionist factions opposed to power sharing with Catholics and, even more vehemently, to any cross-border links with the Irish Republic, had outvoted the Faulkner Unionists to demonstrate that there was no clear Protestant mandate for the British package, although the outline proposals did appear to enjoy an overall majority in Ulster taken as a whole.[14]

The electorate in the Irish Republic had also been sampled in 1973 when Lynch's Fianna Fail government called fresh elections, only to be defeated by an opposition alliance of the Fine Gael and Labour parties. This outcome was seen by some Ulster Unionists, and also by the London government, as an encouraging sign because it relegated to the opposition benches in Dail Eireann the successors to the republican ideals of De Valera. The new prime minister, Liam Cosgrave, the Fine Gael leader, was the son of W. T. Cosgrave, who, in opposition to De Valera, had accepted the original Anglo-Irish Treaty deal and whose forces had won the subsequent Irish civil war. The arrival of the Cosgrave government in Dublin, followed by indications from the Northern Ireland Assembly poll that a bipartisan majority favored the British peace proposals, combined to generate an air of hope that a detailed settlement in Ulster could be worked out, and with the backing of both Dublin and London. Despite the continuing violence on the streets,[15] the stage was set for the most important Anglo-Irish conference in fifty years. In their search for a new political formula in Ulster, many established politicians in Belfast, Dublin, and London had failed to notice that the tribal instincts of Northern Ireland's working-class Protestants were being worked up by extremist leaders, many of whom were prepared to condone the growing violence of the Protestant paramilitary forces.

NOTES

1. *A Record of Constructive Change*, Government of Northern Ireland, August 1971, Cmnd 558.

2. The Widgery Inquiry was subsequently to report that none of the deceased or wounded was proved to have been shot while handling a firearm or bomb. Some were wholly acquitted of complicity in such action; but there were suspicions that others had been firing weapons or handling bombs in the course of the afternoon, and that yet others had been closely supporting them. Dealing with the widely held Catholic view that the British paratroopers had "run amok," Widgery found that there was no general breakdown of discipline. For the most part, the soldiers had acted as they did because they thought that their orders required it. No order and no training could ensure that a soldier would always act wisely, as well as bravely and with initiative. The individual soldier ought not to have to bear the burden of deciding whether to open fire in confusion, such as prevailed on January 30. In the conditions prevailing in Northern Ireland, however, this is often inescapable. If the army had persisted in its "low key" attitude and had not launched a large-scale operation to arrest hooligans, the day might have passed without serious incident. (Edited excerpts from the Report of the Widgery Tribunal, London, HMSO, H.L.101/H.C.220, 1972.)

3. The first border poll, held on March 8, 1973, resulted in 591,820 voting to remain part of the United Kingdom and a mere 6,463 saying that they wanted to join the Irish Republic. The poll was generally boycotted by the Nationalist population.

4. *The Compton Report: Allegations against the Security Forces of Physical Brutality in Northern Ireland*, HMSO, London, Cmnd 4823, 1971.

5. *The Future of Northern Ireland: A Paper for Discussion*, London, HMSO, 1972, (f).

6. Northern Ireland Constitutional Proposals, HMSO, London, Cmnd 5259, 1973, Paragraph 93.

7. Lynch resigned as Taoiseach (prime minister) at the end of 1979 and, after a tightly contested Fianna Fail ballot, he was succeeded by Haughey—whose party lost the June, 1981, general election, to a Fine Gael/Labour alliance supported by a few independent members, but regained power with the support of Independent deputies in the February, 1982, election.

8. *The Future of Northern Ireland*: par. 78.

9. Source: Northern Ireland Office.

10. Sean MacStiofain, David O'Connell, Gerry Adams, Seamus Twomey, Martin McGuinness and Ivor Bell.

11. MacStiofain and McGuinness, together with the former (unified) IRA chief of staff, O'Brady. O'Connell, believed to be MacStiofain's immediate successor as the IRA's military leader, escaped the police swoop on that occasion.

12. As originally provided for under the 1920 Government of Ireland Act, but never implemented.

13. Richard Deutsch and Vivien Magowan, *Northern Ireland: A Chronology of Events* (Belfast: Blackstaff Press, 1972–73), vol. 2, p. 282.

14. By the spring of the following year, when a snap general election was called in Britain, that majority had become a minority, as Ulster candidates opposed to power sharing and the Council of Ireland captured almost 59 percent of the total Ulster vote.

15. The political wing of the Provisionals refused to trade the bullet for the ballot and did not contest the Assembly elections. The Republican clubs did, and this political front for the Official IRA captured a mere 1.81 percent of the popular vote, and not a single Assembly seat. The tiny Communist party did even worse, gaining just 123 votes!

6 Sunningdale and After

The Irish Government fully accepted and solemnly declared that there could be no change in the status of Northern Ireland until a majority of the people of Northern Ireland desired a change in that status.

The British Government solemnly declared that it was, and would remain, its policy to support the wishes of the majority of the people of Northern Ireland. The present status of Northern Ireland is that it is part of the United Kingdom. If, in the future, the majority of the people of Northern Ireland should indicate a wish to become part of a United Ireland, the British Government would support that wish.

These formal declarations, placed not as here but parallel across the page of the final communiqué,[1] in order to demonstrate an equality of commitment, emerged from the Anglo-Irish conference held at Sunningdale in England between representatives of the London and Dublin governments and the three Ulster parties committed to power sharing and a new Council of Ireland. It took place over four days (and one all-night session) at the end of 1973. This summit meeting included the British and Irish prime ministers, leaders of the Official Unionists, the SDLP, and Alliance, and a collection of ministerial colleagues and specialist advisers. It did not include the hard-line Ulster Protestant leaders who were gradually gaining ascendancy with most Northern Protestants.

The Dublin government's solemn declaration was an attempt to reassure anyone open to reasonable persuasion that the Irish Republic accepted, however reluctantly, the existing constitutional status of Ulster, while still harboring an aspiration for national unity. The British declaration was designed to assure both Dublin and Ulster's Catholic Nationalists that London would not stand in the way of eventual Irish unity, provided a majority in Northern Ireland could be persuaded to accept it. Meanwhile, the proposed Council of Ireland was seen as a rather loose and largely consultative cross-border body to encourage harmonious relations between

79

the two parts of Ireland and to advance some useful cooperation in economic, social, and cultural affairs. Importantly, the Dublin side undertook to prosecute, in its jurisdiction, those accused of violence, "however motivated," even if committed in Ulster. This was intended to appease those Ulster Protestants who could not understand, or who claimed that they could not, why courts in the Republic almost invariably refuse to extradite to the North prisoners being sought for crimes allegedly committed there, but who insist that they were guilty, if at all, of "political offenses."

The Sunningdale breakthrough, including an earlier agreement on the composition of a new power-sharing executive in Belfast, was heralded by some as a new dawn in Irish affairs and in Anglo-Irish relations. Edward Heath, the British prime minister, won warm and spontaneous praise when he reported on it to the House of Commons at Westminster. Senator Edward Kennedy in Washington suggested that Whitelaw deserved a Nobel Prize "for his towering success in the cause of peace." But Ulster Protestant factions not represented at Sunningdale saw things in a different light. Paisley termed the package a "massive confidence trick, an experiment to bluff the people," and he claimed that Faulkner had been "out-flanked, out-maneuvred and out-witted." Some of Faulkner's former cabinet colleagues and previous supporters in the Unionist Party called for a special meeting of the all-powerful Unionist Council to ask him to justify decisions he had taken at Sunningdale "in our name but without our authority." Terence O'Neill, the former Ulster premier, thought Sunningdale a "wonderful achievement," but he reflected that a Protestant backlash was likely, adding that "extremists, North and South, have tended to win in the past." The Provisional IRA, in a formal statement, said that the agreement had contributed nothing to peace; "the struggle for freedom will continue until a peace, based on justice, is secured." In the Republic of Ireland the Fianna Fail leader, Lynch, gave a cautious immediate response but observed that the Cosgrave government's solemn declaration could be in conflict with the republic's constitutional claim to the whole island territory of Ireland.

The new Ulster Assembly approved the Sunningdale package by a margin of sixteen votes; the majority in the Dail in Dublin was a mere five. The year 1974 in Ulster was designated as a "Year of Reconciliation," but precisely 179 days later, the fragile attempt to establish a Protestant-Catholic power-sharing structure in Northern Ireland had collapsed, brought down finally by a well-organized, politically motivated industrial strike by Ulster Protestant workers, backed by paramilitary forces, which the British government failed to confront adequately, or in time. In any event, Faulkner had been pushed by the Dublin and London governments to sell too much in one package to a Protestant people with whom he no longer enjoyed anything like majority support.

In Ulster, Protestant extremists and critics of the Sunningdale formula soon merged in a loose amalgam called the United Ulster Unionist Council (UUUC) and effectively joined forces to destroy Sunningdale with Protestant paramilitary factions and the Ulster Workers Council. Faulkner and his acceptance of the Anglo-Irish package were rejected by the Ulster Unionist Council, and he was obliged to resign as party leader. He remained as chief executive in the Assembly, but no longer with any real political base in the constituencies. A premature general election in Britain the following spring was seen there as largely a trial of strength between Heath's Conservative government and trade unions unwilling to accept an incomes policy; in Northern Ireland, it was largely a popular referendum on Sunningdale, and the concept of power-sharing and of links with the Irish Republic was well and truly buried. Anti-Sunningdale candidates won eleven of the twelve Ulster seats at Westminster. This UUUC landslide was resisted only in West Belfast, the political base of the veteran socialist who was then leader of the SDLP, Gerry Fitt. In London the Heath government gave way to a Labour administration, once again under Harold Wilson, and a new Labour secretary of state, Merlyn Rees, was named to oversee Ulster affairs. Others were to follow.

Events were moving quickly, however. As ever, the violence continued, and with some appalling sectarian murders. The Ulster Workers Council, which shared offices in East Belfast with Craig's hardline Vanguard Unionist Progressive party, part of the UUUC alliance, expressed "total dissatisfaction" with Sunningdale, adding in a statement: "Should the wishes of the workers be cast aside, grave industrial consequences will ensue." Less than three weeks later, approximately one-third (308,410) of all Ulster Protestants had signed a petition opposing the Sunningdale package in toto, although an opinion poll one week later showed that the Council of Ireland component, the institutionalized link with the Irish Republic, had generated the greatest Protestant opposition. The poll, conducted for the state-operated British Broadcasting Corporation's (BBC) Belfast region, indicated that 69 percent of the Ulster sample favored giving the new power-sharing executive a chance to

prove itself, whereas a minority 41 percent thought the Council of
Ireland a good idea.

By early in May 1974, the Ulster Workers' Council was threatening a power blackout in the province and possibly an all-out strike if
the executive was not brought down. There followed in rapid suc-
cession partial power cuts, food shortages, long queues at gasoline
stations, which had limited supplies, and the threat of a total breakdown of the sewerage system throughout Belfast. At Westminster,
Prime Minister Wilson declared: "This is not only a political strike;
it is a sectarian strike aimed at destroying decisions taken by this
House," while Gerry Fitt, Faulkner's Catholic deputy in the Ulster
executive, called on Wilson to use the British army to take control
of the power stations and the oil depots and "to maintain the essen-
tials of life in this community." In a developing crisis atmosphere
the Cosgrave government in Dublin recalled most of its army personnel serving with the United Nations peacekeeping forces in the
Middle East, after twenty-seven people had died in two major
bomb explosions in the Irish Republic, assumed to be the work of
Ulster Protestant extremists. More British troops were flown into
Northern Ireland, but London did little to demonstrate that it had
the political will to face the political strike in Ulster head-on, with
military means, if necessary. There were rumblings that senior
British army offiicers were reluctant to confront striking Protestant
workers.[2] Finally, on May 27, British army units were moved into
petrol distribution stations, and the Protestant leadership responded by calling an all-out strike. The power-sharing executive
fell the next day, with Faulkner noting in a resignation statement:
"From the extent of support for the present [industrial] stoppage, it
has become apparent that the degree of consent needed to sustain
the Executive does not now exist." He urged London to open
"some sort of dialogue between Government and those confronting
it."[3] The loyalist hard-liners had won out. The British government
resumed direct rule in the province and, despite a number of
major initiatives since then to break the sectarian logjam, it still
continues in Northern Ireland at this writing. So, too, does the
murderous violence.

Theories abound on the genesis of the Ulster conflict. It has
provided a case study in intercommunal confrontation, which has
attracted political thinkers, sociologists, psychologists, revolutionaries, and even evangelists, and the events of the past decade, and

more, have produced a veritable flood of literature and commentary, some of it of useful scholarship. Long before recent events there, Ireland and its bitter history had come before the eye or the pen of such leaders as Karl Marx and Friedrich Engels, Winston Churchill and Edmund Burke, Mahatma Gandhi, Alexis de Tocqueville and Gustave de Beaumont, Giuseppe Mazzini and Camillo di Cavour. In the sixteenth century, Catholic Spain was interested in an alliance with Irish "rebel" leaders against Tudor England; at the close of the eighteenth, republican France was sending military aid—with little benefit, as it turned out—to Tone's United Irishmen; in the nineteenth century came extensive Irish-American backing for the Fenian revolutionaries; and Nazi Germany's military command studied the possibilities of an Irish landing aimed at Britain's "back door" during World War II. All this interest in a small island country with a total population less than half that of Greater London, or equal to that of Rome and Milan combined, and a land area two-thirds the size of New York State!

The "Irish question" plagued British politics for much of the nineteenth century, and up to 1920; it is again a major unresolved issue in the British political arena, and one that a majority in the three main parties at Westminster would now be glad to be rid of, in almost any circumstances. The Irish themselves have difficulty in explaining it; the English find it an incomprehensible mixture of tribalism and a religious war seemingly without end. Most Irish nationalists worry, deep down, about the political, economic, social, and cultural consequences of the possible absorption of a million reluctant Ulster Protestants in an All-Ireland republic. Honest and impartial observers ask reasonably whether the Ulster problem today is not further away from a solution than when the civil rights campaign exploded in the late 1960s. It is, truly, an intractable problem of majority-minority tensions, which artificial formulas are unlikely immediately to resolve, although unconventional ones just might help toward a long-term resolution. Terence O'Neill, the first important political victim of the civil rights protest, observed publicly before being driven from the premiership: "We have people genuinely trying to be helpful who advocate a kind of reciprocal emasculation. No national anthem or loyal (to the monarch) toasts to offend one side; no outward signs and symbols of nationalism to offend the other. This approach, too, I believe to be misconceived; it is rather like trying to solve the colour problem by spraying everyone a pale shade of brown."

The Irish writer Liam de Paor also touched on the racial parallel. "In Northern Ireland, Catholics are Blacks who happen to have white skins. This is not a truth. It is an over-simplification, and too facile an analogy. But it is a better over-simplification than that which sees the struggle and conflict in Northern Ireland in terms of religion.[4] To de Paor, racial distinction between "colonists and natives is expressed in terms of religion." Others[5] see the conflict in terms of a "battle between two religious systems carried on in the field of politics." Both explanations must sound quite archaic to those removed from the quarrel, given that we are moving toward the end of the second millennium of supposed Christian enlightenment. Others would argue that the two Ulster communities appear to be living still in the Dark Ages, and even earlier, with ordinary charity absent in some inverse ratio to the importance placed on religious identity, or at least professed support for a particular religion. In Ulster today, identity and profession are not always the same thing—with either community. The Reverend Martin Smith, grand master of the Protestant Orange Order, made this point tellingly with his comment:" They [Protestants in Belfast's Shankill area] are Bible lovers even if not Bible readers,"[6] and no doubt many of Ulster's Catholic priests could make parallel observations on some of their own flock. Religion in Ulster is a mark of national identity; those for the Union are Protestant, whereas most Catholics are republicans at heart. To refer again to the Wright argument, there is an essentially religiopolitical conception of the nature of Ulster politics, which places the conflict in terms of the battle between two religious systems carried on in the field of politics. There is effectively a national-political conception of the nature of the conflict. This postulates the Catholic allegiance to a united Ireland and the Protestant loyalty to Britain as two rival and irreconcilable national aspirations.

This association of Ulster Protestantism with support for the Union—and Catholicism with the Irish nationalist aspiration—is at the heart of the matter. It is aggravated by the fact that many Ulster Protestants perceive, and are encouraged by such religious leaders as Paisley so to believe, that an important theological divide is superimposed on the national-political divide. The theological argument rests at the basis of evangelical fundamentalism, and certainly of Paisley's variety, that the Bible contains the one true message available to all who read and study it, in a sense an individualistic interpretation. The Catholic church, in the Paisleyan theory, is simply an unnecessary interventionalist element, with priests imposing themselves to undermine this essential individual liberty and to interpret, or, he would say, often to misrepresent, the true Wisdom, the Word of God, for Catholics grouped in an hierarchial monolith, and with positive political undertones. To this theological argument should be added the traditional fact that, for varying reasons, including in particular the British-imposed Penal Laws in Ireland, Catholic priests have long held an important status as community (in this context, that means political as well) leaders, and it is easy to associate religious commitment with nationalist intent. The situation in parts of Ulster, and predominantly in Belfast, and even more so resulting from major population movements in the recent past, is such that Protestants and Catholics tend increasingly to live isolated one from the other, a situation stemming from intimidation or fears of sectarian mob attacks, fears that are not without good cause. This separation has resulted, inevitably, in perceived notions taking on, in time, the certainty of "facts." It encourages almost spontaneously—and is added to deliberately by partisan leaders, religious and political— the emergence of an accepted body of ideas, myths, and theories that one community holds about the other, whatever the underlying facts. The outcome of this acquired or inspired conventional wisdom is that most Protestants mistrust Catholics, at least collectively, and vice versa. Protestants believe that Catholics are interested ultimately only in undermining the constitutional status of Ulster, of which Protestants, and especially the working class, see themselves as being the automatic defenders.

If some economic components are also added in, the sectarian divide is as complete as it is today in Northern Ireland. The economy of the province is far from buoyant; a decade and more of continuous terrorist violence and sectarian conflict have combined to make Ulster unattractive for foreign investors, despite generous British governmental financial subsidies to new industries in the area. The rate of Ulster unemployment is consistently higher than in the rest of the United Kingdom—as high as one in four of the labor force in some (mainly Catholic) areas—and it is easy to persuade those Ulster Protestants who do not themselves recognize it instinctively that conceding equal rights to Catholics, including more equal access to job opportunities, would damage them economically. Considering the fact that most of their leaders assure them—and most Protestants believe it anyway without much persuasion—that Catholics demanding civil rights will never be satisfied, ultimately, until they have secured national independence for the whole of Ireland, it is easier to appreciate from whence the Protestant intransigence comes, and the rigidity with which it is held. That, today, is at the heart of Protestant resistance to change, to power sharing, and, even more so, to the acceptance of any form of collaboration with the Irish Republic. Ironically, many Protestants would seem to prefer the terrible and violent status quo to any major political changes.

NOTES

1. See appendixes for full official text.
2. This is reminiscent of the"Curragh mutiny." See p. 46.
3. Premier Wilson said of the UWC strike in an interview on the (British) ITN "News at Ten" program: "This is a totally unconstitutional thing which we have never met before in any part of the United Kingdom." See Richard Deutsch and Vivien Magowan, *Northern Ireland: A Chronology of Events* (Belfast: Blackstaff Press, 1968–74), vol. 3, p. 83.
4. Liam de Paor, *Divided Ulster*, (London: Penguin Books, 1970).
5. Frank Wright, "Protestant Ideology and Politics," *Arch. Europ. Sociol.*, 1973, p. 223.
6. Ibid., p. 245.

PART II

Italian Communists

1 What Makes the Italian

Italy was never an easy country to reduce under one rule.

Francesco Guicciardini

Contemporary community cleavage in the Italian state today is based much less on ethnological, cultural, or religious divides but has more of an ideological, socioeconomic, and geographical basis. Yet, a brief look at Italian history is not irrelevant to this study, not least to isolate the inputs of the past that go to make up the Italians of the present, to appreciate why they think and behave as they do, and also to differentiate between them. Later, the cleavage, and some of its causes, will emerge.

Guicciardini reached one conclusion; his Florentine contemporary Niccolò Machiavelli added an explanation, which, in its time at least, was partly true.

It is the [Catholic] Church which has kept, and keeps, Italy divided. No country has ever been united and happy unless the whole has been under the jurisdiction of one republic, or one prince, as has happened in France and Spain. And the reason why Italy is not the same is due entirely to the Church. For, though the Church has its headquarters in Italy and has temporal power, neither its power nor its virtue has been sufficiently great for it to be able to usurp power in Italy and become its leader; nor yet, on the other hand, has it been so weak that it could not, when afraid of losing its dominion over things temporal, call upon one of the [foreign] powers to defend it against an Italian state that had become too powerful. The Church, then, has neither been able to occupy the whole of Italy, nor has it allowed anyone else to occupy it. Consequently, it has been the cause why Italy has never come under one head.[1]

Italy as a unified entity—to the limited extent that it is such today—is a mere 120 years old, and some of its present tensions are those inevitable in a new state and a newer (since 1946) republic. As recently as the middle of the nineteenth century, the Austrians were still in the north (Lombardy-Venetia), the Bourbons were in the south and in Sicily, and Pius IX and his reactionary secretary of state, Cardinal Giacomo Antonelli, held the papal states supported by the French. The leading advocate of orthodox republicanism and national unity was the Genoese, Giuseppe Mazzini, and his underground society, Giovane Italia (Young Italy), was in its day what contemporary observers would describe as a terrorist organization. In Piedmont, the House of Savoy and, in particular, King Emmanuel II's prime minister, Count Camillo di Cavour, shared Mazzini's commitment to Italian unity, but not, of course, his republicanism, and it was Cavour who contrived an alliance with France against Austria. However, Piedmont's policy was seen in most of Italy more as one of annexation than of unification and, following Garibaldi's surprisingly easy taking of Sicily and southern Italy in 1860 (the celebrated Expedition of The Thousand, the famous Garibaldi Red Shirts), most Italians viewed the Piedmontese more as conquerors than liberators. The cession by Austria of Venetia and the final defeat of the papal forces a decade later, with the pope retiring permanently to the Vatican as Italian troops entered Rome (the *Breccia di Porta Pia*), brought about the geographical but not the popular unification of Italy.

In truth, most Italians had never sought actively to unify their country. The risorgimento, or rebirth, was a minority campaign of liberals and progressives among the aristocracy and the educated among the bourgeoisie.[2] The masses remained indifferent, or skeptical, for a deep mistrust of any central authority is inbred in Italians who believe—now as then—that rigid laws and national discipline are for others, not themselves. Machiavelli blamed the church for standing in the way of national unity, for alternatively encouraging some foreign invaders and resisting others down the centuries as it suited best its own (temporal) interests. Yet the church was as much a product of the Italian character as its creator, for have not Italians themselves largely dominated its hierarchical structure for most of two millennia?

Imperial Rome had administratively structured provinces in Britain, Spain, Germany, and Gaul, but Italy itself managed to remain what Barzini[3] referred to as "a vast mosaic of free cities, partly autonomous regions, rebellious mountain tribes, almost independent peoples with their dialects, gods and customs." The Middle Ages were little different. Vast armies from the north

crossed the Alps in the spring when the snows had melted and subjugated the Italians, usually without much resistance and often with splendid public shows of native loyalty to the invaders combined with private plotting to undermine them. Italians joined enthusiastically with the popes against the empire and quickly switched allegiances when the former became too powerful. Italians have seldom been permanently committed Guelphs or Ghibellines. To quote Barzini again:

> Italians have never felt that they were a "new" people, one of those immature and semi-barbaric nations which needed harsh laws and iron discipline to maintain a semblance of civilized order when the Roman Empire disappeared. The Italians felt much too old and wise to become imitation northerners. They clung to the decayed remnants of Roman ways which, like all decayed remnants, were sweet and comfortable enough for them. Neither could they abandon the memory of their past greatness, a memory which was strong even when, in the darkest ages, it was but a dim and fabulous legend. It was not only strong enough to prevent the victory of foreign ideas and institutions, but was also a good substitute for them. The Italians felt themselves sufficiently unified, morally and culturally anyway, to want political and military unification. They were held together by their language, ruins, arts, literature, habits, ruses, the fame of their great men, and the memory of their great saints.[4]

Like Barzini almost five centuries later, Guicciardini, himself no mean survivor under changing regimes, had a perceptive insight into the Italian character, and he had much advice to offer in the art of survival, an art that Italians today acquire not so much from their mother's knee as from an instinct that to them is second nature. There are, to be sure, some exceptions, and Guicciardini, too, had these in mind: "I do not blame those who, enflamed by love of country, defy dangers to establish liberty and popular rule, though I think that what they do is extremely risky. Few revolutions succeed and, when they do, you often discover they do not gain you what you had hoped for, and you condemn yourself to perpetual fear, as the parties you defeated may always regain power and work for your ruin."[5] This philosophy explains much of Italy's history of successful foreign invasions and occupations, princely rivalries internally, and national humiliation through the centuries. Guicciardini's recommended formula for personal survival is equally understood today by Italians: "Those men conduct their affairs well who keep in front of their eyes their own private interest and measure all their actions according to their necessities." As a principle for life, it is as Italian as spaghetti.

This principle is the essential survival kit for all Italians taught to them by their own history. Whatever rendering there may be to God, there is precious little rendering spontaneously to Caesar. Few Italians identify with the state or its supporting and often overbearing bureaucracy unless, of course, they are a part of it, and thus able to use it for their personal gain and advancement. In Italy the state and its institutions are always suspect, and the great mass of Italians feel no need actively to sustain them. They tolerate them because they must (Italians spend more time in queues before official windows and doors, and often to less effect, than any other Europeans), but there is little respect and even less confidence, and the base instinct is to cheat. This is not because Italians are less principled than any others, or less truthful or honest. Their history has shown them how to survive, and largely with their own resources, because their masters did little to help and much to exploit. Nothing much has changed.

Throughout history many Italians understood well that independence and national unity were infinitely preferable to internal fragmentation and foreign tyranny, but they never believed that unity was possible. Today deep down they wish for decent, fair, and efficient rule, for a just society that cherishes all the children of the nation equally, or at least with reasonable equity, but they have little hope that it will come about, so they had best do what they can to look after themselves and their own. They are loyal, but it is a loyalty to family and friend, and to the region of their birth, not to the state or, necessarily, to their country. They are Milanese, Neopolitans, Romans, or whatever, before they are Italians. They are marvelously inventive, frequently highly cultured, mostly hardworking (at least in the North), often generous, courteous, talkative, but careful about what they say in public, warm, emotional, and, almost invariably, disappointed with their lot in life. In a word, they are Italians.

What has gone into making these people? It is generally conceded that Italy attained a unified ethnolinguistic, political, and cultural physiognomy only following the Roman conquest, and detailed knowledge of pre-Roman Italy is limited by the scarcity and unreliability of sources. What is clear is that Italy emerged from a confluence of two great civilizations, Greek and Etruscan. The meeting of these two marked the birth of an Italian civilization

dominated by Rome, which itself was the starting point of civilization in the whole of Western Europe and beyond. Each contributed much to the Italian national character and to the country's
diversity. The early organizational, industrial, and trading patterns
of the Etruscans merged with the cultural and civil enlightenment
of the Greeks. The high point of the Etruscan period constituted
the most important political, economic, and cultural nucleus in the
Italian area, excluding *Magna Graecia* in the south, and Rome
itself was imprinted deeply with Etruscan influences, not the least
in urban planning, architecture, art, technology, and dress. Rome
in turn was to codify laws, end class and opportunity discrimination
(as between plebians and patricians), establish state schools, provide pensions for war veterans, create a fiscal mechanism based on
individual revenue rather than status, and, even in those far-off
days, adopt measures to combat inflation, including price controls.
Rome founded many of Europe's capitals, and the foundations of
Roman legislation can be traced in Anglo-Saxon laws and legislation of the Western world in general. Before the collapse of the
Roman Empire, the power and status of Rome had been enhanced
by the growth of Christianity, which made Rome both the political
and religious center of the civilized world.

The fusion of these Greek and Etruscan inputs gradually made
the Italian whole, but other influences were added through the
centuries, from France, Germany, Austria, Spain, and Arab North
Africa. The result is not homogeneous; Italians in the north demonstrate a practicality and efficiency that is largely an inheritance
from Austro-Hungarian influence; in the south the cultural influences are Greek, Arab, and a carry-over from feudal Spain, the
last in particular injecting a general indolence and disdain for useful and productive occupations. (Italian bureaucracy is filled with
southerners.)

Foreign oppression down through its history, the political duplicity of popes, civil wars, the concentrations of wealth and power in
the hands of the few, and a failure to preserve the political virtues
and the sense of civic responsibility that characterized the early
Romans—all have combined to produce in Italians a dedication to
personal survival at all cost, together with a mistrust of, or general
indifference to, the central state. These characteristics remain today. Northern industrialists cynically describe taxes as something
collected by a bureaucracy based in Rome to be squandered away
in useless investment in the economically depressed south in a
policy dictated more by political considerations than economic

logic. Individual Italians, like most people elsewhere, dislike paying taxes, but Italians go to great extremes and use considerable
inventiveness to avoid paying them. Their motivation is not only to
preserve what wealth they have; it stems equally from a firm conviction that taxation collected will be misspent through bureaucratic inefficiency or political corruption, or most likely both.
Machiavelli advanced "reasons of state" as being the only measure
of political wisdom, and from his standpoint all ethical and religious
criteria were irrelevant. Today's Italians, or most of them anyway,
are convinced that reasons of party politics and the personal advancement and financial gain of leading politicians are the main
measures of political wisdom, and certainly not the betterment of
the state and the well-being of its people. It is an atmosphere and
an attitude not conducive to the emergence of civic spirit or a
public philosophy, and, in Italy, it is not without historical precedent. The nepotism of the past—at which the popes were such
master practitioners that their behavior gave the word its origins—
is the political *clientelismo* of today, and in Italy it is all pervasive.

I will add one final Barzini gem to end this necessarily broad-
brush picture of today's Italians and what has gone into their making, and also to demonstrate that not much has changed through
the years.

Take a small oligarchy of leaders, eternally squabbling among
themselves, frightened for their position and, often enough, for
their lives. Put these leaders above the law and this tends to
make the best of them wary, pitiless, overbearing, unscrupulous
and avaricious. In the old days, such men were courtiers, landowning aristocrats, high dignitaries, and generals; later they
were bankers,[6] shipowners and industrialists; yesterday they
were Fascist chieftains. Today they are the heads of the mass
political parties. . . . When one forgets superficial variations, one
can see that Italian leaders of today behave more or less as their
predecessors have always behaved. They manage Italy as if it
were their own *(cosa nostra);* they carry out vast, ambitious,
impressive political designs which are described as essential to
the welfare of the country, but are brutally and transparently
conceived mainly to reinforce their own power. They use the
people as if they were extras on a Graeco-Roman film set, to be
moved by remote control, to whom nobody explains the plot.
Anything else would be unthinkable.[7]

All Italians can see through this transparency by the light of their own history. However, the rulers, too, are Italian, and they share, to a greater or less degree, the national traits of the ruled; only the vantage points are different.

NOTES

1. Text from Fr. Leslie Walker's translation in *The Discourses of Niccolò Machiavelli* (London: Routledge and Kegan Paul, 1950), based on *Tutte le opere storiche e letterarie di Niccolò Machiavelli*, ed. Guido Mazzoni and Mario Casella (Florence: Barbera, 1929).

2. Revolutionary thought in Italy has invariably come from the so-called intelligentsia. It was so, for example, in the early days of the Socialist party, and many of the ideologists of today's various terrorist organizations are from the same class.

3. Luigi Barzini, *The Italians*, New York: Atheneum, 1964; Bantam ed., 1965, p. 345.

4. Ibid., p. 345.

5. Ricordi Francesco Guicciardini, ed. Raffaele Spongano (Florence: Sansoni, 1951).

6. Italy was the birthplace of modern international banking; for example, Monte dei Paschi di Siena was advertising itself internationally in 1981 as the bank "which is 509 years young," having been founded in 1472—or a couple of decades before the discovery of the Americas.

7. Barzini, *The Italians*, pp. 342–43.

2 Communism and Fascism in Italy

Italy at the time of its geographical unification under the Piedmont monarchy was a tender flower. A political, economic, and social gulf divided the country. No more than 2 percent of its then 26 million people enjoyed electoral rights on the basis of a property suffrage; an estimated four in every five of the population were illiterate, and they worked mainly in agriculture. The peasant masses were predominantly Catholic; the ruling class was generally anticlerical, made up largely of banking and industrial barons from Piedmont and Tuscans steeped in commerce and transportation. The great economic imbalance between north and south, aggravated by the free-trade policies of the early right-wing politicians, led to peasant riots and widespread banditry, which were put down harshly. Centralized rule tended to be authoritarian, even under such relatively moderate leaders as Agostino Depretis, Francesco Crispi, and Giovanni Giolitti. The early bicameral parliaments under the constitutional monarchy—senators appointed by the king, deputies popularly elected but by a mere handful of the people who had the vote—put great emphasis on the need for a national consensus to advance solutions for the many problems facing the country, an attitude that often saw principles giving way to the seen—by the ruling few—national best interest. Many old risorgimento democrats shifted away from Mazzinian republicanism and accepted the monarchist-liberal philosophy. Large coalitions, governments of national unity, became the trend, a tendency mirrored in Italy in most of the three dozen and more governments in Rome since the end of World War II. This trend tended to immobilize the political process, leaving little real opposition within Parliament and establishing a tradition of extraparliamentary activity, which today is all too apparent. In the closing decades of the last century, however, came the emergency of two political movements, one socialist, the other Catholic, which

97

were to dominate Italian politics right up to the present day. The
Italian Socialist party (PSI) was founded in 1892, followed early in
the new century by the rise of a trade-union movement, itself
divided along socialist and Catholic orientations. Meanwhile, the
dark clouds of war were spreading in Europe.

World War I had brought a peace of sorts to Europe, but it had
done much more besides. It had raised the expectations of the
masses, not the least in Italy, which had suffered greatly. More
than half a million Italians had died in the fighting, and a similar
number were left mutilated, and all in a war for which there had
been little popular support—and much opposition—within Italy
itself. The economy was in ruins; inflation was rampant. Soldiers
had come home from the front with more advanced notions of
democracy; the troops had been promised rich rewards for their
suffering, the peasants had been promised land, the unemployed,
jobs. Having emerged from the hell of fighting, they awaited the
manna—impatiently. In Russia, Lenin and his Bolsheviks were
cementing their revolution and holding out the promise of a new
tomorrow of mass equality, the dictatorship of the proletariat, and
their revolutionary example did not go unnoticed elsewhere. The
prewar dreams of a socialist nirvana in Europe had come to naught,
and the continent's socialist parties were in disarray, or worse, rent
in factions mostly agreeing on the need for revolution but in bitter
conflict as to means and also on the precise ends desired.

Perhaps nowhere was this conflict and confusion greater than in
Italy within the PSI. Pietro Nenni, then an emerging personality in
the party and later its leader, recalled the immediate postwar atmosphere of expectation: "All the extraordinary and clamorous
events at the end of 1918 and the beginning of 1919 fired the
imagination, and inspired the hope that the old world was about to
collapse and that humanity was on the threshold of a new era and a
new social order."[1] As early as December 1918, the directorate of
the PSI had called for the establishment of a dictatorship of the
proletariat. Three months later the party in a majority decision
abandoned the Second International in favor of the new Soviet
creation, the Comintern, which before long was dictating its gospel
of pure revolution uncontaminated by reformists, gradualists, or
any others seeking to erode the capitalist house from within a
democratic structure, or waiting for what many Italian socialists
believed then was the inevitable collapse of the capitalist society.
In the shadows, either unnoticed by the warring socialist factions
or ignored by them, the specter of fascism was spreading in Italy.

Benito Mussolini had been expelled from the PSI for campaigning to get Italy into the war, and his postwar appeal to national dignity and awareness, coupled with demands for firm leadership and law and order, took hold with many of the returning soldiers, with industrialists worried by the advance of trade-union "militancy," with conservative peasants, with many of the old-guard politicians alarmed over rising social tensions in the country, and with a Vatican increasingly critical of what it saw as a developing tide of Communist ideology.

In the elections[2] in November 1919, the PSI captured almost one-third of the vote, the first in Italy on the basis of universal (albeit male) suffrage. The nominally nondenominational Italian Popular party, in fact a Catholic political grouping founded earlier the same year by Don Luigi Sturzo and the forerunner of today's Christian Democrats, won 100 seats with just over a fifth of the total vote. The outcome left the former coalition parties virtually impotent because to maintain an administration required either the backing of the increasingly divided socialists or of the populists, and neither formula was likely to make for stable government. The PSI had campaigned in the election on a platform that was ambiguous on the question of revolution and confused on economic and social issues. In capsule, the managers of the PSI were left-wing and prorevolution, although with conflicting ideas on how change should be brought about. The party in parliament was generally reformist, although it made suitable revolutionary noises when they were considered appropriate or thought to be electorally useful. The socialist electorate reflected this divide, although it was more reformist than revolutionary, and many showed a growing acceptance, if not wholly with enthusiasm, of the catchall policies of Mussolini. A notable exception to this socialist profile was the industrialized city and former parliamentary seat of Turin. There the workers were best organized, and the revolutionary zeal was strongest. Factory councils were established as minisoviets, and a young Sicilian hunchback, Antonio Gramsci, was at work trying to educate the masses in revolutionary theory, to prepare them and the PSI leadership for a Communist takeover on the basis of workers' hegemony, a hegemony that he more than any other socialist insisted would have to include the southern peasants.*

Gramsci was among the founding fathers of the Italian Communist party (PCI), its leading ideologist, and, the party today insists,

---

*In the 1919 election, only one in ten of PSI deputies came from the South.

its guiding inspiration ever since. He is for Italian Communists their own messiah, and persistent and, not infrequently, tortuous and often ingenious efforts are made by PCI leaders to demonstrate that the party has never strayed from true Gramscian principles and philosophy. *L'Unita*, the party daily, marked the fortieth anniversary of Gramsci's death with a special issue containing thoughts and tributes by the party's leading faithful, including in particular an interesting contribution by Paolo Bufalini of the PCI's executive committee, which appeared to acknowledge some seen anomalies and then to dismiss them as an "insidious maneuvre" by anti-Communists and on the part of "some left-wing scholars and political figures of Marxist inspiration and socialist orientation."[3] Bufalini noted a criticism (which he repeated but did not satisfactorily answer) that many have directed against the PCI: "Either you Communists are sincere in your present positions on the democratic national road to socialism and political pluralism, in which case you have thrown out Lenin and also Gramsci's conception of the revolution and the State and become a social democratic party that accepts capitalism and seeks to secure a place for itself in the bourgeois power system. Or you are still a revolutionary force, in which case your professions of democratic faith are not sincere and the democrats are quite right not to trust you."[4]

Antonio Gramsci ("He is justly considered, in substance, the real founder" of the PCI[5]), was born in Ales, Sardinia, on January 22, 1891, the fourth of seven children of a minor functionary. A fall as a child left him hunchbacked and in poor and progressively deteriorating health for the remainder of his life. Following early schooling, he left Sardinia for Turin on a scholarship and entered the Faculty of Letters at the university there to study modern philology. One of his first acquaintances, equally impoverished, was Palmiro Togliatti; he was subsequently, like Gramsci himself, to be the PCI representative in Moscow and, later still, the top party leader in Italy. The two students were soon to be joined by two members of the Turin Young Socialist faction, Angelo Tasca and Umberto Terracini, all four regrouping following World War I as members of the editorial board of a new revolutionary publication, *L'Ordine nuovo*, a weekly that first appeared on May Day, 1919.

In his penetrating study of Gramsci, Cammett noted: "This journal is important in the history of the Italian labour movement for two reasons: first, because the men associated with *L'Ordine nuovo* became in time the directing nucleus of the Italian Communist

Party; and second, because the newspaper was a vehicle for Gramsci's campaign to organize Italian soviets *(consigli di fabbrica)*, and the soviet was a crucial issue in the immediate post-war period."[6] It was in the columns of *L'Ordine nuovo* that Gramsci first spelled out his own philosophy of revolution toward workers' hegemony,[7] with an interim period for educating the masses, and also about the need to use the existing parliamentary system if only to prevent power from being seized by others while the revolution was being prepared. Indeed, he himself was elected to Parliament in 1924[8] as a Communist deputy for the Veneto constituency, the PCI having been formed some three years earlier after an open split in socialist ranks at the PSI's 17th congress in Liverno. The long-standing divides within the PSI had become more marked and more open following the Russian Revolution and the social tensions within Italy itself arising from the war, and the editorial columns of *L'Ordine nuovo*[9] were a regular vehicle for Gramscian reflections on syndicalism, maximalism, anarchism, the correct tactics of the revolutionary, Italian nationalism, and socialist attitudes toward the war, but, above all else, his own ideas of the role of intellectuals in the revolutionary movement.

The Liverno congress saw the formal launching of the Italian Communist party. Scheduled originally for Florence, the congress venue was changed under intimidation from Mussolini's Fascists, yet the PSI's deliberations at Liverno paid scant regard to the Fascist threat and concentrated instead on internal wranglings and conflicting attitudes to the Comintern. The party at that time was made up of reformists (basically social democrats) and Marxists of varying hues, including abstentionists, Gramsci's Ordine Nuovo faction, and a few left maximalists. In the final vote to accept the theses of the Communist International the so-called pure Communists were in a minority; they quit the party, adjourned to the Teatro San Marco, and formed the "Communist Party, Italian section of the Third International."[10] This split occurred on January 21, 1921.

The formal birth of the Communist party only reinforced the steady growth of Mussolini's support. Launched in Milan in March 1919, the Fascist movement took on immediately no clear ideological stance, but Mussolini put strong emphasis on outright opposition to socialism and bolshevism and moved skillfully to exploit the discontent and disillusionment felt in Italy. The poor state of the economy, the obvious instability of the parliamentary process, management's concern with the growth of militant trade unionism, popular dissatisfaction with the peace settlement, all coupled with plain irredentist passions, were exploited in a catchall platform that was supported in the streets by armed Fascists *squadristi* attacking socialists and communists alike, indeed without any distinction. Less than two years after the birth of the PCI at Liverno came the Facist March on Rome (October 28, 1922), and Benito Mussolini had taken over the government, soon to convert his rule into an outright dictatorship and Italy into a full-fledged police state. The PCI was forced to go underground; in 1928 Gramsci was sentenced in a show trial before Mussolini's Special Tribunal for the Defense of the State, charged with conspiracy, instigation of civil war, justifying criminal acts, and fomenting class hatred. The prosecutor said of him: "We must prevent this brain from functioning for twenty years," and the tribunal duly obliged, handing down a sentence of twenty years, four months, and five days. Gramsci's by-then-acute ill health was aggravated by his confinement, and the ideological father of the Italian Communist party was dead within ten years.[11] Mussolini was to survive him by eight years, ironically to be executed summarily by Communist partisans on the direct orders of Gramsci's old comrade Togliatti, acting in his capacity, he later told the party newspaper, *L'Unità*, "as head of the Communist Party and vice-premier of Italy." Gramsci did not survive to witness the initially steady and then spectacular growth of the PCI from a membership of a mere few thousand after Liverno to an estimated half million by 1944 to more than one and a half million by the end of World War II, and to a peak of almost two and a quarter million by 1947.[12] The original 15 Communist deputies elected in 1921 had swollen to more than 200 after the 1979 general election for the Chamber of Deputies.

So much for the bare bones of the origins and birth of the Italian Communist party. This is not the place for a detailed history, nor is it germane to this particular study. Equally, it is unprofitable, but interesting, to speculate on what might have been the party's evolution, or indeed its present strength and political status, had its early public life not been choked off by Mussolini's fascism. What is clear today, and there are few in this mass party who would dispute it, is that it was the PCI's campaign against fascism and its uninterrupted existence in Italy during the 1939–45 war (some other parties, including the socialists, were reconstituted in exile) that gave it its national status and, in a sense, established its democratic credentials for many Italians. The mass support the PCI attracted toward the end of the war, and later, was not always for a

Communist party as such, but for the party of the Resistance against fascism—launched formally in 1943 when the Committee of National Liberation (CLN) was formed in Rome by the main political parties, including the Communists. For the party itself, the defeat of the Fascists had, for that moment anyway, a higher priority than revolution, and even the concept of revolution was beginning (whether from genuine conviction or tactical maneuver) to become submerged in an evolutionary doctrine, in large measure to try and ensure that the Communists would not be isolated when the war clouds had passed and constitutional government was restored. The Communist revolutionary doctrine of Liverno was largely overturned, at least temporarily, and on his return from Moscow in March 1944, Togliatti, in his famous *svolta di Salerno*,[13] put the seal on the party's new alliance strategy, no doubt reflecting in part the will of the government in Moscow. Henceforth, the PCI sought to share power with what the Liverno Communists would have (indeed did) labeled as reformists, if not indeed outright revisionists.

However, it was not only the Italian climate that was changing. By 1943 Soviet policy, too, had altered, with the Comintern being dissolved and Stalin apparently accepting a postwar formula of "spheres of influence." Italy very definitely was assigned to the Western sphere, and the Allies were already in the country, even if Fascist remnants and the Germans held the north, albeit under constant harassment by the Resistance. In both Italy and France the Communists proposed governments of national unity. Togliatti himself, to the surprise and great annoyance of many leading PCI activists, had insisted that the war against the Fascist-Nazi alliance must be the first priority, and he said that his Communists were prepared to collaborate with the royal government of Marshal Pietro Badoglio.[14] Significantly, the Badoglio government—which had declared war on Germany after King Victor Emmanuel III's removal of Mussolini, thus gaining for Italy the status of a cobelligerent—had been formally recognized by Moscow two weeks before Togliatti's return.

There were then, in effect, two Italys, the north still under Fascist-Nazi control with Mussolini again free, having been released from prison by German paratroops, and the south under the King and Badoglio. The Rome-based Committee of National Liberation integrated into the second Badoglio government in March 1944 (with Togliatti as one of five vice-premiers), and was under the close supervision of the Allies. The CLN in Milan was largely under the control of the Communists, thousands of whose members were to die in the Resistance. Its leading activists still dreamed that the resistance to fascism could be turned ultimately into a full-scale revolution. Togliatti, however, with the backing of Moscow, had decreed otherwise and, not surprisingly, many hard-line PCI supporters decided then that the great revolutionary opportunity had been lost, and they left the party in total disillusionment. It had been for them too long a road from Liverno, there had been too many turnings; the "revolution now" policy had been well and truly buried, and Gramsci was dead. The PCI, or at least its leadership, was set clearly on its alliance strategy; the so-called New Party concept was to be the new PCI gospel.

NOTES

1. Pietro Nenni, *Storia di quattro anni* (Rome: Einaudi, 1946). p. 6.

2. Fascist candidates collected a mere 4,000 votes, prompting the socialist newspaper *Avanti!*, of which Mussolini was a former editor, to declare that Mussolini was a "political corpse." But the Fascists captured 35 seats in the 1921 elections and 275 parliamentary places in another poll three years later.

3. "Underlying Our Policy," *L'Unità*, April 24, 1977, trans. here as published in the English-language edition of the PCI journal, *The Italian Communist*, April-June 1977, pp. 68–77.

4. Ibid.

5. Ibid.

6. John Cammett, *Antonio Gramsci and the Origins of Italian Communism*, Stanford, Calif.: Stanford University Press, 1979, pp. 71–72.

7. Students of Gramscian thought and writings have always had problems in defining his concept of "hegemony." For Gramsci himself there was a crucial conceptual distinction between power based on "domination" and the exercise of "direction" or "hegemony." His concept, essentially, was that a given group—his own brand of intellectuals, presumably—move to a position of leadership in the political and social arena as the political elites of the workers.

8. He failed to secure election in 1921, the year in which Mussolini entered Parliament.

9. And earlier in the columns of *Il Grido del popolo*.

10. The name was changed in 1943, when the Third International was dissolved, to Partito Communista Italiano (PCI).

11. It was during his period in prison that Gramsci wrote his celebrated *Quaderni del Carcere* on society, philosophy, and history, published in six volumes by Einaudi, Turin, between 1948 and 1951.

12. The PCI's membership was put officially in the *Supplemento all' Almanacco PCI*, 1979, at 1.8 million, roughly one quarter of whom were women.

13. Togliatti returned to Salerno, making it clear that he was prepared to work in alliance with the other parties, and indeed to collaborate with the royal government, while maintaining the Communists' republican commitment.

14. Mussolini, then in a minority in the Grand Council, was arrested under the king's

orders following the landing of the Allies in Sicily. The new government of Marshal Badoglio, made up of military personnel and technicians, negotiated Italy's unconditional surrender on September 3, 1943, and on October 13 declared war on Germany. This government was reconstituted the following April, survived for only eight weeks, and was replaced by succeeding administrations under the old reformist socialist, Ivanoe Bonomi, until the Liberation.

3 The Italian Communist Party (PCI)

More than thirty years after the events, historians and students of Communist party strategy from the fall of Mussolini until and just after the final liberation of Italy are still analyzing and debating why Togliatti changed course on his return from Moscow and, indeed, why the PCI did not act more resolutely to exploit its undoubted leadership of the Resistance. Put crudely, the question is often asked whether the Communists ever had a better opportunity of trying for an actual grab of power, or at the very least demanding a higher price than Togliatti did for Communist backing for a new constitutional order. There is also the related question as to whether the *svolta* was tactical or strategic. Togliatti's policy and his emerging concept of the "New Party" was not understood by the Communist partisans, and certainly it was not willingly accepted by them. There were indications that some Communists saw it as mainly tactical, to be followed by a revolutionary strategy more in keeping with the old Liverno philosophy. That Togliatti himself was aware of this rank-and-file thinking, especially in the north of Italy, was obvious from his warning in August 1946 when he declared: "Whenever we delve into the minds of our comrades, we find the strangest conceptions of what communism should be, conceptions which are difficult to reconcile with our party line. Acceptance of this line is often superficial or formal, or is justified by the same stupid epithets as our opponents use regarding us, 'tactics', 'trickery', 'secret plans', and so forth."[1]

That the *svolta* suited then-current Moscow policy we have seen, but domestic considerations must also have weighed heavily with Togliatti. Italy was effectively two countries prior to the final liberation, and whatever the possibilities of a Communist coup in the north, there was no such prospect in the south, and no inclination by the Communists to split the nation. There were some indications[2] that the question of just such a move by partisans in

106

the north had been raised by the Russians—whether by way of inquiry or encouragement is unclear—but no evidence that the PCI leadership had seriously considered such a prospect. In the climate of post-Fascist Italy, and given the balance of the political forces represented in the Resistance and, more formally, in the CLNs, Togliatti had apparently decided that Italy was not ready for a socialist revolution, and he opted instead for a "progressive democracy", albeit as an interim measure. Of course, a more immediate incentive for Communist moderation at the time was almost certainly Togliatti's knowledge that the Allies would not tolerate a naked bid for power and, following the American landings in Sicily and the move up through the south, the CLN in Rome was virtually answerable to the Allied Military Command. There is ample evidence in official documents, both American and British, now available that the governments in London and Washington were concerned about the Italian Communists' becoming too strong and thus too powerful a political force in postwar Italian politics. The Allies, in any event, demanded a surrender of all weapons by the partisans and the CLNs after the liberation; it is doubtful whether this surrender was totally carried out.[3]

Whatever weight Togliatti, in fact, gave to these and other considerations, not least the Gramscian warnings against a narrow exclusively workers' revolution and the logic of avoiding a head-on confrontation with the powerful Catholic church, it is evident that he molded all party policy to advance his new alliance strategy, his hope of sharing power with the Socialists and the already powerful Christian Democrats. It was in that sense very much the forerunner of the PCI's celebrated *"compromesso storico"* policy that was unveiled in 1973 as something new more than a quarter of a century later. The tangible immediate gains to the PCI of his alliance strategy were less quantifiable. The referendum that abolished the monarchy was a gain of sorts, but almost certainly it would have happened without PCI pressure.[4] The inclusion of the Communists in the second Badoglio administration and the two Bonomi governments between April 1944 and the end of hostilities was by virtue of the party's presence in the CLN; it survived in four more administrations, including the first three governments of the wily Christian Democrat Alcide de Gasperi, but by then even the revolutionary "Northern Wind" had lost much of its force for political and social renewal. With the peace treaty signed in February 1947 and the cold war on the brink, de Gasperi dumped the Communists from the government.[5] Togliatti and the party did not then fully appreciate that this was to be the start of a period of isolation from direct national political office for more than thirty years. The national elections in April 1948 sealed the PCI's fate; the Socialists had split yet again—with the anti-Communist faction moving further to the right—and, immediately more disastrous for Togliatti's party, the Communists had seized power in Czechoslovakia in February, grist to the mill of the "Christ versus Communism" electoral campaign fought in Italy by the Christian Democrats (and the Vatican). A Togliatti-Communist and Nenni-Socialist popular front fought a joint campaign to win 31 percent of the popular vote for the Chamber of Deputies; the Christian Democrats captured an overall majority of the seats with a vote total of 48.5 percent, thus easily reversing the combined Communist/Socialist lead over the Catholic party in the earlier elections for a Constituent Assembly (its powers were limited essentially to preparing a new Italian Constitution).

A perceptive, if wry, comment was made by Calamandrei on the new Constitution, itself a massive, and in parts confused, compromise between the ideologies and visions of the various post-Fascist political factions in Italy. He wrote: "To compensate the left-wing parties for their failure to effect a revolution, the right-wing forces did not oppose the inclusion in the Constitution of the promise of a revolution."[6] One instance will suffice here of the compromise which provided little that was tangible but promised much that was progressive, even revolutionary. Article I of the Constitution was to begin with a sentence noting that "Italy is a workers' republic."[7] This notion fitted the aspirations of Togliatti and Nenni at the time, but not those of the Christian Democrats and the other forces on the right. A compromise was reached, and, in fact, Article I proclaims that "Italy is a democratic republic founded on labour." It does not mean much, if indeed anything, but then it was, and it remains today, enough for the various political forces, including the PCI, to point to the post-Fascist Constitution as a model of their own individual making. The conservative Catholic forces retained the political power; the progressive, if not wholly revolutionary, factions, and most of all the Communists, were left with fine-sounding constitutional declarations.

Even before the 1948 elections, international events had begun to impinge themselves on the position and attitude of the PCI. In 1947 a new international Communist forum, the Cominform, was established in Belgrade, reflecting an early consolidation of the cold war, and both the Italian and French Communist parties were brought to task by Moscow to give an account of their collaborationist stewardship. Ironically, because Yugoslavia was shortly to be drummed out of the movement, it was the Yugoslavs who were set up by the Russians to attack the French and Italian parties. Kardelj and Djilas asked rhetorically (and then answered themselves): "Can it be said that the PCI or the PCF [Parti Communiste Français] have taken clear positions? No, with their theory of popular democracy, they disarmed the masses."[8]

It was made clear to the PCI that the Italian party could not expect to get off lightly with minor self-criticism; what was demanded was a radical change in the party's political line.[9] Back in Rome, the PCI responded to the Soviet demands, and in a manner which implied that Togliatti's own alliance strategy had somehow been a deviationist trick imposed by some PCI fringe elements, and not by the leadership itself. By the end of 1948 the party publication *Rinascita* was declaring:

> In the democratic political and social euphoria of the last months of the war and of the early post-war, it might have seemed to some that a period was opening up in which traditional and class conflicts deriving from the very structure of capitalist society, were being attenuated to the point of permitting a permanent collaboration between political forces different in nature, *operai and lavoratori socialisti* on the one hand, conservative bourgeois members of capitalist society on the other. To others it might have seemed possible, generalising from a transitory experience of a parliamentary type, that these conflicts, although continuing to exist, might be overcome through a system of compromises.[10]

Clearly, the Moscow axis[11] was once more in the ascendancy, no doubt to the relief of many PCI rank-and-file members for whom, as we have seen, the Togliatti alliance strategy had created nothing but confusion, and who believed deep down that the revolution could only be brought about by force. On July 14, just three months after the PCI's electoral debacle, there was an attempt on the life of Togliatti, and armed Communist workers took to the streets, occupied factories, and took command of many local administrative offices. For forty-eight hours it seemed to some that the revolution had come. Union leaders called a general strike, and the whiff of a coup was in the air. Two days and a number of violent deaths later, union leaders called off the stoppage, be it said under direct encouragement by the PCI, and the "threat" had passed. Yet it was not just the threat that had passed in the eyes of many PCI militants. The prospect of violent action to advance a communist revolution had also gone, and with the approval of the party's leadership.

Thereafter, and certainly until the twentieth congress of the Russian party in 1956 and the unmasking of Stalin by Khrushchev, together with the Soviet takeover in Hungary (which Togliatti forced the PCI to support, arguing that the principle of noninterference in the internal affairs of another country could not be absolute), the Italian Communist party concentrated largely on expanding its organizational roots in society and streamlining its internal structure and the quality and geographical representation of its membership. With exceptions, such as the early days of the campaign of peasant occupation of land to back a reform program, opposition to a blatant Christian Democrat gerrymander drive in 1953 to cement itself as a permanent parliamentary majority (the so-called *Legge truffa*), and regular anti-NATO protests, the PCI put its main public emphasis on moderation. At the same time, these exceptions demonstrated the party's capacity, and its willingness when thought necessary, to produce masses of workers on the streets almost instantly, mainly through its then-effective control of CGIL—the Italian Confederation of Labor. These parades of worker solidarity kept a form of revolutionary spirit alive, if not always with the workers, certainly in the eyes of anti-Communists, who were always prepared to think the worst of the PCI's ultimate intentions, a process that many Christian Democrats today still do everything possible to encourage.

Meanwhile, the PCI's steady electoral advance continued, although some contemporary commentators tend to exaggerate it. In fact, for most of the postwar period, the PCI's electoral advance has been rather gradual, although its geographical spread has been impressive. Between 1948 and 1972 the party's share of the popular vote grew by just over 8 percent, or a mean increase from one election to another of about 1.4 percent.[12] The PCI made a major leap forward between 1972 and 1976 when the party's percentage share of the total vote for the Chamber of Deputies rose from 27.2 to 34.4, only to fall back by a significant four percentage points in the national elections in 1979.[13]

While periodic street demonstrations and some tough PCI speeches and writings throughout the 1950s had (or, in any event, were seen to have) a revolutionary air, the party's performance in Parliament, and particularly in the parliamentary committees (where most Italian legislation is processed), was consistently moderate. Togliatti's alliance strategy remained the basic policy sheetanchor, even through much of the 1960s when, at great potential risk to the Communists, the Christian Democrats succeeded in putting together a center-left governing formula with the main body of the Socialist party, thus breaking the ranks of the Italian Left and threatening the Communists with complete isolation.

By the time of the 1968 Soviet invasion of Czechoslovakia to end Dubcek's formula of "socialism with a human face," the Italian party was gradually distancing itself from Moscow, and it roundly condemned the Russian move. By the end of 1979 the PCI was even more forcibly showing its own "Italian face" by attacking the Soviet takeover in Afghanistan when, unlike the 1968 condemnation over Czechoslovakia, there were few signs of much resistance within the party.[14] Togliatti's alliance strategy had long since been joined by the concept of polycentrism to replace the old rigidities of the Cominterm and the hoped-for (by the Russians) conformity of the Cominform. By 1975 the ill-defined (and inaccurate, in my view, if it intends to imply a uniformity of policies and positions in, for example, the Italian, French, and Spanish parties) concept of Eurocommunism had taken root, at least in the media headlines. This development suggests an even further remove between Moscow and the communist parties in Western Europe, but it could be rash to assume that the next logical step is a complete break, at least in the Italian case. As the 1980s approached, the PCI had advanced itself politically to the point of temporary involvement in the "governing majority" in Rome but not actually in the cabinet (only the Italians could invent such refinements). The PCI left the government again in January 1979, complaining through its general secretary, Enrico Berlinguer (like Gramsci, a thoughtful and remote Sardinian) that the Christian Democrats were not prepared to play the coalition game when it came to actual policies. This move was reminiscent of de Gasperi and Togliatti in the immediate postwar era, but the background was frighteningly different this time. Italy was, and remains, plagued with violence, the very state itself seemingly under attack. For the origins, and the Communist response, we must go back a dozen years and more.

NOTES

1. P. A. Allum, *The Italian Communist Party since 1945* (Reading, Eng.: University of Reading Press, 1970), p. 13.

2. Eugenio Reale, *Nascita del Cominform,* Mondadori Editore, Verona: 1958, pp. 119–20.

3. Reports of PCI arms dumps surface periodically—but anything held must be quite obsolete after all this time.

4. The actual vote was close with a margin of only 2 million favoring a republic in a total vote of more than 23 million Italians.

5. It has been argued that de Gasperi held his hand until after the peace treaty so as not to alienate Stalin.

6. Piero Calamandrei, et al., *Dieci anni dopo, 1945–55* (Bari: La Costituzione e la leggi per attuarla, 1955), p. 215.

7. P. Vercellone, "The Italian Constitution of 1947–48," in *The Rebirth of Italy, 1943–50*, ed. S. J. Woolf (London: Longman, 1972), p. 124.

8. Reale, *Nascita del Cominform*, p. 119.

9. Ibid, pp. 139–49.

10. *Sulla nostra politica,* issue no. 5, September-October 1948, p. 331.

11. An interesting American study has argued cogently that PCI behavior can best be understood in terms of the party's pursuits of three basic interests: (1) Development and maintenance of the Communist party itself and its influence over other organizations and groups; (2) Its search for political and social alliances that constitute the core of the *via Italiana al socialismo*—the Italian road to socialism; and (3) maintenance of a close link with the Soviet Union and the International Communist movement. The party has had its "most comfortable and productive period" whenever all three interests coincide. See Donald L. M. Blackmer, "Continuity and Change in Postwar Italian Communism," in *Communism in Italy and France*, eds. Blackmer and Sidney Tarrow (Princeton, N.J.: Princeton University Press, 1975), p. 23.

12. For a detailed analysis see, among other sources, Giacomo Sani, "Mass Support for Italian Communism," in *Eurocommunism: The Italian Case*, eds. Austin Ranney and Giovanni Sartori, (Washington: The American Enterprise Institute for Public Policy Research, 1978) pp. 67–96.

13. This was the PCI's first electoral setback nationally in more than a quarter century.

14. The PCI delegation to the Twenty-sixth Congress of the Soviet party in February 1981 was—uniquely—not led by its secretary-general but by a lower functionary, Giancarlo Pajetta, and Moscow had intimated its displeasure with the Italian party, not the least over its endorsement of the workers' Solidarity movement in Poland.

4 Italian Violence: Origins and Growth

The great themes of the Late 1960s and all the crises associated with, and deriving from, them—crises of religion, family, and institutional values; crises of personal relationships; clashes of old and new ideologies, such as traditional Marxism and neo-Marxism, institutional Catholicism and dissenting Catholicism; and the attempts to develop alternative revolutionary theories different from "official" Marxism—all had much of their origins in Italy in a social group that could not easily be controlled by the Communist party, namely, the students. Indeed, there is evidence that the PCI leadership did not understand the "student movement" and certainly did not initially assign to it any great importance.[1] Yet it was student activism in 1967 that brought on "the awakening of the workers"[2] and the "Hot Autumn" of 1969, after a series of factory clashes in a climate in which traditional trade-union leadership risked losing control over the rank and file, and in many cases actually did lose it. Indeed, few remember now outside Italy that it was the student explosion there which was the forerunner of similar unrest throughout Europe, notably, of course, in France. In Italy the young protagonists did not always have clear social or economic objectives, only a general urge to break away from established traditions, the family, marriage, a home, and a job. According to the sociologist Sabino Acquaviva, "some young people passed from revolt against the family armed with psychological weapons to armed revolt against society."[3]

The period of history in which the young people were living must also be taken into account, and not just the domestic Italian political scene, where any reformist hopes from the center-left governing experiment had quickly faded. Nationalist and often revolutionary struggles in the Third World, including South America and Vietnam, were the backdrop to Che Guevara's dictum to "create two, three, many Vietnams," which was echoed by many

113

Italian students. The OLAS[4] conference in Havana in July 1967 reflected the concept that "it was the duty of every revolutionary to take part in the revolution," a concept that evoked a response in Italy's student youth. The notion of revolutionary violence took hold, in part at least as a reaction to the seen pacifism of the traditional left, especially that of the Communist party. *Potere Operaio* (Workers' Power), the polemical magazine of a workers-cum-students group of the same name formed in the winter of 1966/67, was carrying a clear revolutionary message. "The word peace today has a false ring. There has never been, is not and never will be peace with the bosses."[5] The same message was repeated: "one must not deceive oneself nor deceive the masses on the possibility of obtaining recognition of even their most elementary rights peacefully and democratically. . . . The masses must be constantly ready to confront their enemies' aggression under whatever guise it appears, opposing violence with violence.[6]

The origins of the Italian student movement are both interesting and ironic. It had its birth at Trento, at the time arguably the most conservative stronghold of traditional Christian Democracy in Italy. Indeed, the provincial DC group had encouraged the establishment of a higher institute for social sciences in the expectation that this addition to the local university would, in time, turn out a stream of sociologists as part of a new management elite, but of course within the existing system. The outcome was something quite different, and thousands of young people reached political and sometimes revolutionary maturity in these same Trento halls—among them Renato Curcio and his subsequent wife, Margherita Cagol, considered among the original founders of the Red Brigade terrorists. The institute at Trento throughout 1967 produced a never-ending stream of processions, demonstrations, assemblies, and political meetings, together with a rash of crudely duplicated ideological pamphlets. An anti-American demonstration of solidarity with the people of Vietnam led the authorities to call in the police. This campus confrontation between students and the established forces of order was to be quickly followed in other European universities. Some latter-day Italian students, with a touch of pride almost, point to Trento as the European pacesetter of the movement, albeit at that time a movement roused by fiery ideological rhetoric and outright condemnation of the status quo, but without any violent revolutionary commitment. The great debates began within the university, which many students viewed increasingly as being a mere transmission belt for the ideology of the ruling class, a process of educating new disciples of the old order.

Such labels as "reformist" and "revisionist" were directed angrily against the Communist party, which was seen as "the principal enemy to be defeated at the mass level in order to restore a revolutionary character to the struggles of the masses."[7] A democratic university in a capitalist society was viewed as an anachronism, if not indeed an impossibility, prompting the notion that one should not fight for the university but against it, the start of the students' struggle against what was termed "academic authoritarianism." Curcio himself launched the idea of the "negative university," in which critical thought could be developed. "Counter-lectures" were arranged to coincide with official lectures on the same subject, counter-courses analyzing the state of development of capitalist society and its "contradictions," together with programs on the Chinese revolution and the thoughts of Chairman Mao. Pamphlets praised the Chinese example, emphasizing that attaining a true egalitarian society would be no overnight affair but rather a long and arduous process. "It is not the Cuban but the Chinese example which we have before us; that is, the organisation of a happy land can not be achieved through two years of struggle, but is possible through forty years of resistance."[8] The movement's new magazine, *Lavoro Politico*, with Curcio himself as one of the editors, concerned itself largely with the "degeneration" of an Italian Communist party increasingly committed to its alliance strategy. Yet the movement continued to oppose "philo-Castroism and tactical adventurism . . . [by those who advocate] armed action in Italy. . . . [These people are only] petit bourgeois in search of emotional experiences, not revolutionary proletarians."[9] Curcio, and certainly the top leaders who were to come after him in the Red Brigades, were seen to change this philosophy dramatically, and indeed by the spring of 1969 he himself left Trento, having the previous winter formally joined the new Communist party (Marxist-Leninist), a breakaway faction founded in Pisa by ex-militants of the PCI opposed to Togliatti's "New Party" concept and the whole destalinization process that the Kremlin had unleashed in 1956 at the Twentieth Congress. However, Curcio was not to remain long in its ranks, and he soon moved to Milan to exploit the revolutionary potential of the workers there more than student militancy in the universities.

The Trento explosion was no isolated event. Throughout Italy more and more young people approached the end of the 1960s in a mood of growing frustration over the apparent inability of the "system" and the old-guard political parties to tackle the fundamental economic and social problems facing the country. The more extreme considered it a matter of indifference rather than inability; the more perceptive saw it as a failure of the ruling elite to understand the problem, let alone solve it. Christian Democrat nepotism and, worse, downright corruption remained after thirty years the order of the political day. Parliament continued to churn out new legislation,[10] but it contained little touching on the major problems: the depressed south, penal reform, education, health, and the housing shortage, among others. The so-called *leggine*—literally hundreds of them in any given Parliament—generally advanced narrow sectional interests whose satisfaction was necessary to hold votes for the DC. As often as not, these legislative proposals were not attacked by the Communists because the PCI was trying to hold its left while moving closer to the middle ground and thus was afraid to alienate any sectional groups that might eventually be persuaded to leave traditional DC ranks and vote Communist. The political parties, including the Communists, used Parliament because "it was the only game in town." Seemingly angry Communist interventions on the floor of Parliament were intended primarily for the electorate outside; inside in the parliamentary committees, where most Italian legislation is actually thrashed out, the PCI, on average, either endorsed approximately three in every four proposed measures or let them through by abstaining. The big debates, such as those on the annual budget or the even more regular governmental crises, brought out the big party political personalities, but usually with more heat than light.

In the country the "economic miracle" of the late 1950s and early 1960s had moved on and in truth had either left unchanged vast parts of Italy's south or helped to create new social tensions. The vast flight from the land to the towns and cities (more than two in five of the working population were engaged in agriculture in 1950, but the figure had slumped to below 20 percent twenty years later) was inevitably on a south-north axis, and industrial Turin became the fourth largest "southern city" after Naples, Palermo, and Bari. Families that had survived for generations on the edge of the productive economy were suddenly, and with understandable trauma, thrust into an industrial civilization, a whole new world, and their eyes were opened to new living standards, which they sought, and, in corollary, to trade-union and political power, which they demanded. Yet for all too many of them there was no cornucopia on the streets of Milan, Turin, or Rome; all they found was a largely unplanned and shamefully inadequate physical and social infrastructure.

The outcome was not just the slum ghettos and the ghetto mentality but human fodder for the revolutionary notions then taking hold. Support for the parliamentary opposition was seen by many as offering no real way out of the impasse because the PCI had gone "respectable" with its emphasis on moderation so as not to alienate potential electoral supporters, a policy that was paralleled broadly in the official labor movement, and especially in the powerful CGIL. The old alliance between the historic left and those in opposition to the system broke apart, and the vacuum gave birth to the extraparliamentary left in Italy in a climate fertile to nourish the revolutionary seeds that militant workers and student activists were already sowing. In approximately one year starting in the autumn of 1968, a rash of new and often overlapping militant organizations surfaced with their accompanying propaganda vehicles. Principal among them were La Classe, uniting militants of Potere Operaio (formed originally in Tuscany in the winter of 1966/67) including Tony Negri[11] with student militants in Milan, Turin, and Rome, among whom were Oreste Scalzone and Franco Piperno,[12] and their journal of the same name; Lotta Continua and its own publication; the Gruppo dell'Apartamento in Reggio Emilia, remnants of which were subsequently to join with Curcio and his followers to form the Sinistra Proletaria; the Gruppo Armato Proletario, or GAP; and the Metropolitan Political Collective (Collettivo Politico Metropolitano, or CPM), which first surfaced in September 1969, launched by militant workers in a number of major Italian industrial undertakings—including Pirelli, Alfa-Romeo, SIT Siemens, and IBM—and some student leaders.

The professed themes of all these groups, to the extent that they could be understood from the often tortuous and complex phraseology of their publications and communiqués, combined in a relatively simple message: the capitalists and the established political power brokers were seeking to maintain their traditional hegemony in Italian society by joining forces with, or at the very least exploiting, the growing moderation of the Communist party (and its backers in the trade-union federation, CGIL), which was intent on entering the governing majority. The top union leaders, it was claimed, no longer adequately represented the views and felt needs of the workers and, fundamentally, the "system" could only be changed through revolution; the concept of violence was no longer excluded. In the summer of 1969 at Turin a number of these groupings, including La Classe, Potere Operaio Toscano, Lotta Continua, and student militants from the city came together in an effort to unite in a national revolutionary organization under a common political program. The aim was "to accelerate the destruction of [the] counter-revolutionary control of the unions and the parties on the class movements; to link and organise the avant garde groups, developing proletarian unity in the struggle."[13] A total break with the unions was required to achieve this objective, to be understood not as a "generic overthrow" but as a "political rejection" of the unions as a "means of mediation in the class struggle."[14]

The not-unrelated background to all this worker-student activity was the situation inside many of the factories. Union struggles were becoming more bitter leading up to the "Hot Autumn" of 1969. Workers were in revolt. The unions were being criticized and bypassed, their tactics debated and condemned. Whereas the official union demands were concentrated largely on wage levels, the autonomous groups were putting forward proposals on a much wider front, including shorter working hours, a reexamination of piecework with a view to its elimination, and health and recreational facilities in the factories. Increased worker militancy took on many until then unconventional forms: wildcat strikes, department and works assemblies, the blocking of merchandise, sabotage, and absenteeism. This new protest reflected the demands of the CPM for more organization to radicalize the struggle and to achieve the maximum level of confrontation, thus encouraging the political growth of the masses, a high degree of independence from the so-called revisionist trade unions, and the transformation of the class struggle into a generalized social struggle.

In a report[15] on the public order situation in the city, the prefect of Milan, Libero Mazza, noted on December 22, 1970, to the government in Rome that the CPM "had recently announced the formation of groups called Red Brigades to be sent to factories with the declared aim of promoting worker autonomy from the traditional party and union organizations." It seemed that, to the CPM, the class struggle could no longer be contained within the established unions and the PCI, but it had to be turned into a direct armed clash with guerrilla warfare and secrecy as chosen weapons. At a conference held at Chiavari near Genoa at the end of 1969, CPM leaders, among them Curcio, Corrado Simoni, and Franco Troiano, the stage was set for a long struggle. "It is not a question of winning suddenly and conquering everything, but of growing in a long period of struggle." The movement was intended "for the liberation of the proletariat from bourgeois hegemony which is manifested in the political institutions (state, parties, unions, legal system, etc.), in the economic institutions (the entire capitalist apparatus of production and distribution), in the cultural institutions (the dominant ideology in all its manifestations) and in the regulatory bodies (bourgeois customs and morals)." In order to reach this objective, it was necessary to "pull down the whole system of exploitation and set up a different social system."

Nor was the Communist party spared criticism. The PCI "is deaf, limits itself to backing union initiatives . . . sets up *L'Unità* as a union [news]paper, and takes an essentially moderate position in individual situations."[16] The proletariat must, therefore, carry on the class struggle directly, almost as if it were a war. The "revisionists" were viewed as undertaking the defense of the values of the ruling class, parliamentary democracy, independence, industrial development, and national unity. To the militant CPM, the time had come for urban guerrilla warfare; the organization of violence had become an essential component in the class struggle. The enemy would have to be attacked using hit-and-run tactics. The initial target area was to be the industrial triangle of Milan, Turin, and Genoa. The movement used its occasional "struggle leaflet" entitled *Sinistra Proletaria* both to whip up worker agitation and to advocate unity between the various revolutionary factions, and indeed later the CPM itself took on the name Sinistra Proletaria, and the struggle leaflet was replaced in 1971 by a new paper, *Nova Resistenza*. This had as its symbol the significant addition of a rifle to the traditional Communist hammer and sickle; the gun had well and truly appeared on the Italian scene.

NOTES

1. "The Italian Road to Socialism," an interview by Eric Hobsbawm with Giorgio Napolitano of the PCI, London, 1977: "We did not at first understand the significance and implications of the explosive growth of the student population."

2. Giovanni Russo, in *Eurocommunism: Myth or Reality*, eds. Paolo Filo della Torre, Edward Mortimer, and Jonathan Story, (London: Penguin Books, 1979), p. 71.

3. Sabino Acquaviva, *Guerriglia e guerra revoluzionaria in Italia* (Milan: Rizzoli, 1979), p. 20.

4. Organizzazione Liberazione America Sud.

5. *Potere operaio*, no. 3, July 1967.

6. Ibid., no. 6, October 1967.

7. *Lavoro Politico*, October 1967.

8. R. Curcio and M. Rostagno, "Proposta di foglio di lavoro," a pamphlet of the time.

9. *Lavoro Politico*, November 1967.

10. In the twenty years from 1948 to 1968, for example, the Italian Parliament approved more than 8,000 laws, an annual average of 400 compared with representative averages, rounded, of 100 in England, 150 in France, 290 in Sweden, 30 in Ireland, and 50 in India. Details are found in Guiseppe Di Palma's *Surviving without Governing* (Berkeley and Los Angeles, Calif.: University of California Press, 1977), pp. 41–42.

11. Acquitted in April 1980 of involvement in the kidnapping and assassination of former Prime Minister Aldo Moro, but held on numerous other terrorist charges.

12. A teacher of physics at the University of Calabria who was extradited from France in 1979 to face Italian charges of alleged armed insurrection against the state.

13. "Documento dell'assemblea operai-studenti," reported in *Quindici*, no. 19, August 1969.

14. Guido Viale, Giorni di lotta alla Fiat, an ideological tract of the time.

15. An Italian news media report. This was the first public reference to the Red Brigades by official sources.

16. Reports and quotations of the Chiavari declaration, and arising from the meeting, are taken from the pamphlet "Frutto di un lavoro collettivo," quoted in *Brigate Rosse*, ed. Soccorso Rosso, (Milan: Feltrinelli, 1977).

5 A Climate for Violence

Economic and social conditions in Italy at the time provided an ideal background for recruitment to revolutionary concepts and even for the direct use of violence. The process of industrialization and, as noted earlier, the "economic miracle" had not altered substantially the traditional gap between rich and poor, between those with regular work and those committed, it seemed, to permanent unemployment, between (as a generality) northern well-being and southern poverty. The universities were turning out more and more graduates, but the system was not capable of providing corresponding expanding employment opportunities. Wider educational opportunities, whatever the underlying improvement in quality, had created higher expectations. At a different level, the vast shifts in population from the south to the north, from agriculture to the overcrowded towns and cities, resulted inevitably in increasing the catchment area for recruits to advance the new "social order." Solitude and segregation faced the newcomers to the industrial locales; people were uprooted from their own cultural environment, left largely on their own on the peripheries of the great cities, taken away from the rules of social, cultural, and religious behavior that had been their inheritance. They were unable to draw much from the new industrial culture save the philosophy of consumption. The inevitable results were overcrowding and ghettos, exploitation and promiscuity—the ideal backdrop for the recruitment of guerrillas and, immediately and more directly, for an explosion of ordinary crime. At a time when common violence was spreading,[1] others were planning to destablize the whole system, and revolutionary violence often allied itself, and in part merged with, ordinary criminal violence in the creation of a psychological climate of revolt. Slogans spread by revolutionary pamphlets provided an inspiration of sorts for ordinary crime, including demands for expropriations, sabotage, the destruction of

cars owned by the wealthy classes, damage to shops, the occupation of houses, and the destruction of electric and telephone bills.
Revolutionary violence and ordinary criminality met in a murky
and gray area, combining to confuse the authorities as to precise
motivations and creating fear in the people as a whole that law and
order was breaking down. It produced a response from the political
right, from neo-Fascist elements always ready to exploit what they
professed to see as a society becoming an inevitable victim to
creeping communism. As with the Mussolini *squadristi* of the
1920s, neo-Fascists took to the street, sometimes with the connivance of the security forces. The police regularly met demonstrations and processions, particularly those organized by the left, with
a security overkill, a not unusual phenomenon in a democratic
society faced with problems that the administrative process ne-
glects, or fails to comprehend, and is only too responsive, because
of electoral considerations, to global, shrill, and unspecific demands for the maintenance of law and order. In turn, this overkill
aggravated the problem and produced more recruits for the cause
of violence and revolutionary change. Curcio, for example, who in
the 1967–68 period was arguing in *Lavoro Politico* against a strategy of armed fight, was by the summer of 1970 a committed revolutionary, dedicated to clandestine operations against the state and
its institutions, backed by the gun. For thousands more, worker
militants, students, and elements in the defined "intelligentia"
class, there appeared to be a declining place for the democratic
order. The clandestine life seemed to have its own myths: of
menaces, of the escapee, of the prisoner, of the alternation between the fear of death and the often irresponsible playing at being
guerrillas. The underground way of life isolated many from a community structure that they had rejected, making them part of a
secret society that approved of segregation and cut them off from
any links with compromise. The transition to armed underground
struggle was a result of their rejection of a society that could not, to
their lights, satisfy even their minimal needs and aspirations.
Hence was born a kind of moral justification for armed revolt.

One of the theorists of the revolutionary movement, Professor
Sergio Bologna,[2] had this comment: "A year ago in the Movement
there were many people ready to dissent from the armed party;
nowadays the subject is not discussed because nobody is ready to
say 'no' clearly to the armed party. I don't say that many approve of
the armed party or are ready to join it; I say that there are very few
people who think that some sort of proletarian violence can be

avoided. This is why the request made to us by the Communist party to declare ourselves against any form of violence is not accepted." Whether Bologna exaggerated the extent and uniformity of outlook of those who thought that some sort of proletarian violence was inevitable is arguable, and already there were signs of a growing divide in revolutionary ranks, a divide essentially between those who could be loosely described as Italian Bolsheviks and others committed to mass but largely democratic action. The position of *Potere Operaio* in September 1971 was rather ambiguous: "We are not interested in city guerrilla warfare but in the growing movement aimed at the organization and arming of the masses." By November 1973 this criticism had hardened: "It is not possible to delegate an objective to a separate body or to any other instrument . . . what we do not accept from the comrades in the Red Brigades is their accepting service, indeed their ardour in fighting for a structure which they believe to be already the armed party of workers autonomy." However, the revolutionary elite in the Red Brigades were already in the ascendancy; the masses, as Marx and Lenin had earlier defined, would follow suit, or perhaps be made to in the overall interests of the revolution.

The two-year interval covered by this evolution within the ranks of *Potere Operaio* saw the first kidnapping by the Red Brigades. It is appropriate to interject here some observations on the historic leaders of the terrorist movement and seek, using mainly their own declarations, to determine more precisely their ideological stance and their professed objectives. It is necessary, however, to add two important qualifications. Firstly, the authenticity of all statements and communiqués purporting to have come from the BR[3] throughout much of the violent 1970s and still continuing in Italy have not been independently established, given the nature of the organization; secondly, now that the original leaders are either behind bars or dead, there is inevitably a high level of speculation, and within the security forces too, concerning both the identity and precise long-term objectives of present BR leaders. On this latter point inferential conclusions from earlier statements are, in all probability, close to the mark, but they remain inferential; a similar cautionary note should be sounded on official assertions and mere speculation, concerning international links between the BR and terrorist groups elsewhere in Europe, but principally in West Germany and France or, indeed, of feeder lines to the movement from Eastern Europe.[4] Given the present international traffic in arms, a Czech-made gun found in a BR hideout uncovered by the police in

Rome, or on a captured IRA fighter in Belfast, or with a Basque nationalist in Bilbao does not prove very much and certainly does not justify any substantive conclusions.

NOTES

1. In 1961 there were (figures rounded) 890,000 reported crimes in Italy. In subsequent years the total had increased to 1,015,000 (1970), 1,800,000 (1974), and 2,039,000 (1979). Related to the particular years of the buildup through industrial unrest to revolutionary violence, Italian crime figures were: 1,700 per 100,000 population (1969), advancing by 11 percent in 1970, by 22 percent in 1971, again eleven percent in 1972, twelve percent in 1973, 13 percent in 1974, and yet another 11 percent rise, to 3,650 per 100,000 in 1975. Source: Italian Interior Ministry.

2. In *Potere Operaio*, of which he was a director and a collaborator with Tony Negri on many books and polemical writings.

3. All further references to the Red Brigades appear as BR, reflecting the Italian name, Brigate Rosse.

4. President Sandro Pertini, himself an old-guard Socialist, asserted in an interview on French television in January 1981, that the "sanctuaries" of Italian terrorism were outside the country, and he implied that he had the Soviet Union in mind. Moscow demanded an explanation; the Rome government said that it had no firm evidence for the president's assertion.

6 The Red Brigades (BR)

Who were the early BR leaders? Quickly, if negatively, can be dismissed what they were not, certainly not obsessives with nothing but terrorism and murder on their minds. Nor were they social outcasts, although they were clearly misfits in the society into which they were born, reared, and had their early education. On the contrary, they came mainly from bourgeois backgrounds and demonstrated considerable intellectual and at times political abilities. Their early manifesto, the widely published *Risoluzione Strategica*, was a carefully analyzed assessment of the national and international political situation, of the Italian security and penal structure, and of the state of the capitalist society in Italy, including its more obvious imperfections, extremes, and excesses, and all in a society permeated extensively by nepotism, indifference, and often downright discrimination. The BR case was argued cogently and with clarity, but most of all with extreme dogmatism. Any other analysis, it was argued, could only be a deliberate error by those who were essentially pillars of a corrupt economic and social system, its primary beneficiaries, and, hence, custodians and defenders of the status quo. However extremely stated, the BR's analysis did not merely represent the opinions of its own elite; much of it was, and remains today, reflected widely in the population—which of course is not the same as saying that any extensive popular support existed, or does today, for the subsequent methods of the movement in seeking "to smash the system."

I will give a few brief leadership profiles, starting first with Renato Curcio himself. Born into a bourgeois family, he had a Catholic education and joined the Gruppo Trentino dell'Intesa Universitaria, a mainly Catholic student group. As noted earlier, he entered the Institute of Social Sciences at Trento and advanced with impressive academic success before ultimately launching his "counter-lectures" strategy and finally quitting the university with-

125

out formally graduating. He married Margherita Cagol, with him among the first of the BR activists. About her he wrote tenderly to his mother, Yolanda (with whom he maintained a regular correspondence, including information on how his own revolutionary ideas were developing): "Margherita is magnificent. Every day I discover more and more why it is beautiful and important to have her by my side."[1] His wife's sister, Milena, was to say of Margherita that if she took a certain path it was because she was convinced it was the right one, and she followed it through. Once she had made her choice, she had no more doubts; it was others who were wrong. She had a very strong, decided character. At a certain moment she knew what she willed, and she willed it to the end—Milena remembered her saying once, "to death."[2] This statement proved prophetic, for Margherita died in a shoot-out with the police in Milan in 1975 at a house where a kidnapped industrialist was being held.[3] A BR communiqué distributed in Milan the same afternoon (May 6) to mark her death stated: "Mara, a flower has budded, and the Red Brigades will go on tending this flower until victory."

Alberto Franceschini, who had earlier formed his own Marxist Gruppo dell'Appartamento, was also among the first BR leaders. The son of an anti-fascist who had been interned for a period in Auschwitz during World War II and was later to become a minor Communist party functionary, Alberto himself became involved in political activity in the ranks of the Communist youth movement, the FGCI. He later quit (and dropped out of the university), declaring that he could not go on living with the system; to do so would not be honest with himself or with the party. He joined Curcio in Milan.

Roberto Ognibene, whose political activity switched from the Socialist to the Communist camp, was the son of a local government official in Reggio Emilia. At school, by all accounts, he was an outstanding student, although more interested in absolutism than reform. During the years of contestation in the schools he advanced his own revolutionary thoughts and ideas. He rejected the school system, claiming that it did not offer children an adequate maturity. On the contrary, it inhibited them from taking an interest in their real problems. He considered the system of marks and oral examinations as a "barbarous means for educating a youngster."[4] He was convinced of the correctness of his own interpretation and believed that school was a product of a kind of society that would have to be destroyed. He, too, went to Milan to join Curcio.

Finally, completing the first elite of the BR, there was Giorgio Semeria, again from a bourgeois family, his father being a manager with SIT Siemens, his mother a schoolteacher. She was to say of her son that "he had the habit of taking everything he did terribly seriously."[5] Giorgio had been associated with a number of revolutionary groupings prior to joining with Curcio and the BR. At the time of his arrest in Milan in 1976, police said that he had a document noting that "the choice has been made to attack people instead of things." This statement was presumably a reference to the initial BR policy of directing their actions at property, especially that of the multinationals, which the movement viewed as representatives of world capitalism.

The BR's first known kidnapping took place in Milan in March 1972, when Idalgo Macchiarini, a manager with SIT Siemens, was held briefly and put on "proletarian trial." The movement's first killings did not occur until just over two years later, the victims being two officials of the Padua office of the neo-Fascist MSI party. Thereafter, terrorism continued with a real vengeance for the remainder of the decade and beyond into the 1980s.

An examination of the growth of terrorism in Italy should not be undertaken in isolation from domestic political events there throughout the 1970s. Indeed, it is reasonable to assume that the increased militancy of the BR paralleled political developments, most especially the Communist party's apparent coming closer to participation in the governmental process. Equally, such political developments provide at least part of the explanation for the escalation of violence from the neo-Fascist right, violence that was intended to reverse this advance by the PCI and also to discredit the Communists, whose attitude to violence, as seen by the electorate, has not always been unambiguous. The alliance strategy of Togliatti's "New Party" has earlier been highlighted, but it was not until the autumn of 1973[6] that its updated version, at least in terminology, took shape. At that time Enrico Berlinguer unveiled the *compromesso storico,* or "historic compromise," concept in some writings that took note of the military coup in Chile against the Allende regime and, by inference, of the fact that Italy, despite its fairly rapid secularization, still remained heavily Catholic and that Catholic and Socialist traditions confronted each other there. Fifty-one percent of the popular vote, argued Berlinguer, would not be sufficient for the left under the PCI to form a government, thus starkly excluding, for the foreseeable future in any event, a governing alternative without the Christian Democrats.

It could not be an alternative, he reasoned, but an alliance. Revolutionary change was excluded. Not surprisingly, therefore, the armed militants stepped up their campaign. By the time of the local government elections in 1975, the PCI had made substantial electoral advances, with left-wing administrations taking over in Milan, Venice, Florence, Naples, and Turin: Genoa already had such an administration, whereas Bologna continued to be governed by a Communist-Socialist alliance, as it had been for decades. This 1975 electoral advance was consolidated for the PCI in the premature general election in June the following year after the Socialists had finally decided that the center-left formula had failed. Later, and after prolonged and mostly private negotiations, the Communists advanced another step toward power, or at the very least to the ending of political discrimination against them, when the party agreed to support, through a policy of abstention, a Christian Democrat minority government under Giulio Andreotti. This decision opened a new political phase categorized with customary Italian inventiveness as one of "not no-confidence." It marked an important milestone for the PCI by ending, albeit not wholly, that party's isolation from direct political power for more than thirty years since its expulsion from government by Alcide de Gasperi. By 1978 the PCI had advanced ever further, joining with other parties in the so-called constitutional arc in signing a multilateral programmatic agreement, which a restructured Andreotti government was to administer. The agreement brought the PCI even closer to power, but at some cost. The Communists were obliged to agree to a number of Christian Democrat proposals, including enhanced powers of arrest by the police and the setting up of special prisons to house "political detainees"—little more than a euphemism for leading BR activists. The unions had to promise to deliver on a limited incomes policy. By March 1978 the former prime minister, Aldo Moro, then president of the Christian Democrats, had, through a combination of subtle diplomacy, linquistic ingenuity and a measure of old-fashioned political duplicity, succeeded in persuading his own party to accept the PCI into the "governing majority,"[7] a kind of political halfway house invented by Italians in answer to the question as to when an Opposition is not an Opposition. The answer, it seemed, was when the PCI was in the governing majority, although not formally in the government in constitutional terms and, therefore, unrepresented in the cabinet. The BR decided to go after the architect of this particular compromise, and in a daring move its members kidnapped and subsequently assassinated Moro.

NOTES

1. A. Silj, *Mai piu senza fucile* (Florence: Vallecchi, 1977), p. 63.

2. Interview with the magazine *Europeo*, June 20, 1975.

3. Earlier that year, Margherita with other armed supporters freed her husband from the prison at Casale Monferrato, where he was being held following his arrest the previous September.

4. Silj, *Mai piu senza fucile* p. 25.

5. Giorgio Bocca. *Il terrorismo Italiano*, (Milan: Rizzoli, 1978), p. 9.

6. Enrico Berlinguer, *"Riflessioni sull'Italia dopo i Fatti del Cile,"* three articles published in *Rinascita*, September 28, October 5, and October 12, 1973.

7. This particular formula collapsed on January 26, 1979, when Berlinguer told the other parties that, after a careful examination of the facts, the PCI had reached the conclusion that its continued presence in the majority had become impossible. He charged the Andreotti administration with, among other things, a campaign to portray the PCI *"as ideologically and politically responsible for terrorism"* and with a failure to implement agreed programs. In fact, Berlinguer and the PCI leadership had come under growing rank-and-file pressure to distance themselves from the DC, but in the subsequent (again) premature general election the PCI suffered a significant reversal. [author's italics]

7 Terrorism in the 1970s

Now that I have filled in this essential political backdrop,—
essential, that is, to understand better the evolution of tactics and
militancy both by the BR and by other emerging terrorist groups—
I want to go back to the early 1970s. The BR militants started with
the premise that an internal Italian crisis was in progress, and that
it was fundamentally structural. It was leading capitalism to ally
itself with the parliamentary Left, guaranteed by the consent of the
masses. The purpose of such an alliance, as analyzed by BR leaders, was to put off the end of the capitalist system, which, however,
could be advanced if the proletariat choose the path of armed
struggle. In order to put this struggle into effect, it was necessary
to implant deeply into the working class the historical necessity for
armed action; to break "corporative links" between the directing
class and the workers' organizations; to strike directly at the government and oppose every attempt to put the "historic compromise" into practice. Throughout the embattled 1970s the objectives of terrorists appeared to change little, but their operations
and tactics altered considerably and gained growing militancy from
the time of their first real "political" kidnapping. This involved the
taking of the procurator-general in Genoa, Mario Sossi, who was
captured by a BR commando unit on April 18, 1974.[1] Sossi was
known within the "New Left" as "doctor handcuffs" for the zeal
with which, it was claimed, he prosecuted extremists. He was,
according to a press communiqué left for journalists in a telephone
kiosk in Genoa, "a basic pawn on the chessboard of the counter-
revolution, a fanatical persecutor of the working class." Sossi faced
a "proletarian trial" during which his disclosures, spontaneous or
induced, seemed to throw strong doubts on the independence of
the Italian judiciary and to include other unsavory political tidbits
of innuendo touching on people in the higher echelons of government power. The BR demanded, with the claimed backing of

Sossi, the release of a number of "political prisoners," and their release was ordered, but, after Sossi's was freed, the order was immediately rescinded through the agency of the Genoa magistrate, Francesco Coco. About two years later, in June 1976, Coco and his two bodyguards were gunned down in broad daylight. This incident provided the BR with its revenge.

Long before, however, indeed soon after the release of Sossi, the militant movement suffered its own first major setback with the arrest of both Curcio and Franceschini,[2] resulting from the infiltration of BR ranks by Silvano Girotto, a former Franciscan friar with a questionable background as a mercenary (in Algeria) and a guerrilla (in Bolivia and Chile). Girotto was later to write in his political defense.[3] "With foolish irresponsibility you are facilitating the progress of the fascist scum. . . . enclosed in your ivory tower of illusions, feverishly possessed by sacred fury against everything and everyone, you failed to interpret correctly even the repudiation expressed with extreme clarity by the very people you claim to be the advance guard of, namely the working class." The capture of top BR leaders and other suspects did nothing, however, to reduce the activities of the movement, or its obvious growing efficiency. The range of victims, too, was widened, whether for kidnapping and show trials, knee-capping,[4] or assassination, to take in journalists, magistrates, doctors, police, and prison officers. The BR was to declare subsequently that the political role of the press and the mass media in general was to mobilize the masses permanently in a reactionary manner, to organize a consensus for the physical destruction of the "enemies" of democracy. "The regime's press is always at the service of the class enemy (the bourgeoisie); falsehood and mystification are its rule."[5] It was not perhaps a wholly original analysis; more than fifty years earlier Antonio Gramsci had written in the Socialist Party journal *Avanti:* "The bourgeois worker should always know the bourgeois newspaper (no matter its complexion) is an instrument of struggle impelled by ideas and interests which are contrary to his own. Everything it prints is constantly influenced by one idea, that of serving the ruling class, which translates itself into one fact, that of combatting the working class." Nothing much had seemingly changed in half a century, except perhaps the definition of the middle class.

The increased daring of the BR, the widening of its list of victims, and its overall organizational efficiency may have stemmed from a growing number of recruits, but more likely it came from the skills and fanatical commitment of its new leaders—those who replaced Curcio, his immediate deputy, Fabrizio Pelli (captured in September 1974), Franceschini, Cagol, and the others. Curcio himself was to say at the time of his second arrest: "With my capture, the BR have simply lost a man, but there are many of us, you can not even imagine how many, of all kinds, from all classes and social extraction and position."[6] He was also to observe, during his subsequent trial, in a direct reference to the taking of Aldo Moro: "We didn't do things on such a large scale—a view echoed in part by the mother of Cagol, who said in an interview: "The new BR are a different matter." More and more the BR movement became a tightly organized body split into small cells of a few members each, and with minimal contact between them. So-called columns were based principally in Milan, Turin, Genoa, Rome, and Naples. Private estimates by the Italian security authorities, whatever their accuracy, put the number of BR activists at no more than 500, perhaps only a dozen to twenty of whom would act as assassins, although several thousand might be "passive sympathizers."[7] Cristoforo Piancone, a BR activist arrested in 1978, quoted a total membership of 1,500, whereas Giorgio Bocca[8] estimated the number of Italian terrorists in all groups and movements, and not just the BR, at about 3,000. He went on to observe that this figure "is respectable when we consider that this was the number of all Italian partisans between September 1943 and March 1944, before the great increase in the spring of the latter year." The BR itself has noted what is perhaps its greatest strength. "The revolutionary movement has a strength that the traditional means of repression do not succeed in touching, because of the guerrilla fighters' capacity to live among the workers in the big industrial centers, among the proletarian masses of students and the emarginated of the workers in the suburbs and in the prisons. There they make themselves both clandestine and incapable of being discovered."[9]

By the middle of 1978 approximately 250 alleged BR members were in jail, either under sentence or awaiting trial. The number still free then and now, whatever the precise total, was clearly adequate to continue efficiently the reign of terror. The publication of communiqués, often with supporting photographs, in several cities, and quickly following individual incidents, demonstrated the skills and organization acquired by the movement. One of their (abandoned) hideouts uncovered in Rome contained a "manual of behaviour" laying down the careful and discreet personal conduct to be adopted by activists. Secret official reports were also found, suggesting that the BR had infiltrated the Interior and Justice

Ministries and the ranks of the police; earlier there had been sug-
gestions, based on circumstantial evidence and inferential conclusions, that some magistrates might even be sympathetic to the BR
cause, and a number of lawyers did represent themselves as being
acceptable intermediaries between the authorities and the terrorists.

I now return to an informal chronology of events following the
first BR kidnapping, that of Idalgo Macchiarini in 1972, the taking
of Sossi in 1974, and the movement's first killings the same year.
The following year marked the official birth of "Eurocommunism,"[10] and with it the BR stepped up its attacks, criminal and
verbal, on the political parties, but mainly the PCI and its allies in
the trade-union movement. A BR communiqué released to the
press in February 1975 noted that "the counter-revolutionary
forces active in the country today are in the process of carrying out
a white putsch *(colpo bianco)* in the true sense, following the
instructions of [U.S. President] Ford and [Secretary of State] Kissinger. . . . We have, in other words, reached the point in which the
dramatic crisis of the bourgeoisie's hegemony over the proletariat
results in the terroristic use of the state's entire apparatus of coer-
cion. The campaign of public order deliberately prepared and
launched in recent months, especially by the Christian Democrats,
demonstrates this. The working-class movement . . . must put on
the agenda the need for the historic breach with the Christian
Democrats and the defeat of the strategy of compromize. It must
put on the agenda the question of power and the dictatorship of the
proletariat." In a January 1976 communiqué, the BR had returned
to the attack specifically against the Communist party: "Berlinguer's ultrarevisionists have long renounced organising the working-
class struggle in the field of resistance and the class war in return
for a warm seat in the armchairs at the sidelines of power. By the
obscene practice of 'compromise' with the soft-line Christian Democrat rulers and the 'corporative pact' with wealthy industrialists
such as Agnelli [head of the Fiat company], they too seek the
defeat of the revolutionary tensions which permeate and stir the
working class."

The increasing shrillness of these BR communiqués was accompanied by further outbursts of terrorist activity and by some moves
to organize a combined front with other revolutionary groups. The
right-wing Christian Democrat leader of the town council in Milan,
Massimo de Carolis, was knee-capped, as were Enrico Boffa, a
manager with the Singer Company, and Vincenzo Casabona, per-

sonnel manager of Ansaldo Nucleare. Another victim was a Fiat medical doctor, Lugi Solera. Meanwhile, evidence emerged that a number of NAP (Nucleo Armato Proletario) followers had joined forces with the BR in a seemingly informal alliance that also embraced elements in the GAP (Gruppo Armato Proletario), formed by the millionaire property and publishing entrepreneur, Giangiacomo Feltrinelli. The latter's imagination had been fired by the rise to power of Fidel Castro in Cuba, and he was to die violently when, according to police, he blew himself up with a bomb he was planting at an electric installation near Milan in 1972.

By May 1976 the authorities were ready to proceed with the trial in Turin of some of the top BR activists then in custody; less ready were ordinary Italians to serve on the jury, primarily because of threats emanating from the BR. Shortly after the trial opened, Fulvio Croce, chairman of the Turin judiciary council charged with the defense of the accused, was murdered and, as noted earlier, weeks later Francesco Coco was gunned down with his bodyguards. In the Turin courtroom the BR accused hurled abuse at the entire judicial system, insisted on their right to be considered not ordinary criminals but prisoners of war, and threatened that in the course of time their prosecutors would themselves be tried for "war crimes."

All the while, violent acts continued throughout Italy on virtually a daily basis, with only the more notorious getting mass-media coverage. The official trade unions continued to organize work stoppages to protest against the growing violence, but support for these protests declined from a public that seemed increasingly apathetic to violence against a system and its institutions, from which very many Italians felt isolated. The political parties made regular and noisy demands for tougher measures to maintain "law and order," and the neo-Fascists were openly harkening back to the Mussolini era. The PCI demanded more action by the government, but the party was, characteristically, reluctant to join in voting tougher security measures, being more ready to address blanket criticism against the Christian Democrats and their three decades of inefficient and corrupt rule, which, said the PCI, was largely responsible for the climate of terrorism.

The actual or imagined international links of the BR also began to get emphasis, sometimes from politicians but mainly in the news media. The fact that both Moscow and the BR were opposed to the new concept of Eurocommunism produced some sinister notions that perhaps the Soviet Union was somehow behind the Italian terrorists. Weapons used in the assassination of the judge, Coco, were Czech-made, whereas Curcio had Czechoslovak visas in both his real and his fake passports when arrested the second time. Francesco Cossiga, interior minister at the time, told Parliament in November 1977 that there appeared to be some connection between the BR and the West German Baader-Meinhof terrorist faction. The following year police in Milan found copies of a sixty-page booklet in which the BR compared their struggle with that of the Red Army group in West Germany and the Armed Nuclei for the People's Autonomy (NAPAP) in France and urged greater cooperation on an international level. A Fiat executive kidnapped by the BR told a Turin court that one of his captors had said that he had undergone guerrilla training abroad, and the Italian and West German media reported that such a training camp did, in fact, exist near Karlovy Vary in Czechoslovakia. German-born Petra Krause, an Italian citizen by marriage, was extradited from custody in Switzerland on charges of setting fire to an electronics factory near Milan. She had been charged in Switzerland with participation in bombing attacks, supplying arms to Baader-Meinhof supporters, and organizing a Zurich anarchist group in thefts of ammunition, explosives, and weapons from Swiss military armories. Weapons used by the BR in Turin were said officially to have been linked with these thefts, and two Swiss anarchists who were charged along with Krause admitted supplying arms to "foreign terrorists." The international conspiracy theory gradually took shape in Italy, although the published evidence was rather flimsy. Paolo Bufalini, one of the top Italian Communist leaders, thought that Italian terrorism was an indigenous phenomenon, but he did not exclude intervention by foreign forces or groups, perhaps reactionary ones. "These latter would be interested, in this phase of Italian politics especially, in disestablishing Italian democracy and impeding the present democratic unitary process from going ahead,"[11] wrote Bufalini.

For a while it seemed in Italy almost more important to establish some international links with the BR than to actually capture the movement's new leaders and resolutely prosecute the old guard awaiting trial. The law-enforcement agencies of the state appeared incapable of making significant inroads in BR ranks; the Christian Democratic politicians were too busy either trying to prop up successive weak governments or endeavoring to make new alliances short of actually sharing power directly with the Communists. Then, dramatically, the complacency was shattered, temporarily at least, by the BR's blockbuster, the kidnapping on March 16, 1978, of Aldo Moro. Suddenly, Italy appeared to be thrown into total turmoil with the basic institutions of the state under attack. Could it survive under such a terrorist fusillade?

NOTES

1. There had been numerous other BR actions in the previous two years: the kidnapping of union official Bruno Labate, Alfa Romeo manager Michele Mincuzzi, and Fiat personnel manager Ettore Amerio, all three charged at their "trials" with exploiting the working class. However, the taking of Sossi could be considered, and was in fact by the authorities, as the BR's first direct assault against the state.

2. Sossi was later to identify Franceschini as one of his captors.

3. In an "Open letter to the BR," photocopies of which were distributed to news agencies and selective journalists both in Turin and Milan.

4. Shooting victims in the legs, but with no intention that they should die. The process of knee-capping was started in Ireland by the IRA.

5. Communiqué no. 6 during the Moro affair (see below).

6. V. Tassandori, *BR imputazione banda armata* (Milan: Garzanti, 1977), p. 246.

7. A phrase and a number used frequently by officials of the Italian Ministry of the Interior in private briefings for foreign embassies in Rome and quoted in unofficial documents produced by their governments. See, for example, a briefing document, *Italy: Red Brigade*, June 1978, prepared by the British Foreign and Commonwealth Office.

8. Giorgio Bocca, *Il terrorismo Italiano* (Milan: Rizzoli, 1978), p. 110.

9. "Risoluzione della direzione strategica delle Brigate Rosse," published in Italian newspapers on April 5, 1978.

10. Authorship of the word *Eurocommunism* has been attributed to the Yugoslav journalist, Frane Barbieri in an article in *Giornale nuovo*, published on June 26, 1975, a few days before a joint declaration by Enrico Berlinguer and the Spanish Communist leader, Santiago Carrillo, launched the concept. It appeared to be reaffirmed later that same year (November 17) in another joint statement, this time by the Italian and French Communist parties.

11. Paolo Bufalini, *Terrorismo e Democrazia* (Rome: Editori Riuniti, 1978), p. 19.

8 The Murder of Compromise

Early in the morning on Thursday, March 16, 1978, Aldo Moro, five times prime minister of Italy and president of the Christian Democrat party, was being driven to Parliament under the surveillance of a five-man bodyguard. Parliament was meeting to approve a new government under the premiership of Giulio Andreotti, with the unique support of the Communist party, which, it seemed, had finally come in from the political cold. Andreotti, the caretaker prime minister, was to retain that post, but it was Moro who had plotted the compromise with the Communists and who, in a marathon talking session, had finally persuaded the DC to accept it, albeit with considerable reluctance on the part of many of his party's deputies and senators. Bringing the PCI into the "government majority" had been Moro's personal achievement, just as more than fifteen years earlier he had masterminded that other historic turning in postwar Italian politics, the center-left governing formula that had ended the isolation of the Socialists. To many observers, not the least perhaps in Washington, Bonn, and London, it seemed that now the full realization of the *compromesso storico* might be just around the corner, and that the largest Communist party in the West was about to share directly in the government of a strategically important member of the North Atlantic Treaty Organization. The deal with the PCI had finally been clinched a little more than forty-eight hours before Aldo Moro left his home in a northern suburb of Rome to go to Parliament. He never got there.

In a daring and ruthlessly efficient ambush by BR commando units, Moro was kidnapped and his bodyguards were gunned down on the street. The veteran republican party leader, the late Ugo La Malfa, was quick to declare: "Without doubt we are now in a state of war . . . the terrorists want to destroy the democratic state."[1] The democratic state reacted, although none too quickly or

efficiently in the view of the present writer, who was based in
Rome at the time. Roadblocks supported by police and army units
were thrown up around the city, but the terrorists spirited their
celebrated prisoner away. He was heard from two days later when
the first of a series of "Moro communiqués" was released to the
mass media. Like others over the following eight weeks, it was not
always crystal clear in its language or explicit in its references.
Moro, declared communiqué no. 1, was "the indisputable strategist of the Christian Democrat regime which has opposed the Italian
people for thirty years." He had been kidnapped by the BR, the
communiqué said, and his bodyguard, "composed of five agents of
the notorious special branch," had been killed.

The most obvious objective of the Moro kidnapping was to try to
stifle at birth the new governing majority and with it the prospect
of the PCI's cherished *compromesso*. However, an important and,
in the long run, perhaps more significant motive was to strike a
direct blow at the Christian Democrats and to unveil in public,
using the "testimony" of Moro himself—whether extracted or
volunteered—the party's dirty political linen, and to do so before a
public which, essentially, was prepared to believe the worst about
its political leaders and about a system of government from which
most felt isolated. The Christian Democrats were, said the BR
communiqué, in the process of implementing a plan of "transformation in the European area of the obsolete nation-states of
liberal stamp into imperialist states of the multinationals," a plan
being maneuvered, it was claimed, by the major imperial powers.
"This ambitious plan, in order to be able to succeed, requires one
essential prerequisite: the creation of political, economic and military personnel to implement it. During recent years this political
personnel, inseparately linked to imperialist circles, has assumed a
leading role in all the parties of the so-called constitutional arc
('arco costituzionale'), but has its maximum concentration . . . in
the Christian Democrat Party." Moro personally was characterized
as being "the political godfather and most faithful executant of the
directives issued by the imperialist centers of power."

The communiqué continued:

> In the framework of the strategic unit of the imperialist states,
> the major powers at the head of the hierarchical chain require
> the Christian Democrats to function as the national political pole
> of the counter-revolution. It is the machine of Christian Demo-
> crat power, transformed and "renewed", and the new regime

imposed by it, which should propel the reconversion of the nation-state into the effective link in the imperialist chain, thus enabling the savage economic policies and profound institutional changes, openly repressive in character, requested by the strong partners in the chain—the United States and the Federal Republic of Germany—to be implemented.

In a second communiqué the BR returned directly to the attack on Moro, who, it was claimed, in encouraging the formation of the center-left governing formula in 1963, had furthered an American attempt "to recover the 'left-wing' fringe of the Italian bourgeoisie by the incorporation of the Socialist (PSI) in the government," with the result of further dividing the working-class movement. The BR's demands, whatever their ultimate intentions, were made clear, namely the release from prison of thirteen "Communist prisoners," including Curcio, Franceschini, and Ognibene, in exchange for Moro, who, in any event, was to face "proletarian trial."

For the BR more was involved than just the spectacular kidnapping of Moro. For weeks the terrorists had the news media at their mercy ready and only too willing to provide immediate and extensive exposure to BR statements and demands. The movement succeeded in making the established security forces of the state look inefficient and, at times, plain stupid. False trails were plotted to send the police and the army on useless searches while, with obvious efficiency and daring, vehicles used by the BR in grabbing Moro were gradually returned to the immediate area of the kidnapping, despite extensive police presence in the zone. A message purporting to come from the terrorists sent hundreds of police, army personnel, frogmen, and others to a frozen lake up in the Apennine mountains—another false alarm.

The political forces, too, often appeared in disarray or, at best, unsure how to respond, and it appeared that the BR were not only holding Moro but were also, and efficiently, holding the nation for ransom. The pope issued an appeal to the terrorists to show mercy and release their prisoner, as did Kurt Waldheim, the Secretary-General of the United Nations, but to no avail. Almost continuous police and military roadblocks and the searching of houses and apartments in many parts of the country not only added to the near-chaos that is normal Italian urban traffic but also antagonized a great many people who, noticeably, had more sympathy for the murdered bodyguards and their families than for Moro and the politicians. As the immediate shock of the initial act gave way to reflection, the big question was whether the political forces would capitulate, would give into the terrorists' demands for the release of prisoners. The first political party to weaken, indeed substantially the only one that did so during the long ordeal, were the Socialists under their new secretary, Bettino Craxi, who was prepared to offer a deal, or at least to consider it.[2] The Communists stood firm, insisting that there could be no surrender to the agents of violence. One of the PCI's elder statesmen, the late Giorgio Amendola, had earlier stated that "the criminal actions of the so-called BR, every act of violence, no matter under what colour it attempts to hide itself, is invariably an act which serves fascism."[3] Paolo Bufalini, reflecting on the Moro case, was to write:

> One thing is certain, that we find ourselves faced by barbarous methods. Absolute firmness is essential in opposing the BR. If the blackmail is yielded to—and in a case so high in level and so great in scale—the way would be opened to the dissolution of the State, or in any event to a recognised situation of military conflict which would involve great consequences. . . . The popular masses and all citizens will certainly continue to make a valuable contribution to the public security forces, the police and soldiers engaged against terrorism. . . . The most important contribution is the political and moral isolation of the BR and their sympathisers and supporters, in order to deprive them of every alibi, every external collaboration and every point of support.[4]

On balance, the ranks of Christian Democracy, too, held firm, although there were some potential supporters of compromise. The party's then secretary, Benigno Zaccagnini, a moderate and humane man, sought to harmonize conflicting views from within the party, and also from Moro's wife and family who, understandably, were more concerned with securing his release than with any political consequences stemming from a deal with the terrorists. Lights burned bright into the night in the various party headquarters in Rome while the BR held the media headlines with their stream of communiqués, demands, allegations against the ruling elite, and reports of the progress of Moro's "proletarian trial." The political Right called for tougher measures against the unseen enemy. Antiterrorist security advisers came to Italy from other European countries with help to track down the BR leaders, but with little apparent success. By the time of the BR's communiqué no. 4, Aldo Moro was talking through a memorandum that his captors said he had personally drawn up. He accused much of the ruling elite in Italy. Andreotti was described as a "cool-headed director, inscrutable, without a heart, without a trace of human compassion . . . of whose orders the others are all merely obedient executors." Those who knew the then prime minister thought privately that the description was not too wide of the mark, but none of the top DC leaders wanted to say very much on the record, for none knew who would next be named by the BR or in further extracts from Moro's alleged memorandum. Against a background of some fairly sensational acts of political corruption in Italy, disclosures by the BR were inclined to be believed, no matter how far-fetched they sounded on first reading. Moro went on to insist, or at least to have claimed on his behalf, that he was unwilling to pay the price personally for the errors of the whole governing class. "They are bringing forward accusations which concern everyone, but I am called to pay the price for them personally, with consequences which it is not difficult to imagine."

The national tension and the agony of Moro dragged slowly on. The release of BR communiqué no. 6 in mid-April headlined that "Aldo Moro is guilty, and has therefore been condemned to death." Some three weeks and three communiqués later, the BR said: "We have nothing further to say in words to the DC, to its government and to the accomplices who uphold it [in power]. The only language which the servants of imperialism have shown that they understand is that of arms, and it is this language which the proletariat is learning to speak. We therefore bring to its conclusion the battle begun on March 16, by carrying out the sentence to which Aldo Moro has been condemned."

The body of the DC president was found on May 9, as a final mockery it seemed to the state and its forces, abandoned in the trunk of a small Renault car parked in Via Michelangelo Caetani in the historic center of Rome and roughly midway between the party headquarters of the Christian Democrats and the Communists. Apart from taking the life of a distinguished politician, the BR had clearly won the propaganda war and had demonstrated an organizational and operative efficiency which, however temporarily, proved to surpass that of the security forces, albeit in a situation in which the advantage must inevitably be with the terrorists. Yet the immediate balance sheet also demonstrated, and it was a sizable achievement, that the political forces in the country generally held firm, refused to be intimidated, and rejected making a deal, which, recalling the Sossi-Coco affair, the BR would, in all probability, not have delivered on anyway. The terrorists had unquestionably unbalanced the Italian state and its institutions but had not succeeded in pulling them down, and they themselves were left inevitably with two significant questions: firstly, what form would a new spectacular have to take to be seen as an "appropriate" encore to the Moro affair; and, secondly, did the whole affair itself, whatever the immediate trauma, alter significantly anything in Italy's unbalanced society or advance the revolutionary purpose of the extremists?

The second question is the easier—and the answer is no. The first must inevitably await events, and even an upstage on the Moro kidnapping and assassination cannot be excluded. A judge with special responsibility for top-security prisons, Giovanni D'Urso, was kidnapped in December 1980 and, like Moro, put on "proletarian trial" by the BR. He was released after thirty-four days, however, the terrorists having secured a partial victory in that some (but not all) Italian newspapers responded to their demands to publish a lengthy statement incorporating the views of the *Brigatisti*, both in jail and at large. The security forces, for their part, were not without some success either, and during 1980 about 700 terrorist suspects were detained. General Umberto Cappuzzo, the head of the paramilitary police force, the 85,000-strong Carabinieri, expressed the view the following year that terrorism in Italy was no longer so much a police problem as a political and social one. "The solid image of terrorism is cracking,"[5] he claimed, under the police onslaught. The authorities could rightly claim a remarkable security coup in the Dozier case. James Dozier, the senior American NATO general based in Italy, was kidnapped by the Red Brigades from his apartment in Verona just before Christmas, 1981, and released unharmed some 42 days later when a ten-man police commando unit raided a flat in suburban Padua. They captured alive five terrorists. Within days of Dozier's release, some 260 arrest warrants had been issued for terrorist suspects based largely on information gained from the "Padua five." It might, however, be rash to assume, as was general in the Italian and European media, that the Dozier case had broken the terrorists; their demise had been reported prematurely in the past.

Cappuzzo was on much safer ground, however, in the view of this writer, with his opinion that the active terrorists "may be only a few hundred," but that their sympathizers, who enable them to operate, are many more.

That is why it is not a question of simple repression any more. We have got to make the young believe in democracy, to see that violence doesn't lead to reform, and *that minorities do have a chance of becoming majorities* [author's italics]. . . . It is the classic Maoist doctrine of the fish in the water. The terrorists swim in these waters of sympathisers. We may be successful fishermen, but what we have to do is remove the water. . . . If the politicians can see this, and bring in measures to ensure that terrorism, defeated once, doesn't just spring up again in another form, the problem can be solved.

I now return to the immediate aftermath of the Moro killing. Some tentative signs had then surfaced of dissent within revolutionary ranks. One such dissident published his views in a polemical and often rambling presentation in the columns of *Lotta Continua*:[6]

This battle represents the apex of the strategic undertaking of the armed struggle. It represents the highest example of what levels of power, defiance of the State, ransoming of power the proletariat can achieve by using the principal instrument in its struggle—organization. That is what the Moro operation achieved for the Italian revolutionary movement. Fine, but after having demonstrated what power can be achieved, it is essential to look back, and to make sure that this "concentration" and "school" of power-potential was really made up from the whole proletarian movement.

This dissenting voice appeared to argue that isolated acts of terrorism coupled with narrow, and essentially individualistic, demands—for example, the release of prisoners for the freedom of Moro—did not advance the interests of the working class. A quoted instance of what would be more advantageous was the use of terrorist power to "destroy an electronic checking and spying unit used against the working-class in a factory." From their maximum security prison, Curcio and the "foundation group" of the BR provided its dismissive reply to such doubts and seemingly counterrevolutionary assertions.[7] In a reply directed to the "whole revolutionary movement," the BR noted sarcastically that summer was the time of the mosquito, and that "just as irritating as the mosquito, there are felt the stings . . . of those who, in the service of the imperialist counter-revolutionaries, buzz around the guerrilla band. . . . Every revolution inevitably drags along in its wake slime and trash of every kind." They were certainly not ready for compromise.

Within Communist party ranks, another compromise, the *compromesso storico*, had come under increasing pressure. Many rank-and-file members could not understand the need to make a deal in government with, to them, the long-hated Christian Democrats. Was the PCI, they asked, a party of proletarian struggle or a party of compromise? All the while the party's leadership was stung continuously by needling assertions, often from within its own ranks, that the PCI had lost its revolutionary ways and, even more so, by the insistence by the BR that they were the true Communist combatants; all BR communiqués ended with the assertion *per il comunismo*, an association of words that produced its own embarrassment for Berlinguer and his party. Some Italian socialists, too, entered the fray, although probably more for electoral than ideological reasons. *Mondo Operaio*, the PSI's cultural review, suggested that Gramsci's hegemony of the working-class, to which the PCI insisted it was still committed, was not an alternative to the "dictatorship of the proletariat" but rather a prerequisite for its realization. One of the PCI's old guard, Pietro Ingrao, who had become Speaker of the Chamber of Deputies in Rome following the Communists' successes in the 1976 general election and who was known to be no committed enthusiast of Berlinguer's *compromesso* policy, later acknowledged that perhaps not all PCI policies and programs were along uninterrupted Gramscian lines. Soundings to PCI party headquarters from the constituencies suggested, at best, considerable confusion over Berlinguer's policies and, at worst, downright disquiet, which, inevitably, increased when the PCI's arrival into the governing majority showed party members no obvious gains. Instead, the party was seen to be pressing the trade unions to sell a government "austerity programme" to the workers as a necessary measure to overcome yet another economic crisis, this time partly a consequence of sharply higher oil prices.

Perhaps above all, the PCI showed signs of losing its grip on, or at least its appeal to, the young generation, even prior to the taking of Aldo Moro. This loss created a vacuum, which, in one sense, the BR was able to exploit indirectly, and which others were in a position to channel more directly into a kind of loose metamorphosis that was revolutionary but not committed solely, or even predominantly, to violence. This loose force had emerged in 1977 in a kind of rebirth of the earlier student crisis.[8] The PCI, moving closer to government, was trying publicly to ride two horses simultaneously, terming itself "the party of struggle and of government." This delicate process resulted in the Communists permitting opposition to grow on their left, mainly from young people and students and the ranks of the chronically unemployed, categories that, for all the fine declarations, have long since been largely ignored (and continue so today) both by successive governments and by the trade unions. In this latter regard, it was interesting that one of Italy's leading trade unionists, Luciano Lama, the secretary-general of GGIL, visited the University of Rome to speak with students on the invitation of the PCI. He was shouted down and had to be virtually smuggled out of the campus, and the police were called in to deal with a near-riot situation after some shots were fired from the crowd. Major protest demonstrations and discussion sit-ins followed in a number of centers during 1977, notably two very big rallies—in Rome and in the Communist stronghold of Bologna. The former resulted in widespread disturbances, and again with gunfire from the crowd, while at Bologna a young student, Francesco Lorusso, was killed during a battle with the Carabinieri, and the city was for a while in a state of semisiege.

The spectacle of Bologna, the established showplace of Communist administration, being apparently unable to maintain ordinary law and order was particularly sensitive for the PCI—a situation that not unnaturally delighted some extremist leaders who had helped to bring it about. Matters were not improved when the PCI daily, *L'Unita*, echoed the minister of the interior by labeling the students and young people in Bologna as "Fascist." A follow-up demonstration in the same city later that year produced a massive crowd, variously estimated at between 40,000 and 80,000, this time a mainly peaceful demonstration, which, more importantly, resolved into a form of impromptu debate between the so-called armed party declaring a commitment to outright violence against the state and its institutions and a majority demanding radical change but not that bought with the barrel of a gun. Too late perhaps, as one analysis of the 1979 general election outcome can indicate, the PCI's central leadership woke up to the fact that a vast reservoir of discontent existed among the youth and the unemployed. This discontent was not just directed against lack of jobs and the defects in the educational system but against a host of other concerns—environmental damage from largely unplanned industrialization, inadequate health and social services, inequalities in income, massive tax evasion by the wealthy—in total over the failure of the system in Italy to evolve into a progressive and fully participative democracy operating within contemporary social and human values, a society capable of fulfilling the rapidly changing standards and expectations of a younger generation.

This potentially explosive situation could, in the long hual, prove an even greater problem than the terrorists of the BR—or those from the neo-Fascist ranks, notably *Tertsa Positione*. Italy today is not only a vast arena of protest, but it is one that is structured on differing levels with different objectives and prepared to use differing means. Notoriously, at the top are the BR, but below them come the lesser terrorists, such as the extremists in NAP and similar organizations. Further down the scale of protest are the *autonomi*, in part coordinated somewhat loosely by a reformed Lotta Continua, and a myriad of other student and militant worker factions besides, many of whom surface briefly with a claim of responsibility for some particular violent action and then are not heard from perhaps for months. During the year of the Moro kidnapping, 1978, reports[9] show the existence by name within Italy of 209 "terrorist groups" (against, incidentally, only 76 the previous year), 181 said to be classified as "left" and 28 as "right."

This frightening potpourri, including its supporters and passive sympathizers, is, in Italy, the real minority today, and the country and its established political forces have yet to demonstrate any potential to persuade it to follow along constitutional lines, or even as a start to understand and appreciate the forces and the expectations behind it. Italy is now well beyond the stage of conventional social protest of the 1970s; it is bordering precariously on the verge of social breakdown in many of the larger towns and cities. This condition must be looked at against the country's recurring political crises and the vast economic divide that still separates the nation between north and south. The recipe for orderly change— and speedily before a form of national rigor mortis sets in—is not easy to set down. One encouraging ingredient remains, and it is the remarkable fact, and a characteristic of most Italians, however temporarily pessimistic they may be, that those who bemoan the system and its deficiencies the most are also those who express a sort of fatalistic acceptance that somehow it will survive.

Notes

1. *Financial Times*, London: March 17, 1978, and other newspapers.

2. In some measure Craxi was influenced by an earlier episode in which the son of Francesco De Martino, his immediate predecessor as party secretary, was kidnapped and later released in circumstances that have never been documented publicly. Also, Craxi may have feared isolation in a DC/PCI alliance.

3. In an interview with the Milan-based newspaper *Corriere della Sera*.

4. Paolo Bufalini, *Terrorismo e Democrazia* (Rome: Editori Riuniti, 1978), p. 16–17.

5. Interview with the *Financial Times*, London, February 3, 1981.

6. *Lotta Continua*, July 25, 1979.

7. *Lotta Continua*, August 11, 1979.

8. For a more detailed account, see Giovanni Russo's contribution to *Eurocommunism: Myth or Reality*, eds. della Torre et al. (London: Penguin, 1979), pp. 94–96.

9. PCI's Sezione Problemi dello Stato's publication, *Attentati e Violenza nel 1978*, pp. 10–11.

PART III

The Turks in Cyprus

1 Early History of Cyprus

The situation which Turkey is striving to create in Cyprus closely resembles the Irish problem. The native population has been driven from a part of the island, and their lands have been seized. The intention is to have only Turks in the occupied area, thus creating another Ulster within Cyprus. The analogy will become a homology if the partition of Cyprus results in the Turkish section being linked with Turkey. A "Republic of Turkey and Northern Cyprus" will create endless trouble because the expelled population will strike back eventually.

P. N. Vanezis,

Cyprus: The Unfinished Agony

Cyprus, like Ireland, is a small country, although even smaller, and at the other end of Europe. Most Cypriots, however, see themselves more positively, pointing to their island as being the third largest (after Sicily and Sardinia) in the Mediterranean. Cyprus has a land area of just about three-fifths that of Ulster and a total population less than half that of the Irish province. The two islands, however, do have much that is common, at least at first glance. There are religious differences in Cyprus between Christians and Moslems; there are racial differences between Greeks and (implanted) Turks; there are differences of language,[1] although many educated Turks can speak Greek, and, similarly, some Greeks know the Turkish-Cypriot dialect—which is different from the language of the Turkish mainland. English is, for all practical purposes, the lingua franca throughout Ireland today, and it is also in wide use in Cyprus, but not among the peasants. Ireland was partitioned formally by the 1920 Government of Ireland Act; Cyprus now has de facto partition following an invasion by the Turkish army from the mainland in 1974. Both islands secured a measure of independence from the same colonial power, Britain, after a bloody campaign of violence, albeit relatively short-lived in Cyprus. Arguably, both national "minorities," the Ulster Protestants and the Turkish-Cypriots, would have been perfectly content with

151

the maintenance of the colonial status quo. Neither island has found peace.

First, briefly, I will give some essential history, in the context of which to establish the arrival of the Greeks in Cyprus and, very much later, the Turks. The origins of Neolithic settlements in Cyprus (or Asy, as it was originally known) are unclear. The earliest known settlements, on the basis of remains of beehive-shaped hut dwellings discovered at Khirokiyia, close to what is today the port town of Limassol, date from about 5800 B.C. Stone vases and crudely shaped implements of bone and obsidian suggest some contact with Asia Minor. More concretely established, at around 2500 B.C., is the discovery of copper—with which the island's name is associated—and, over the next millennium and more, the introduction of bronze, which put Cyprus on the map for the attention of rival East Mediterranean peoples, notably the Egyptians. They were not colonists in that they made no obvious attempt to populate Cyprus, merely to exact tribute. The real colonists were first the Greeks and later the Phoenicians. Greeks from Mycenae reached the island late in the Bronze Age and established settlements, bringing with them a religion, language, and way of life that, ultimately, became the basis of Greek-Cypriot culture. This development, important in the context of contemporary politics, is often misrepresented in an ingenious attempt to suggest that there are valid grounds for Cyprus to be restored to Greek hegemony;[2] it never was a part of ancient Greece, however. The early settlers were not bent on any expansion of their own land but simply were in search of a new home, particularly after the fall of the Mycenaean empire.

Again there is some parallel with early Irish history in that the first Greeks, like the Celts, established a system of area kingdoms, generally autonomous settlements each with its own ruler, a pattern that the Phoenicians followed, although their motivation was largely commercial, and they sought to exploit the island's strategic position on the sea routes between Greece and the Levant. Their major early stronghold was at Kition, the present-day Larnaca, and for about three centuries Phoenicians and Greeks lived side by side in Cyprus and generally at peace, although both were under the tutelage of Egypt and, later, of Assyria and Persia. Evagoras, king of Salamis (ca. 435–374 B.C.), was the first native Cypriot to attempt to unify the island. He failed but he did much to promote Greek culture at his court and also to popularize the Greek alphabet and Greek coinage. Unification came with the Egyptian

Ptolemies who, in the third century B.C., abolished the kingships in Cyprus. For the next two thousand years and more, the small island experienced a long line of changing rulers—the Romans,[3] the Byzantines, the Lusignans, the Venetians, the Turks, and, from 1878 until 1960, when it secured independence, the British.

The decline and fall of these empires in the roulette of history in which Cyprus was a mere subjugated pawn is not directly germane to this study, but it is necessary to look at the end of the Venetian Period (1489–1571). The Ottoman Empire had by then been expanding fast in the East. The fall of Constantinople and the submission of the Egyptian Mamelukes gave the Ottomans unfettered control over the Eastern Mediterranean—with the exception of Cyprus itself. The rest was inevitable. In 1570, Sultan Selim II demanded the cession of the island to Turkey, the Venetians refused, and the Turks invaded massively and, interestingly in view of today's intercommunal tensions, without any recorded resistance from the native population. The Venetian occupiers did, however, resist fiercely, but they were overwhelmed finally at Famagusta, although not before the Italian general Marcantonio Bragadino and his relatively small garrison had taken about 80,000 Turkish lives.

The Cypriots, for their part, had no good cause for loving the Venetians, and they welcomed the Turks not least in the knowledge that the Ottomans, unlike their Latin rulers, recognized the Orthodox church. Indeed, one of the first administrative acts of the new rulers was to restore the archbishopric. The feudal system was abolished, and most Greek-Cypriots must have thought that their political and religious deliverance had come. Yet the restoration of the archbishopric was not so much an act of religious liberalism on the part of the Ottomans as a recognition that the church could become part of the new administrative process on the island and could collect taxes for Turkey. The Cypriots again had their religious freedom, but they were obliged to pay for it.

There was nothing particularly distinguished about Turkish rule, but the island's implanted minority were, of course, identified directly with the Ottoman rulers, whereas Greek-Cypriots were simply subjects of the sultan. The Greek revolution against Turkish rule, two and a half centuries later, was to find an emotional echo with Greek-Cypriots, and the Turks, fearing a spreading of the rebellion, reacted brutally, the grand vizier summarily executing leading Greek-Cypriot churchmen, including the archbishop. This quickly brought the island's majority into line, but at the price of its total alienation from Turkish rule. It also provided one of the more grisly episodes of "Turkish barbarism" for future Greek-Cypriot school textbooks, which still today put considerable historical emphasis on the sufferings endured by Greeks under the Turks.[4]

By the 1870s, Turkish rule itself was on the defensive, and not only in Cyprus. Turkey was on the verge of national bankruptcy as a result of seemingly unending wars in a vain attempt to hold together a crumbling empire. Cyprus was ceded to Britain (through the Anglo-Turkish Convention, 1878) in return for promised British support in the event of a Russian invasion of Turkey. In the process Turkish-Cypriots lost their special status and became, together with the island's majority, mere colonial subjects. Their defensiveness against the more populous Greek-Cypriots, when it was not outright resentment, stems from that moment.

NOTES

1. Few Irish people today use Gaelic as their first language, but many, including some Protestants, have a working knowledge of it.

2. The island's Greek-speaking people have always seen themselves as being part of the Hellenic world, which is not quite the same thing, but the cultural and emotional pull of this felt association has been a powerful drive in the campaign for *Enosis*.

3. Cicero was military governor of Cyprus for a period when the island was a Roman province. Caesar then returned it to the Ptolemies as a favor to one of their more celebrated daughters, his mistress Cleopatra. The island returned to imperial Roman rule after her death.

4. Barbara Hodge and G. L. Lewis, "Cyprus School History Textbooks: A Study in Education for International Misunderstanding," Parliamentary Group for World Government, 1966.

2 British Rule in Cyprus

Cyprus, in truth, commands the curve of Turkey's southern shore, and if ever the island were in the possession of a country with a system of government unfriendly to her, the consequences to Turkey could be fatal.

Sir Anthony Eden, 1956.

Britain had, until the mid-1950s shown little real inclination to surrender sovereignty over Cyprus. On the contrary, it seemed that the island was one of those places in the minds of the colonial administrators reflected in another House of Commons intervention: "It has always been understood and agreed that there are certain territories in the [British] Commonwealth which, owing to their particular circumstances, can never expect to be fully independent. . . . The question of the abrogation of British sovereignty can not arise. . . . British sovereignty will remain."[1] It was not so understood by Greek-Cypriots, and Britain's seen strategic interests in the overall context of British Middle East policies were, understandably, much less important to the Greeks than their own desire for *Enosis*—the union of Cyprus with Greece. Greek-Cypriots had welcomed British rule in 1878, not only seeing it as a release from Turkish domination but believing it to be a potential stepping-stone to ultimate union with Greece. After all, the British, who had taken the Ionian Islands from the French (who, in their turn, had seized them from the Venetians) had voluntarily handed them to Greece. It was a good omen,[2] thought Greek-Cypriots, and on a periodic, though initially nonviolent, basis they reminded their new colonial masters that *Enosis* was their final objective, not independence. Turkish-Cypriots reacted to these pro-*Enosis* demands by arguing that Cyprus should be returned to Turkey if ever the British were to leave. The Turkish-Cypriot leadership had never indicated that it would settle for minority status; instead, its case was that Cyprus had two separate communities and not, in conventional terms, a majority and a minority.

155

Thus, in 1882, when the British set up a legislative council for the island, the Turkish side expressed little interest, seeing it merely as a minor legislative body in which Greek-Cypriots would be dominant.

In any event, a not unusual colonial hybrid administration was established combining elected with appointed members, but with effective power still residing in the British colonial administrator. Appointees, when combined with the Turkish members, equalled in number the Greek-Cypriot representatives, and the administrator had a casting vote. The colonial official could, of course, also act unilaterally through virtual decree law. This legislative balance remained, in a sense, at the heart of the British administration for the next eighty years, and a pattern emerged of the British authorities using the Turks, or at the very least exploiting their fears, to hold back, and eventually to try to put down militarily, Greek-Cypriots' aspiration for *Enosis*. On the wider diplomatic front, the British argument necessarily changed in keeping with altered political and strategic circumstances. Initially, it was said that *Enosis* was impossible because Britain had a treaty obligation to return the island to Turkey in the event of a British withdrawal. Following Britain's formal annexation of Cyprus in 1914 and Turkey's acceptance of this in the Lausanne Treaty (1923),[3] the British argument against *Enosis* was that Britain's military-strategic needs in the area required British control in Cyprus. Later still, when military considerations became somewhat less pressing, London insisted that *Enosis* could not be conceded because the Turkish-Cypriots would not accept it and would demand partition. This changing rationale did not impress Greek-Cypriots.

By 1931 their frustrations had reached such a point that a mob set fire to Government House in Nicosia, the first violent offensive in support of union with Greece. The British reacted with a degree of military force and administrative repression that combined to sow the seeds of a guerrilla struggle, culminating in the 1955–59 Ethniki Organosis Kyprion Agoniston (EOKA) campaign and a patched-together independence settlement—but not *Enosis*. It is useful to detail the British response in order to understand the speed with which anticolonial sentiment mounted on the Greek-Cypriot side. Law and internal order was restored with additional British troops being called in from Egypt. Two senior bishops were banished from the island, together with other religious and community leaders. About two thousand Greek-Cypriots were either imprisoned or heavily fined, and a collective fine of £66,000, a massive figure in those days in a relatively impoverished country, was imposed on the majority community to meet the cost of damage. Constitutional government was suspended, the Legislative Council was abolished, all political parties were banned, and censorship was imposed on the local press. For the next seventeen years the British governor ruled by decree. By any criteria, the British used a sledgehammer to crack a not too large, if obdurate, nut.

NOTES

1. Henry Hopkinson, British minister of state for colonial affairs.

2. The British takeover of Cyprus was welcomed in a speech by the then bishop of Kition, whose reported initial address to the first British high commissioner included in part: "We accept the change of government in as much as we trust that Great Britain will help Cyprus, as it did the Ionian Islands, to be united with Mother Greece, with which it is naturally connected." See Robert Stephens, *Cyprus: A Place of Arms* (London: Pall Mall, 1966), p. 70.

3. In view of subsequent events in an independent Cyprus, it is interesting to note that the Lausanne settlement provided for the Greek and Turkish populations of Turkey and Greece respectively, to be exchanged, except for the Greeks in Istanbul and the Turks of western Thrace. This compulsory exchange involved about two million people—a massive two-way exodus of human suffering.

3 Grivas and Makarios

I swear in the name of the Holy Trinity to keep secret all I know or come to know about the cause of *Enosis*, even under torture or at the cost of my life. I shall obey without question the instructions given to me at all times.

On the testimony of the Greek-Cypriot guerrilla leader, George Grivas,[1] twelve people signed that oath in Athens at a secret meeting in March 1953. They included Archbishop Makarios, head of the Greek Orthodox church on the island. Indeed, from the very beginning the Greek-Cypriot pro-*Enosis* campaign of the 1950s was something of a "holy alliance" between Makarios and Grivas, two men who claimed to serve a common cause but who seldom made common cause, each using and tolerating the other, the one Grivas, the military leader, the other Makarios, the religious leader and political strategist. In Cyprus, and not for the first time in Britain's decolonization process, the nationalist political leader was to emerge on top.[2]

Makarios (family name, Mouskos) was born in 1913 in the village of Panayia, near Paphos, in the west of the island, the son of a mountain shepherd. He joined the priesthood at Kykko Monastery, high in the Cyprus Troodos mountains, then and now one of the more celebrated monasteries in the Orthodox world. The young Mouskas progressed well at his studies, was sent for further scholarship to Athens, and later went to Boston University, where he was when made a bishop even before finishing his studies. By 1950 he had become archbishop, at thirty-seven the youngest ever recorded in Orthodox annals. By tradition he was also ethnarch, thus combining the national and religious leadership of the Greek-Cypriot community. On his election he pledged publicly "to work for the birth of our national freedom" and "never to waiver from our policy of annexing Cyprus to Mother Greece."[3] It was a pledge that many Turkish-Cypriots would never allow him to forget, and an acute embarrassment to himself when, subsequently, he sought to shift ground away from *Enosis* and toward self-determination and the establishment of an independent republic of Cyprus. Less than three years later he was in Athens taking another oath (see above) translating his undertaking into a commitment, however reluctantly at first, to the use of physical force to advance political ends.

Already, there had emerged to mastermind the guerrilla side of the *Enosis* struggle a fiercely anti-Communist Cypriot, George Grivas. About fifteen years older than Makarios, Grivas was born in eastern Cyprus in the village of Trikomo near to Famagusta. Following some early schooling at the Pancyprian Gymnasium in Nicosia, he joined the military academy in Athens and later served in the abortive Asia Minor campaign against the Turks, collecting a small war wound and a captaincy at the age of twenty-six. The Greek army at peace sent a number of its officers to France for military studies, including young Captain Grivas, who was attached briefly to the Ecole de Tir and the Ecole d'Infanterie at Versailles. The Italian invasion of Greece in 1940 saw Grivas as a lieutenant colonel attached to the General Staff, and subsequently he was placed in charge of the Second Army Division fighting in the mountains.[4] When Hitler's forces joined the Italians, Greece capitulated, and Grivas, by his own account,[5] set up a "private army" to harass the invaders while avoiding direct association with the Greek Communist resistance movement. His "private army," at most a few hundred men scattered among private houses in and around Athens, claimed deeds of valor and military successes that neither the British forces helping the Communist nor the Greek government in exile in Cairo nor, for that matter, independent chroniclers, have ever managed to document. Grivas recorded bitterly of being variously ignored, let down, and upsupported and of how, he claimed, the British were deceived and generally duped by the Communists. "They neither foresaw nor cared what would happen at the end of the war."[6]

In the aftermath of the bloody Greek civil war and the final defeat of the Communists, Grivas retired on pension from the army and began to think again of his native Cyprus. By then (1948), Britain was still saying "never" to full independence, and Grivas unfolded his ideas for an armed struggle on the island to the brother of one of his former "private army" colleagues, a Cypriot lawyer named Christodolous Papadopoulos, who, more significantly, was also a confidant of Makarios. Contacts were made with some exiled Cypriot leaders who reported that the demand for *Enosis* was still very much alive and growing, despite the best efforts of the colonial British to erode the aspiration. It was decided that Grivas himself should visit Cyprus "to study the situation and prepare the revolution in my own time."[7] He arrived openly in July 1951 and stayed at the Nicosia home of his doctor brother, Michael, from which base he traveled extensively throughout the island. He also met with Archbishop Makarios, to whom he explained his tentative plans for a guerrilla campaign. Eighteen months later they met again, this time in Athens in the oath-taking ceremony to advance the cause of union with Greece. The campaign, planned in detail largely by Grivas, was to be a two-pronged affair, a guerrilla campaign in the mountains but also with small teams of trained saboteurs working in the principal towns to attack British forces—both in their personnel and through their security infrastructure. The Greek-Cypriot church, in the person of Makarios, agreed to supply money to procure arms and other equipment.

Makarios initially was skeptical, however, in part because he doubted whether the Greek-Cypriot population would rise in support of such an armed campaign; also he then believed that diplomatic pressure by Greece at the United Nations could, in turn, persuade Britain to concede self-determination to Cyprus, and self-determination in the mind of the archbishop was still synonymous with *Enosis*. Not for the first time, Makarios failed to consider the Turkish-Cypriot minority, especially at a time when Britain was beginning to come under pressure from the Turkish government in Ankara either to maintain the status quo in Cyprus or, alternatively, to partition the island between Turks and Greeks.

The guerrillas' starting armory was not impressive. Paid for with money made available through Makarios, a small shipment of arms arrived clandestinely on March 2, 1954, off the Cyprus coast near Paphos and was landed for storage in the village of Khlorakas. It consisted of 3 Bren guns, 3 Beretta machine guns ("one in poor condition"), 4 Thompson submachine guns (for years the favorite weapon in the armory of the Irish Republican Army), 17 automatics, 47 rifles, 7 revolvers, 32,150 rounds of ammunition of varying calibers, 290 hand grenades, and approximately 20 kilos of explosives.[8] A second small-boat load, dispatched from Greece the following October, was intercepted by the British, but they failed to intercept Grivas, who arrived in Cyprus—this time clandestinely—some weeks later to personally lead the anti-British campaign of violence under the nom de querre "Dighenis," the legendary Greek hero. After midnight on March 31, 1955, the first terrorist bombs exploded in Cyprus. Before the final independence settlement was signed in London in 1959, more than 500 people had died in the campaign, almost half of them civilians. Total fatalities included more than sixty Turkish-Cypriots. The seeds of the post independence confrontation had taken root.

The process of germination was helped by other factors, too, and more of a diplomatic variety. By the early 1950s, Britain's Middle East strategy was running into difficulties in the face of rising Arab nationalism. In Egypt, King Farouk had been forced to abdicate, and a young army officer, Gamal Abdel Nasser, at the head of a military regime, quickly became an inspiration for nationalist movements elsewhere in the Middle East. Greece and Turkey had, by then, both joined the North Atlantic Treaty Organization (NATO), and Turkey's final acceptance as a fully fledged and strategically important member of the Western Alliance came with its inclusion in the five-nation Baghdad Pact (Britain, Iran, Iraq, Pakistan, and Turkey). This pact emerged in 1955, largely on a British initiative, but with considerable inputs from Washington, notably by the then U.S. secretary of state, John Foster Dulles. Washington wanted to complete the encirclement of the Soviet Union and saw in Turkey a vital link in the chain, together with Iran and Pakistan. All of this increased the importance of Turkey in the diplomatic scales as weighed in Britain and the United States.

In the summer of 1954, Nasser's brand of Arab nationalism had taken such hold that Britain agreed to withdraw its troops from the Suez Canal Zone, replacing them with civilian technicians, and to transfer the British Middle East Land and Air Headquarters[9] to Cyprus. This move could hardly have been welcomed by Greek-Cypriots, who saw the transfer as a further consolidation of the British presence in, and hold over, the island. Their forebodings were increased when the London government offered a new Constitution for the island, which, in terms of the reality of power, promised less to the Cypriots than they had earlier rejected. It was in conjunction with this new plan that the British junior minister, Henry Hopkinson, made the statement, quoted earlier, to the effect that there were certain territories that could never expect to be fully independent "owing to their particular circumstances." Wise politicians tend to avoid commitments to *never*, and Hopkinson's declaration only fueled the fires of nationalism, or rather *Enosisism*, in Cyprus, a process added to by the intervention in the British House of Commons by Selwyn Lloyd, then minister of state at the Foreign Office. He asserted that British sovereignty over Cyprus was essential if the country was to fulfil its obligations to the Arab states, to NATO, and to the United Nations. To both Makarios and Grivas, Britain was fast closing off options to any form of meaningful independence for Cyprus. It was the perfect climate to persuade those in any lingering doubt that nothing but violence would shake the British.

Meanwhile, a new government under Field Marshal Alexander Papagos, a staunch anti-Communist and formerly commander in chief of the Greek army, had come to power in Athens. Papagos, while in opposition at the head of the rightist Greek Rally, had been sounded out by both Grivas and Makarios separately on his attitude to a "liberation struggle." It was, initially at least, wholly negative. Papagos had no wish to clash with Britain, an old and valued Greek ally, and, in any event, his government had decided to take the Cyprus issue directly to the United Nations General Assembly, despite Britain's insistence that Cyprus was an internal affair of the United Kingdom government and not germane to the UN. In the diplomatic buildup to the planned UN initiative, Athens was anxious to win friends and concluded that an outbreak of anti-British violence on the island would not help. Nonetheless, the record shows that, during this period, Grivas had secured arms and had had them shipped to Cyprus, almost certainly with the knowledge—or at very least the strong suspicions—of the government in Athens. When the recourse to the UN failed, Makarios reported to Grivas[10] that all restrictions had been lifted by Athens to his planned campaign in Cyprus, and the issue between the two men became one of selecting the most appropriate date to launch the anti-British offensive. The archbishop favored March 25, 1955, the anniversary of Greek independence. Grivas, never one to be dictated to on matters of military strategy and timing, set the date for six days later. It was then that the first bombs launched the EOKA campaign, and "Dighenis," alias Grivas, published its "First Revolutionary Leaflet" (See appendix B).

NOTES

1. *Memoirs*, Ed. Charles Foley, (London: Longman, 1964), p. 20.

2. In Ireland, Eamon De Valera had earlier emerged as head of government and subsequently as president; the guerrilla leader, Michael Collins, was killed in an ambush during a civil war fought in Ireland over the terms on the Independence settlement with Britain.

3. Oath taken on his election (October 20, 1950), as reported in the local media.

4. Grivas, *Memoirs*, p. 4. Never one to avoid extravagant claims, especially in military matters, Grivas wrote of his part in the campaign: "Not only did we hold the Italian army, but we succeeded in throwing enormously superior forces back across the border as we fought our way slowly forwards through the wild, mountainous frontier region into Albania. That winter the World watched Greece in admiration and wonder."

5. Ibid., p. 5.

6. Ibid., p. 6.

7. Ibid., p. 13.

8. Ibid., pp. 21-22.

9. With the move went the "Head of the Political Division of the British Middle East Office and Political Adviser to the Commanders in Chief Middle East," a diplomat named John Pack who was destined later to enter the Irish imbroglio as British ambassador in Dublin.

10. Grivas, *Memoirs*, p. 29

4　The Anti-British Campaign

"The attack," wrote Grivas, "took the world by surprise; but none were more shocked than the British officials who ran Cyprus. Both they and their military advisers appeared stunned and panic-stricken; absurd efforts were made to recruit Cypriot civil servants into a special constabulary to guard government buildings, and pathetic bleats of protest and condemnation were broadcast. . . . Unlike Makarios, I did not expect an early solution from Britain or the United Nations."[1] The events of the night of March 31, 1955, had, in fact, produced mixed reactions in Cyprus. The British authorities thought that it might be an isolated action by pro-*Enosis* fanatics, although the revolutionary leaflet caused an initial ripple of concern. The resident British community did not disturb greatly their leisurely routine, the Turkish-Cypriot leadership on the island took note, the island's powerful Communist party (AKEL) was critical, while the predominantly Greek-Cypriot commercial establishment expressed concern both at the likely cost of the resultant publicity to the tourist industry and at the fact that Greek-Cypriots, not the British, might have to pay for much of the bomb damage. At first, it was mainly the students at the Pancyprian Gymnasium, then a citadel of Greek nationalism, who registered a noisy welcome for the start of the EOKA campaign. (Many of the same students were later to join the Grivas movement although they were still in their teens). Speculation centered inevitably on the identity of "Dighenis," but this remained a secret for barely the first month of the guerrilla campaign, until the leadership of Grivas was disclosed in a broadcast from Moscow over the "Free Greek Radio," the mouthpiece of the Greek Communists, who had good reason to uncover the identity of their old adversary of civil-war days. British intelligence took note, and sought to get, from Grivas's wife in Athens, some of the old clothes worn by him in order to set tracker dogs on his trail in the mountains.[2] On June 19, about ten weeks after Grivas had launched his anti-British

164

campaign, EOKA claimed its first victim, a police constable killed in an explosion at the Nicosia police headquarters. He was a Turkish-Cypriot. This incident was the start of an all-out guerrilla war against the occupying British, but its leader was also giving notice that it also meant death to any Turkish-Cypriot who got in the way. The Turkish-Cypriot response was to launch their own counterattack, Volkan,[3] an underground organization, which, unlike EOKA, the British authorities initially ignored. Volkan's emergence could hardly have been without the knowledge of the government in Ankara. Its first public leaflet was explicit: "If the Greeks touch a Turk, whether a Government official, a policeman, or a civilian, we will take immediate action. Volkan is growing stronger every day."[4]

What was certainly growing stronger daily was an embryo civil war atmosphere on the small island, albeit one concealed initially by the Greek-Cypriots' confrontation directly with the British. Anthony Eden, the British prime minister, whatever his faults as a statesman—and most agree that the 1956 Suez adventure was not his finest hour—did, in fact, see—unlike Makarios or Grivas—that the real barrier to *Enosis* would prove ultimately not to be the British government but the government in Ankara. His memoirs recall that in 1955 he was concerned over what he considered to be Turkey's official passivity over the Cyprus question. In the light of this, he had welcomed warnings in the Turkish press that a form of autonomy for Cyprus, which opened the door to *Enosis*, would mean that Britain's alliance with Turkey would have no more than paper value. He commented directly: "It is well that they (the Turks) should speak out, because it is the truth that the Turks will never let the Greeks have Cyprus."[5]

The formal Greek appeal to the United Nations in the autumn of 1954 did cause Ankara to give a higher diplomatic priority to the Cyprus question. The Turkish assumption remained that the British would stay on in Cyprus, that "never" in terms of full independence meant just that. Yet Turkey wanted a fallback position just in case, and it took the line that, in the event of British withdrawal, the island should revert to Turkish sovereignty—a questionable argument, to say the last, because Turkey had effectively surrendered all sovereignty over Cyprus in the Lausanne Treaty.[6] However, with the *Enosis* sentiment gaining ground with Greek-Cypriots, Ankara, with some none-too-subtle prompting by Britain, also advanced the notion that the answer to *Enosis* would be partition, what became known as *Double Enosis*. Turkey was then, and remains today, locked into the Eastern Mediterranean by the myriads of Greek islands in the Aegean, and its southern coast is a mere forty miles from Cyprus and could well feel threatened in the event of the island's falling into the direct domain of Athens. To the extent that this was not fully appreciated by Ankara, and the evidence shows that it largely was, the British sought to emphasize the point, while also considering Britain's own regional defense objectives. Eden was to say of Cyprus: "I regarded our alliance with Turkey as the key first consideration in our policy in that part of the world."[7]

Britain's preoccupation with the importance of Turkey and London's professed concern for the Turkish-Cypriots[8] was, of course, seen by Greeks and Greek-Cypriots alike as a policy that was far from evenhanded. The British government went a step further in alienating Greek opinion when, within three months of the launching of the EOKA offensive, it invited Greece and Turkey to a conference in London, ostensibly to discuss defense and related matters touching on the East Mediterranean theater but, in reality, for tripartite talks on Cyprus. This conference marked the first formal and direct entry of Turkey into the Cyprus affair, and its presence brought a howl of protect from Makarios, and a more subdued but equally critical response from Athens, over the exclusion of any representative of the Greek-Cypriots. The conference was timed quite deliberately to try to head off a further Greek approach to the United Nations on the question of self-determination for Cyprus. Makarios urged Greece not to attend it. Athens rejected his appeal, and he told a press conference: "We unhesitatingly believe that the convocation of a conference constitutes a trap and a means of delay [by Britain], with the purpose of undermining Greece's appeal to the United Nations and of entangling the matter in complicated patterns whence it will not be easy for it to be extracted."[9]

The London conference was deadlocked by the Greek and Turkish foreign ministers' maintaining, respectively, their already known positions for and against self-determination on the basis of new British proposals. These provided for an assembly in Cyprus with an elected majority. It would have limited powers, and none touching on defense, foreign policy, and security; control in these key areas was reserved to the British governor. A proportion of seats in the proposed assembly would be allotted to the Turkish minority—a form of enforced power-sharing, albeit with limited power to share. Part of the British package was to include a special development plan including, on the direct suggestion of Eden, the provision on the island of an institution of university status, linked with one or more of the existing universities in Britain, "which would help to wean the Cypriots away from the cultural attraction of Athens."[10]

What finally killed any hope of compromise in London was something quite different from the British proposals, and quite sinister, and it is still talked about today by both sides in Cyprus. The Turkish minister, Fatin Rustu Zorlu, was incensed (perhaps diplomatically embarrassed, too) by a remark from the Greek side to the effect that there did not appear to be much popular feeling in Turkey on the Cyprus issue. Zorlu responded with a cable to Ankara suggesting a popular demonstration, although under the circumstances the suggestion may well have been read as an order. In any event, he got a strong response. On September 5 an explosion damaged the Turkish consulate in Salonika and, emotionally much more important for Turks, the adjoining home, the birthplace of Mustafa Kemal Atatürk, the father of the modern Turkish nation. Who caused the explosions was never established conclusively, or at least not publicly, but, in the light of immediately subsequent happenings, suspicions fell inevitably on agents provocateurs. Twenty-four hours later, on the night of September 6–7, major anti-Greek riots erupted in three principal Turkish cities. An acknowledged British expert on Turkey described the scene after stating his own belief that "there has never been a spontaneous riot in the whole of Turkish history."[11]

> The rioters travelled in lorries and had lists of addresses to visit. But soon the amateurs took over, and what had begun as anti-Greek, became anti-minority, then anti-foreign, ending as anti-rich. Churches, houses, and shops were sacked; there was much looting, but more wanton destruction. Istiklal Caddesi, formerly the Grande Rue de Pera, the main shopping street of Istanbul, was littered with the wreckage of furniture, refrigerators, and radios. The police were slow to realize that the planned demonstration had changed its nature; by the time they and the military intervened, the damage was done. Three thousand people were arrested, but subsequently released.

About ten years later, when Turkey threatened to invade postindependence Cyprus in support of the island's Turkish-Cypriots, the then prime minister in Ankara, the ordinarily moderate Suat Hayri Urguplu, a nonparty candidate heading an interim administration, commented: "If a single Turk is killed in Cyprus, I cannot give any guarantee about what may happen in Istanbul. I fear another incident like that of September 6–7."[12]

The Turkish government apologized formally to Greece and offered compensation for damaged Greek property, but the damage to community relations, especially in Istanbul where the Greek community was concentrated, was quickly reflected in Cyprus itself. Greek-Turkish relations slumped, and Athens withdrew its military personnel from the NATO base at Ismir[13] on Turkey's Aegean coast. The London conference dispersed, and Makarios publicly rejected the British proposals, adding a thinly veiled call for all Greek-Cypriots to support the anti-British offensive of Grivas and EOKA.

The guerrilla leader himself was quick to respond, with more bombings and attacks on the British military and the local police. The ranks of the latter gradually became depleted through resignations resulting from EOKA intimidation,[14] and some police officers actually joined the guerrillas in the mountains. The British authorities moved to fill the growing gap in police ranks by recruiting Turkish-Cypriots as special constables, thus adding a direct intercommunal component to what had started out as a Greek-Cypriot offensive against British authority. Britain's own ignominious debacle in the 1956 Suez crisis was then only a year away, and when it came it reinforced the hard-liners in the ruling Conservative party in London who insisted that Britain could not be pushed around indefinitely by what they termed terrorists fronting as nationalists. The line would have to be held in Cyprus, if only to reassure Britain's remaining friends in the Middle East.

The big military stick was about to be unsheathed in the island to crush rebellion. There was to be, as promised before and since in other rebellious British colonies and appendages, including Northern Ireland, a "military solution." On the diplomatic front Eden promised to continue with efforts to find a political solution, portraying his government as something of an honest broker between two valued NATO allies, Greece and Turkey, and trying hard to hold the ring in Cyprus against an eruption of racial violence.

Following the breakdown of the London conference, Field Marshal Sir John Harding was appointed governor in Cyprus, replacing Sir Robert Armitage, who was withdrawn from the island even before his successor had arrived—a studied reflection on the part of his political masters of his inability to deal with the terrorist situation. Harding talked tough, promising an early military victory against EOKA,[15] but also offering to talk with Makarios. They met shortly after his arrival, and Harding emphasized that British policy over Cyprus would inevitably be dictated by wider regional considerations, and particularly British commitments in the Middle East. The two men were soon in detailed talks in the context of Britain's possibly granting "a wide measure of self-government to Cyprus," but leaving unclear the key issue of self-determination— on which the London attitude could be summarized, alternatively, as leaving the door open or not closing it. However, the olive branch came from an iron fist, and Harding, in parallel, declared a state of emergency with more than seventy new regulations. They included the death penalty for anyone caught carrying arms, life imprisonment for those found in possession of explosives or involved in acts of sabotage, and a host of other provisions, such as the prohibition of public meetings, the banning of all strikes, collective fines on towns and villages suspected of harboring EOKA terrorists, deportations, and the right to flog youths under eighteen years of age. More troops were called into Cyprus, the police, both regular and auxiliary, being merged with the expanded army, and a full-scale search was launched to find Grivas and his armed supporters. The security buildup on the island, from a base figure of approximately 4,000 troops when the EOKA campaign first started, was to continue steadily over the next four years to reach close to 30,000. Against that force Grivas could command no more than a couple of hundred men, permanently or semiregularly under arms, but sympathizers were everywhere, including those in police ranks. Grivas himself was to make the important point that, in Cyprus, Britain was facing "not a handful of insurrectionists, but the whole people,"[16] albeit the whole of the Greek-Cypriot community. His concurrent claim that the Cyprus struggle "was unique in motive, psychology and circumstance" was open to greater doubt, but it reflected well Grivas's overhanging ego and his supreme faith both in the justness of his cause and in his own ability to succeed, whatever the odds.

On the political front Harding did appear to be making some progress in his talks with Makarios during late 1955 and early the following year. The Greek-Cypriot leader showed signs that he might be prepared to go along with British ideas for a period of internal self-government, but he wanted assurances that the way would eventually be opened to unfettered self-determination. By February 1956 the Harding-Makarios dialogue seemed to have reached the point of a possible breakthrough, and the British colonial secretary, Alan Lennox-Boyd, flew from London to join the talks. Dramatically, just twelve days later, British security forces detained the archbishop as he was about to board an aircraft for Athens and London, served him with a deportation order, and bundled him off, together with Bishop Kyprianos of Kyrenia (his public demand had long been *"Enosis* and only *Enosis"* immediately and unconditionally), to an internment retreat—in fact, the governor's summer residence on Mahe, capital of the Seychelles Islands in the Indian Ocean.

Why the deportations, and so suddenly and at a point when there were grounds for optimism that an agreed interim settlement might be in sight? Even at this point removed, no one involved officially in the Cyprus problem at the time has thrown much real light on this question. Eden implied[17] that he was quite prepared for a showdown with Makarios even before Lennox-Boyd had left London for Nicosia, and the security forces in Cyprus believed increasingly, and rightly, that the archbishop was in collusion with Grivas and the EOKA guerrillas. Harding himself had become frustrated because each time he secured London approval of a new concession to Makarios, the archbishop came back with a fresh demand. Also, Eden's Conservative government was then well to the right of center in terms of its seen foreign-policy options, an attitude partly inherent in the character of many senior ministers, but also, perhaps, a fairly natural response to a series of British setbacks in the Middle East. The latest reversal had been the sudden dismissal by the young King Hussein of Glubb Pasha, the British commander of the Arab League, following nationalist riots in Jordan against Britain's attempt to bring that country into the Baghdad Pact. It seemed, in London at least, that holding on to Cyprus was now essential, whatever the cost.

The immediate cost was considerable, with Greek riots against the deportations outside the British embassy in Athens and the withdrawal of the Greek ambassador from London. On the island Grivas now had a free hand, and even more popular Greek-Cypriot support while, diplomatically, Harding and the British government were left with no one with whom they could negotiate. Harding had hoped for the emergence of some "moderate" Greek-Cypriot leaders, but none emerged, largely because no one was prepared to sit down with the governor while the archbishop was detained in the Seychelles and, in the unlikely event that someone should have considered such a move, the fear of certain reprisals by EOKA would have inhibited it. Harding's security forces were displaying posters offering rewards for information against EOKA, the price on Grivas himself being £10,000, but the political vacuum was well illustrated by a cartoon in a British newspaper offering a reward of £5,000 for "political moderates" in Cyprus. There were no takers.

The security forces, once again enlarged, did have some successes, but at a sizable cost in alienating the local population. Intensive house searches, abrupt street arrests, a flood of detention orders, collective fines on towns refusing to disclose information on EOKA activities—all combined to drive the Greek-Cypriot community further into the arms of Grivas. Young British conscripts doing their (at that time) two-year compulsory stint in the armed forces had little commitment to the antiterrorist campaign. British police, imported on financially rewarding contracts to augment the local police, lacked knowledge of either the locale or the language, and, in terms of gathering important intelligence data, they were virtually useless. In addition, their street patrols in groups of three or four, provided easy targets for the gunmen, and usually each group was given armed cover by one or more Turkish-Cypriot police officers, again further identifying the Turkish-Cypriot community with the British colonial administration. The government in Turkey hailed the deportation of Makarios and the others as a long overdue firm measure, a sentiment echoed by a number of Conservative speakers in the British Parliament at Westminster.

Yet the London government realized that the political vacuum could not be allowed to last indefinitely if there were to be any hopes of defusing the violence in Cyprus itself. Six months after the deportation of Makarios, a distinguished British judge, Lord Cyril John Radcliffe, was asked to suggest a formula for new constitutional proposals.

NOTES

1. Grivas, *Memoirs*, ed. Charles Foley (London: Longman, 1964), p. 20.
2. W. Byford-Jones, *Grivas and the Story of EOKA* (London: Robert Hale, 1959), pp. 47–48.
3. "The Volcano," later to become TMT, the Turkish defense organization.
4. Charles Foley, *Island in Revolt* (London: Longman, 1962), p. 33.
5. *Full Circle: The Memoirs of Sir Anthony Eden* (London: Cassell, 1960), pp. 394–415.
6. Ibid., p. 400. Zorlu, the Turkish foreign minister, hinted that any change in the status of Cyprus would amount to a revision of the Treaty of Lausanne and open the way to Turkish counterclaims against Greece in Thrace and the Dodecanese.
7. Ibid., p. 414.

8. Ibid., p. 396: "The Turkish-speaking Cypriots were strongly opposed to union with Greece. In early 1955 their passions were not yet inflamed, for the Turk is slow to anger, but once roused, he is implacable. Graeco-Turkish racial conflict on the island was a far greater danger than anything EOKA terrorism could contrive. The British Government had to try to suppress terrorism before it led to widespread racial conflict, and to seek a political solution which would give the people of Cyprus as a whole scope to govern themselves. Communist Cypriots fished in these troubled waters."

9. Ibid., p. 339.

10. Ibid., p. 398.

11. Geoffrey Lewis, *Modern Turkey* (London: Ernest Been, 1974), pp. 147–48.

12. Ibid., p. 148. Urguplu's intemperate remark was attacked sharply by President Cemal Gursel: "I cannot imagine what possessed the Prime Minister to talk like this. Turkey is not a tribe, it is a state. . . . It is distressing to be reminded of the events of September 6–7."

13. Ironically, the scene of the massacre of Turks by Greek forces almost forty years earlier.

14. A similar form of intimidation has been used widely by the IRA against Catholic members of the Ulster police.

15. Grivas, *Memoirs*, p. 45. "My opponent was to be Field-Marshal Sir John Harding, who had commanded British troops in North Africa, Italy, Germany, and the Far East. . . . He was, in fact, the leading British soldier of his day, and no higher compliment could have been paid us than to send against our tiny force a man with so great a reputation and so brilliant a career."

16. Ibid., p. 45.

17. Eden, *Full Circle*, pp. 411–12.

5 The Road to London

It is important to set out here precise terms of reference because they demonstrated the state and the priorities of official British thinking on Cyprus at the time. Equally, his own report provided a concise and accurate statement of just what it was the Turkish-Cypriots were seeking, and their demands are much the same today. Radcliffe was asked to make recommendations as to the form of a new constitution for Cyprus, which would be consistent with the following requirements:

a. That during the period of the Constitution, Cyprus is to remain under British sovereignty;
b. That the use of Cyprus as a [military] base is necessary for the fulfilment by Her Majesty's Government of its international obligations and for the defence of British interests in the Middle East and the interests of other Powers allied or associated with the United Kingdom;
c. That all matters relating to external affairs, defence, and internal security, are retained in the hands of Her Majesty's Government or the Governor;
d. That, subject to this, the Constitution is to be based on the principles of liberal democracy and is to confer a wide measure of responsible self-government on elected representatives of the people of Cyprus, but is, at the same time, to contain such reservations, provisions, and guarantees as may be necessary to give a just protection to the special interests of the various communities, religions, and races in the island.[1]

Radcliffe's proposals, as his report made clear, were his own. They could not have been otherwise because his mission was ignored by Greek-Cypriots, owing to the deportation of Makarios. He did, however, have direct contact with the Turkish-Cypriot leadership under Fazil Kütchük. His report noted in part: "Every-

173

one knows that Cyprus is not homogeneous. Taking the figures of
the 1946 Census . . . the population of the island is formed, as to
about eighty per cent of Greek-Cypriots [and] as to about eighteen
per cent of Turkish-Cypriots." Having excluded the remaining
minorities, British residents, Armenians, and Maronites, who, in
fact, asked him for no special constitutional privileges or protections, Radcliffe continued:

> The problem comes down to the political relations between
> these two communities. . . . I have given my best consideration
> to the claim put before me on behalf of the Turkish-Cypriot
> community that they should be accorded political representation
> equal to that of the Greek-Cypriot community. If I do not accept
> it, I do not think it is out of any lack of respect for the misgivings
> that lie behind it. But this is a claim by 18 per cent of a popula-
> tion to share political power equally with 80 per cent, and, if it is
> to be given effect to, I think that it must be made good on one of
> two possible grounds. Either it is consistent with the principles
> of a constitution based on liberal and democratic conceptions
> that political power should be balanced this way, or no other
> means than the creation of such political equilibrium will be
> effective to protect the essential interests of the community from
> oppression by the weight of the majority. I do not feel that I can
> stand firmly on either of these propositions.
> The first embodies the idea of a federation rather than a
> unitary state. It would be natural enough to accord to members
> of a federation equality of representation in the federal body,
> regardless of the numerical proportions of the populations of the
> territories they represent. But can Cyprus be organised as a
> federation in this way? I do not think so. There is no pattern of
> territorial separation between the two communities and, apart
> from other objections, federation of communities which does not
> involve also federation of territories, seems to me a very difficult
> constitutional form. If it is said that what is proposed is, in
> reality, nothing more than a system of functional representation,
> the function in this case being the community life and organisa-
> tion and nothing else, I find myself baffled in an attempt to
> visualise how an effective executive government for Cyprus is to
> be thrown up by a system in which political power is to remain
> permanently divided in equal shares between two opposed com-
> munities. Either there is stagnation in political life, with the
> frustration that accompanies it, or some small minority group
> acquires an artificial weight by being able to hold the balance
> between the two main groups. . . . My conclusion is that it can
> not be in the interests of Cyprus as a whole that the constitution

should be formed on the basis of equal political representation for the Greek and Turkish-Cypriot communities.

Does the second ground lead to a different result? I do not think so. To give an equal political strength in a unitary state to two communities which have such a marked inequality in numbers—an inequality which, so far as signs go, is as likely to increase as decrease—is to deny to the majority of the population over the whole field of self-government, the power to have its will reflected in effective action. Yet it might well be right to insist on this denial if the Constitution could not be equipped with any other effective means of securing the smaller communities in the possession of their essential special interests. Not only do I think that it can be equipped with such means by placing these interests under the protection of independent tribunals with appropriate powers and relying only to a limited extent on direct political devices, but I think that the "legalist" solution on which this depends, is, in fact, better suited to provide the protection that is required, and it does not have the effect of denying the validity of the majority principle over a field much wider than that with which special community interests are truly concerned.[2]

The Radcliffe constitutional package offered Greek-Cypriots a majority in an elected assembly, with the proviso that a two-thirds majority of the assembly's Turkish members would be necessary to amend legislation touching on Turkish communal affairs. The minority was to have a member in the cabinet ex officio to look after Turkish-Cypriot matters, and with a budget. Ensured Turkish-Cypriot communal rights would be determined, if challenged, both by a supreme court and a special tribunal of guarantee, the membership of both bodies being balanced equally as between the two communities, but with each having a neutral head.

The proposals were rejected by both Greece and the Greek-Cypriots; Makarios refused to consider any such document as long as he was being detained. The British government did not help matters by suggesting in the House of Commons, when the Radcliffe package was unveiled, that to concede self-determination to the Cypriot majority, which, of course, Radcliffe had specifically excluded, given his terms of reference, would result inevitably in partition. The reasoning was that in a free vote Greek-Cypriots would undoubtedly opt for *Enosis* and the Turkish-Cypriots for partition, and, it was suggested, equity implied that one community could not be given a free vote without an equal opportunity being afforded to the other. It was the first time on the official

British record that the word *partition* had been injected into the Cyprus question, and neither the Turks on the island nor the government in Ankara were prepared to ever again drop the notion entirely. Turkish policy from that time forward was designed, at least in part, to undermine the basic objection advanced by Radcliffe to the concept of a federal solution, through working, in fact, to bring about "a pattern of territorial separation" between the two communities. Radcliffe could not find such a pattern in 1956; the invading Turkish army was to establish it approximately eighteen years later and to force Greek-Cypriots, even before the death of Makarios in 1977, to accept, however reluctantly and for however long, the principle of a federal settlement in Cyprus—or else none.

Following Radcliffe's proposal, there was something of a diplomatic hiatus. At the start of 1957, Eden resigned and was replaced as prime minister of Harold Macmillan. In February the United Nations Political Committee rejected both partition and self-determination as solutions in Cyprus and adopted instead a vaguely worded Indian resolution calling for negotiations, a call that the British interpreted as meaning tripartite talks between London, Athens, and Ankara. Greece, however, chose to consider it a signal for direct peace negotiations between the British authorities and the Greek-Cypriots, in essence a renewal of the earlier Harding-Makarios dialogue. Grivas, under pressure from Athens, agreed to a temporary cease-fire, provided Makarios was released to join negotiations. The British cabinet divided on the question, but Macmillan won the day and offered to end the archbishop's exile, but with a ban on his immediate return to the island. The diplomatic situation over Cyprus was now clear-cut. The British wanted to keep Turkey in the negotiations and to exclude the Greek-Cypriots; Greece demanded that Makarios be present and Turkey excluded.

Harding was replaced as governor by Hugh Foot—a civil servant with a known liberal streak taking over from a tough-minded soldier—and the possible significance was not lost in Ankara. Turkey feared that, with Makarios released and with a liberal in the governor's residence in Nicosia, Britain might try for a fast settlement in Cyprus at Ankara's expense. As with the infamous anti-Greek riots in Turkey coinciding with the earlier London conference, Ankara decided that a show of strength was needed by the Turkish-Cypriots in Cyprus. Intercommunal rioting broke out on the island designed to demonstrate that Turkish and Greek-Cypriots could not live harmoniously together. By early 1958, intercommunal tensions were at a high pitch. Grivas had again ordered EOKA explosions and sabotage and was soon to reject, or rather to ignore, a dramatic offer from Foot to meet the guerrilla leader unarmed and alone.

In London Macmillan unfolded another British settlement plan, which was partly Radcliffe's ideas, partly ideas advanced by Foot, and partly Colonial Office inputs, the last advocating a direct Turkish (with Greece and Britain) role in a proposed seven-year self-government experiment, which might be followed by a full surrender of British sovereignty if all sides then agreed, in itself an unlikely prospect.

The Turkish government was delighted. It now could add the prospect of a direct internal role in ruling Cyprus to its earlier gain of securing direct participation in the tripartite discussions on the island's future. Greece and Makarios were furious, the latter dismissing the suggestion of accepting a partnership with the Turkish-Cypriot community at the price of what he termed "a triple condominium." Instead, he shifted his traditional ground away from self-determination, the established euphemism for *Enosis*, and in favor of outright independence. Whether a tactical or strategic move, this change was to win for Makarios the support of most of the emerging independent countries at the United Nations.

Britain, too, was putting a changed emphasis on its post-Suez military requirements. The Macmillan government, overriding initial military opposition, concluded that control over the whole of Cyprus for defense purposes was no longer necessary. London's needs, it appeared, could be adequately met by having base facilities on the island, and preferably bases surrounded not by a hostile local population but by a people grateful for their independence. The international climate, too, was influencing events. The Soviet invasion of Hungary in 1956 had sharpened the cold war, and NATO was anxious to be rid of the thorny Cyprus problem, which involved two important members, Turkey and Greece, confronting each other to the detriment of the alliance's capabilities in the Mediterranean zone. Additionally, in internal British politics, the largely bipartisan policy over Cyprus was cracking, with the opposition Labour party coming out in general support of the notion of an independent state of Cyprus. The stage was set for a deal.

Grivas still had to be satisfied, however, and he opposed any solution that excluded *Enosis*. He was then directing guerrilla operations from a hideout in Limassol and coming under heavy pressure both from the Athens government and from Makarios to cease the terror campaign in order to facilitate moves for a peaceful solution, but without being told much about what diplomatic moves were in progress. He became progressively more suspicious and more angry, relaying his mounting concern in several notes and letters through the Greek consulate in Nicosia, both to Makarios and to the Greek foreign minister, Evangelos Averoff.[3] They responded with assurances that there was no need for concern and that tension on the island should be reduced, but they provided no hard diplomatic information. Instead, Grivas found that new weapons promised from Greece, with the knowledge of the government there, failed to arrive. In fact, Grivas, the EOKA leader, was being kept quite deliberately in the diplomatic dark.

Early in December 1958 the United Nations was once again occupied with the Cyprus problem, but still without a General Assembly majority for self-determination or independence. Through a British initiative,[4] Averoff had a private meeting in New York with his Turkish opposite number, Zorlu, and the two men agreed to try to secure a settlement in direct bilateral negotiations. Averoff consulted Makarios back in Athens, the British were kept informed, and Grivas was told nothing of any substance. Less than a fortnight later, Averoff and Zorlu were back in talks, this time during a NATO ministerial council meeting in Paris. The discussions continued through Christmas and into the New Year, until, by February, a formal meeting took place in Zurich at which the two ministers were joined by their respective prime ministers, Constantine Karamanlis and Adnan Menderes. Within a week an outline agreement had been hammered out, and Averoff and Zorlu flew to London to discuss it with the British. There was no direct Greek-Cypriot or Turkish-Cypriot representation at Zurich, an absence that was to loom large in the future when Makarios claimed that he had not been consulted on the settlement details and, ultimately, he was effectively to disown them.

From Zurich the scene moved to London with a conference at Lancaster House on February 17, this time with Makarios and Kütchük representing their respective communities. They were there to sign, not to negotiate. The three sovereign governments had already reached broad agreement; what they wanted simply were the initials of the Cypriot leaders, not their opinions. Makarios hesitated, but Karamanlis made it plain that he stood behind the settlement terms, and he did not conceal his view that the Greek-Cypriots could depend on no further diplomatic or other backing from Athens if Makarios rejected the package.

Makarios signed and hurried off a personal note to Grivas saying: "Accept my warm congratulations for your splendid achievements and the heroic spirit which you injected into the people. To-day's happy consummation is primarily due to your efforts. I feel sure that you will now agree that it is time for a strong statement of support for the agreement from EOKA. This will show the unity of the national front to everyone.[5]

No such unity was shown, however. Grivas was never formally to endorse the Zurich and London agreements, or to accept the fact that they opened up, in the words of Makarios, the way toward creating "a little Greece at the end of the Mediterranean."[6] Later, he was even to suggest collusion between the British and Greek governments—and also involving sources close to Makarios himself—aimed at disclosing his final Nicosia hideout to the British army, so that he might be captured before the agreed cease-fire on both sides.

The arrangement reached at Zurich and London, incorporating special provisions for British military bases on the island, had four components:

1. A draft Constitution for the new independent Republic of Cyprus;
2. A Treaty of Guarantee between Cyprus, Britain, Greece, and Turkey;
3. A Treaty of Alliance between Cyprus, Greece, and Turkey; and
4. A Treaty of Establishment between Cyprus, Britain, Greece, and Turkey.

The Constitution consisted essentially of four sets of provisions. The first of these recognized to each of the two island communities a separate existence; the second contained constitutional devices assuring the participation of each community in the exercise of the functions of government, while seeking, in a number of matters, to avoid Greek-Cypriot supremacy and assuring also partial administrative autonomy to each community; the third set forth the human rights and fundamental freedoms in the Constitution; and the last group of provisions constituted a complex system of guarantees of the supremacy of the Constitution.

Through the arrangement as a whole, Turkish-Cypriots had secured much that Lord Radcliffe would have denied them and, in general, were given access on a ratio of 30 to 70 percent (against an actual population ratio of about 20 to 80 percent) to jobs at virtually every level, including cabinet posts. However, the convention of collective cabinet responsibility was to be notional; Greek-Cypriot ministers would be answerable to the Republic's president, who would be of the majority community, whereas their Turkish-Cypriot ministerial colleagues answered to the vice-president, a Turkish-Cypriot who was assigned extensive powers to veto legislation. The president and vice-president, who each could act separately on a wide variety of issues, were to be elected separately by their respective communities. Each community would have its own communal chamber, apart from its representation in the central House of Representatives, each language had equal status under the constitution, and each group was permitted to fly the flag of its respective "fatherland," Greece or Turkey. A subsequent United Nations report[7] was to summarize the situation succinctly thus; "The general effect . . . was to make most of the major affairs of the state subject to the agreement of the representatives of both the Greek and Turkish communities, either by joint decision or by the renunciation of the right of veto. The negative side of this situation is that it can invite deadlock on any of the questions concerned when the two communities have sharply differing views on them."

The Treaty of Guarantee effectively blocked—at least theoretically—for all time (both the Treaty of Guarantee and the Treaty of Alliance were included in the Basic Articles of the Constitution "and could not, in any way, be amended, either by variation, addition or repeal") either *Enosis* or partition, and it gave to Britain, Greece, and Turkey, acting together or, in circumstances of disagreement, separately, the right to intervene militarily to reestablish constitutional order should it be disturbed, as in fact was to happen in 1974. The Treaty of Alliance gave both Greece and Turkey an armed presence on the island because it provided for the basing on Cyprus of Greek and Turkish military contingents, numbering, respectively, 950 and 650 officers and soldiers. These contingents were to provide an immediate military guarantee to the infant republic and also to undertake the training of its new army, the numerical upper limit of which was set at 2,000 to be divided, in this instance, on a sixty-to-forty ratio between Greek-Cypriots and Turkish-Cypriots. Finally, the Treaty of Establishment provided Britain with full control, including sovereignty, over two military bases in Cyprus, covering a combined area of ninety-nine square miles.

These were the terms of the Cyprus independence package that

Makarios reluctantly accepted and Grivas rejected. By no stretch of the imagination could it be described as "full and unfettered" independence, and the ink was hardly dry when the archbishop was heard first to mutter about, and then openly to declare that he had signed under duress. The constitution was never submitted to a referendum in Cyprus, and, for the purposes of Makarios's subsequent strategy and tactics, this was probably a wise move, nor did Karamanlis do as he had undertaken—namely, to consult the Greek Parliament before signing. Yet Makarios, too, had promised a referendum. The detention camps in Cyprus were thrown open to release their EOKA heroes, but none got such a welcome as did Makarios on his return to Nicosia. Grivas got safe conduct to Athens and a hero's welcome there.

NOTES

1. *Constitutional Proposals for Cyprus*, (Radcliffe Report) HMSO, London, Cmnd. 42, 1956.
2. Ibid.
3. George Grivas, *Memoirs*, ed. Charles Foley (London: Longman, 1964), pp. 180–82.
4. Hugh Foot, *A Start to Freedom*, (London: Hodder and Stoughton, 1964), pp. 176–77.
5. Grivas, *Memoirs*, p. 190.
6. Ibid, pp. 194–98. (An interesting parallel with Ireland is the conflicting attitudes to the Anglo-Irish Treaty in 1921, which split the republican movement and sparked the civil war. Speaking of the compromise agreement with Britain, Michael Collins, the military leader, told the political leader, De Valera, that the treaty "gives Ireland freedom, not the ultimate freedom that all nations desire . . . but the freedom to achieve it." De Valera thought otherwise at the time.)
7. *Report of the UN Mediator on Cyprus, Galo Plaza, to the Secretary-General*, March 1965, par. 30.

6   Short-lived Independence

The Republic of Cyprus was born on August 16, 1960, with Makarios as president[1] and Kütchük, at least nominally, his deputy as vice-president. Cyprus joined the United Nations, became a member of the Council of Europe, and demonstrated that no ill will was held against London by also joining the British Commonwealth. In the elections to the new House of Representatives, the Popular Front supporting Makarios secured thirty of the thirty-five seats available to Greek-Cypriots, the archbishop having handed, in a pre-electoral deal, the other five to AKEL, the large pro-Moscow Communist party. All fifteen Turkish seats went to Kütchük's Turkish National party. Makarios went on record as saying that he had accepted the Zurich and London settlement package under duress and that *Enosis* was still his ultimate aim; in response the Turkish members of the House refused to congratulate him on his accession to the presidency, an initial sour note that was to set the intercommunal pattern for the future. Cabinet meetings were conducted generally in English, a language common to most leading members of both communities but not, unfortunately, to the Swiss-educated Kütchük who, apart from Turkish, felt more at home with French, and some early misunderstandings stemmed from language difficulties. More importantly, however, Turkish-Cypriot ministers suspected that the cabinet was being used simply as a rubber stamp for decisions that were reached earlier by their Greek-Cypriot colleagues, who, of course, had the majority vote.

In essence, the Turkish-Cypriots felt that, whatever the constitutional package, they were being excluded from government. True, they enjoyed considerable blocking powers over legislation, but the general atmosphere of suspicion and mistrust did nothing to help improve intercommunal relations, and major arguments soon surfaced. The Greek-Cypriots complained that the constitutional provisions and safeguards were too rigid. They charged the Turkish-Cypriots with refusing to permit ordinary government to function in the hope, according to the majority, that the entire constitutional edifice would collapse and give Turkey an excuse to intervene militarily under the Treaty of Guarantee. Not unnaturally, the Turkish-Cypriots put a different interpretation on events. They charged Makarios with trying to erode their rights and safeguards won at Zurich and London and, in particular, claimed that the archbishop sought to deal with them as a mere minority and not, as they themselves insisted, as "co-founders" of the new republic. They alleged that Turkish-Cypriots were not getting their approved share of civil-service jobs, and the majority answered that too few sufficiently qualified candidates were available. Numerous civil-service appointments were challenged before the Supreme Constitutional Court under its neutral president, a West German, Professor Ernst Forsthoff, who was later to resign abruptly and to claim that Makarios "wanted to remove all constitutional rights from Turkish-Cypriots."[2]

The independence agreement that was to have resolved the Cyprus problem had, in many ways, actually made it worse. Freed finally from direct British influence, Greek-Cypriots felt that, for the first time in their history, they were rulers of the island, and they intended to exercise their mandate fully. Yet, they found themselves confronted by Turkish-Cypriots intent on insisting on the strict letter of a rigid constitutional law. Not surprisingly, perhaps, the majority resorted to duplicity and intrigue. Makarios tried to make good in government practice what Zurich and London had denied him—namely, a pattern of government where the majority will prevailed, albeit with some guarantee for the minority. Later, this intrigue was extended to securing arms clandestinely in order to be better able to resist any Turkish invasion, and the Turkish-Cypriots did the same in preparation not against any invasion threat but in readiness should the majority attack.

The first three years of independence were stormy. Conflicts over relatively unimportant issues gave way to confrontation on two basic issues, taxation and the creation of racially separate municipalities in the island's five main towns—Nicosia, Limassol, Famagusta, Larnaca, and Paphos—as provided for in the constitution.[3] Makarios saw, rightly, that separate municipalities could be a partitionist move by the Turks, and he rejected them, claiming that the two communities did not live in clearly delineated locations and that the organizational problem of determining such communal separation would be impossible. Instead, he proposed an experiment in jointly operated municipalities, but the Turkish-Cypriots rejected the idea after an initial period of wavering. A constitutional deadlock ensued. In parallel, there was a refusal by Kütchük, in keeping with a strict interpretation of the constitution, to accept a pattern of island-wide taxation, rather than having each community making payments to its own communal chamber. The outcome was to deprive the central government of taxation revenue and to make the operations of local government virtually impossible.

Makarios then moved to try unilaterally to break this constitutional impasse based on an uncharted law of necessity, but the only outcome was a further aggravation of intercommunal tensions and, by the end of 1963, outright intercommunal violence. The history of the events of this period has been written selectively by each side, and it forms part of the considerable propaganda files that each maintains today. Yet enough of the basic facts exist for an impartial observer to distinguish the essential components. The record shows that the archbishop proposed[4] to his vice-president a list of thirteen amendments to the constitution (See appendix C), the effect of which would have been to make government more workable, but also to undermine significantly many of the finely balanced protections given to Turkish-Cypriots. In retrospect, one can only guess at the archbishop's motives, but it could hardly have been a surprise to him when the minority rejected the amendments, as did the government in Ankara. He continued to insist that his sole concern was to make government workable, although many of his own Greek-Cypriot admirers have since questioned his wisdom in presenting such dramatic changes in a single package, and without any real prior negotiations with Kütchük.[5]

The Turkish rejection was followed almost immediately by an outbreak of intercommunal violence. Both community leaders had tolerated, if not actively encouraged, the buildup of well-armed illegal groups, and the clashes just before Christmas were encouraged by elements not far removed from the leadership on each side of the racial divide. Starting first in Nicosia, the violence spread quickly to other Cypriot towns and resulted in massacres on both sides. On Christmas Eve, Turkish military jets flew warning sorties over parts of Cyprus, adding to the state of developing panic and alerting the major powers to a possible Turkish invasion. The British government moved troops out of its Cyprus bases to police an eventually agreed cease-fire, but not before thousands of Turkish-Cypriots evacuated from their homes in mixed villages and crowded into "no-go" enclaves, which were quickly barricaded against attack and guarded by armed personnel. Confronting them were similar Greek-Cypriot barricades and their supporting irregular forces. Kütchük was shortly to announce that "the Cyprus Republic is dead." Turkish-Cypriot leaders withdrew from the central administration, as did their representatives on public bodies, the courts, and the civil service. The central government, now exclusively in Greek-Cypriot hands, threw an economic blockade around the main Turkish enclaves, but principally in Nicosia, and for a long period no "strategic materials," including building requisites and cement, were allowed through. The majority controlled the ports and the airport; the minority retaliated by refusing entry to their enclaves by Greek-Cypriots "for security reasons."

Meanwhile, back to Cyprus had come the old guerrilla leader, Grivas, to take charge of the Greek-Cypriot National Guard, and he was later to assemble some of his old comrades into EOKA B units to advance the cause of *Enosis* again and virtually to confront Makarios. Few constitutional formulas granted by Britain or another colonial power were to be so stillborn, and over this small island, Turkey and Greece, both members of NATO, had come very close to all-out war. Makarios, who had rejected an American proposal for a NATO peacekeeping force in 1964 in favor of a UN presence, was soon flirting with the Soviets for support against Turkey, although he was generally careful to follow his declared policy of nonalignment. In Washington there was highly colorful talk of "a Mediterranean Cuba." In Cyprus itself Makarios was shopping for arms, including, ominously, ground-to-air missiles.[6] He was also in collusion with the government of George Papandreou in Athens, who proposed[7] a plan to infiltrate mainland Greek regular army forces into the island. Behind their barricades Turkish-Cypriot leaders moved in cooperation with Turkey to improve their own defenses through clandestine landings of troops and arms at numerous small inlets along the northeastern panhandle.

On the international front, and more visibly, diplomatic efforts were at work to try to defuse the developing Cyprus crisis. The Lyndon Johnson administration moved early in 1964 to block what Washington believed was an imminent Turkish invasion. The U.S. president wrote to Turkey's prime minister, Ismet Inonu, warning "in all candor" (see Appendix D for full text) that American-supplied weapons could not be used by Turkey for an invasion of

Cyprus, adding that any such excursion could undermine NATO's commitment to go to Turkey's aid in the event of an attack by her vast neighbor to the north, the Soviet Union. That intervention held Turkey's hand, but a British initiative with a special London conference failed to bring the two Cypriot sides together. Washington then moved again with some shuttle diplomacy by its special mediator, Dean Acheson, who proposed, eventually, that Greece should have Cyprus, but not all of it (*Enosis*); Turkey was to have a major military base in the north of the island, together with two or more Turkish-Cypriot cantons (partition), and also the small Greek island of Kastellorizon off the Turkish mainland. This package had been prompted by growing fears in Washington that Makarios, under internal pressure from the Communists of AKEL, was getting too close to Moscow[8] and that the Soviets might gain a foothold on Cyprus. Hence emerged the plan to lock Cyprus into the staunch NATO ally, Greece.

The Acheson plan got nowhere, essentially because, by then, the Turkish government was incensed over the direct Johnson intervention and the sharpness of tone in his letter to Inonu. This intervention had sparked considerable anti-American sentiment in Turkey, and no government in Ankara wanted to be seen doing Washington's bidding. Another attempt, along similar lines, to break the Cyprus stalemate was to come five months after the military coup (April 1967) in Greece in bilateral talks between Athens and Ankara, but it, too, failed. That same year there was further intercommunal violence in Cyprus, and again Turkey threatened invasion. Washington intervened once more and pressurized the junta in Athens to withdraw its "illegal" forces in Cyprus, including, notably, Grivas.[9] Intense diplomatic pressure by Washington and London in Athens, Ankara, and Nicosia, but also through the UN in New York, finally persuaded the two factions on the island to open intercommunal talks under UN auspices in a bid to reach an internal settlement.[10] They were to last on and off through more than two hundred meetings, and, at times, they appeared to come close to outline agreements, despite regular mutual recriminations and allegations that one or the other side was not acting in good faith. Makarios believed that he could wear down the economically disadvantaged Turks behind their barricades; Denkthas and his supporters remained set on a partitionist course and hoped, no doubt, that some miscalculation by Greece or the Greek-Cypriots, or both, might finally give Turkey the excuse to invade.

Coinciding with the start of the intercommunal talks, Makarios had appeared to give some ground on the *Enosis* question. He talked about the need for a "realistic appraisal" of the whole Cyprus question, and he pointed out that a solution must be sought within the limits of what was feasible, and that, he said, did not always coincide with what was desirable. This formula of words, however, whatever the intention, satisfied no one. Ankara and the Turkish-Cypriots read it as one more illustration "of the priest talking with two tongues," while the junta in Athens heard a different message and thought that the archbishop was trying to distance himself from their military regime. Some young Greek officers with the Cypriot National Guard felt that the archbishop was turning his back on the "national ideal," while Grivas and EOKA B charged less ambiguously that he had sold out on *Enosis*. The Greek colonels' regime believed that it was Makarios in person who was preventing a satisfactory settlement over Cyprus between Athens and Ankara, and this belief took on an element of "certainty" with most Greek-Cypriots when Makarios survived a number of attempts on his life. In July 1974 the archbishop wrote personally to the Greek president, General Phaedon Ghizikis:

I am sorry to say, Mr. President, that the roots of the troubles are very deep, and they stretch from Athens. The Tree of Evil is nurtured and grows there. . . . To spell it out in more precise terms, I would say that the higher echelons of the military regime in Athens supports and directs the activities of the terrorist organization, known as EOKA B. This explains the participation of the officers of the [Greek-Cypriot] National Guard in the illegal acts and the conspiracies. . . . Documents recently discovered and seized from EOKA B leaders prove this. . . . I can not say that I hold a particularly warm place in my heart for military regimes and particularly for that of Greece, the cradle of democracy. . . . I have often felt—and even brushed against—the invisible hand that reaches out from Athens to wipe me out.[11]

NOTES

1. In the presidential election Makarios was opposed on a thinly veiled pro-*Enosis* ticket by John Clerides, who won 72,000 votes against just double that number for Makarios, but the challenge showed up an embryo split in the ranks of the island's majority population.

2. Interview given at Heidelberg to United Press International and reported on December 30, 1963. A claim of about two thousand legal challenges concerning civil service

appointments was attributed to Professor Forsthoff, but court records show that the Supreme Constitutional Court during its active life of twenty-eight months delivered *judgment* in only one hundred and twenty-three cases, a small minority only dealing with civil service cases. Total cases *filed* with the court, according to official records, were seven hundred and sixty-one.

3. Article 173, Par. 1: "Separate municipalities shall be created in the five largest towns of the Republic . . . by the Turkish inhabitants thereof, provided that the President and Vice-President . . . shall, within four years of the date of the coming into operation of this Constitution, examine the question whether or not this separation of municipalities in the aforesaid towns shall continue."

4. Disclosed publicly on November 30, 1963.

5. Polyvois G. Polyviou, *Cyprus: The Tragedy and the Challenge* (London: John Swain, 1975), p. 30: "The writer's personal view, however, is that putting forward all 13 proposals simultaneously may have been a mistake and a tactical miscalculation." For a similar viewpoint, see P. N. Vanezis, *Cyprus: The Unfinished Agony* (London: Abelard Schuman, 1977), p. 27.

6. In Andreas Papandreou, *Democracy at Gunpoint* (London: Deutsch, 1971), p. 206, the son of the then Greek prime minister reports that in 1965 Makarios had disclosed that Petros Garoufalias, the Greek minister of national defence, had prevented such missiles from reaching Cyprus under instructions from the U.S. government and without the knowledge of his own prime minister Andreas Papandreou—an office to which Andreas himself was elected in late 1981.

7. Ibid., p. 100: "This was my father's proposal, and Makarios accepted it. A clandestine operation then began on a huge scale—of nightly shipments of arms and troops, of volunteers who arrived in Cyprus in civilian clothes and then joined their Cypriot units. . . . No less than 20,000 officers and men, fully equipped, were shipped to Cyprus. They provided a decisive defensive force that prevented the Turks from being able to promenade to Cyprus. And they strengthened the Greek government's bargaining position in Washington and at the UN in New York.

8. Makarios visited Moscow in the spring of 1971.

9. He returned once again in 1971 and regrouped his EOKA B pro-*Enosis* faction. He died three years later at Limassol.

10. Glafcos Clerides, son of John Clerides who had challenged Makarios in the first presidential election, headed the Greek-Cypriot negotiating team; Rauf Denktash led the Turkish-Cypriot side and later became president of the self-proclaimed Turkish Federated State of Cyprus.

11. Peter Modinos, *The Events in Cyprus* (Paris: American Hellenic Institute, 1974), p. 6.

7 The Coup . . . and the Invasion

The "invisible hand" arrived with more substance just two weeks later, shortly before eight o'clock in the morning. A column of Soviet-made T-54 tanks surrounded the Presidential Palace in Nicosia and started to pound the yellow sandstone building. A factory siren, the prearranged signal, sent armored cars and trucks filled with Greek-officered units of the local National Guard racing through the streets of Nicosia to take over key buildings, including the offices of the Cyprus Broadcasting Corporation (CBC). Makarios was inside the palace talking with some schoolchildren visiting from Cairo, and subsequent indications were to suggest that killing him was the primary aim of the coup, and not necessarily toppling the whole government or taking over a large part of the island. Within an hour of the arrival of the tanks, CBC announced that Makarios was dead, and the message was flashed around the world. It was untrue. The archbishop, with three bodyguards, had slipped out a back door and commandeered a passing car, which was driven—with Makarios lying on the floor—to the village police station at Klerou, not far from the capital. The police sergeant provided his own car to take the president and his guards to Kykko Monastery and from there, via his own birthplace at Panayia, to Paphos. There he used a small transmitter to urge his people to defend their country, freedom, and democracy. He was then lifted by a UN helicopter to one of the British military bases and flown to London by way of an overnight stop on the island of Malta. The following day he was in New York to address the United Nations.

The Greek officers behind the coup named a local journalist, Nicos Sampson, as president. Sampson, an EOKA comrade of Grivas and the man who had personally led at least one murderous assault against Turkish-Cypriots a few years earlier, went on television to assure the island's minority that they had nothing to fear. What had happened, he said, was a domestic Greek-Cypriot affair,

189

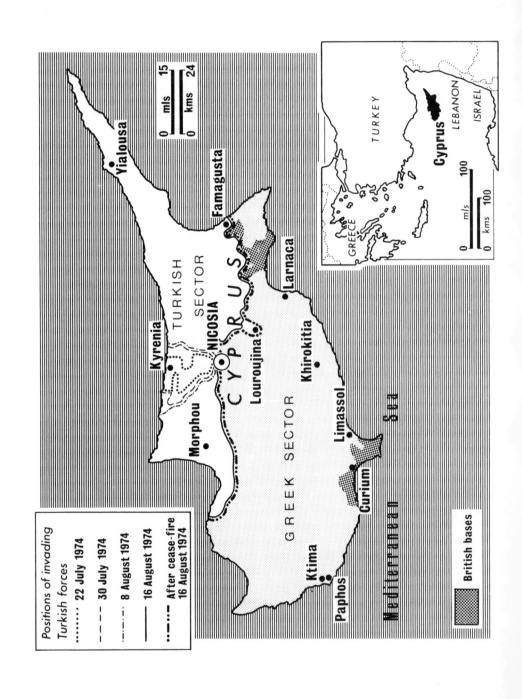

Positions of invading
Turkish forces

······ 22 July 1974
– – – 30 July 1974
–·–·– 8 August 1974
——— 16 August 1974
–··–··– After cease-fire
16 August 1974

Vialousa

Famagusta

Kyrenia

TURKISH SECTOR

NICOSIA

Larnaca

Louroujina

Morphou

C Y P R U S

Khirokitia

GREEK SECTOR

Limassol

Curium

Ktima

Paphos

Mediterranean Sea

British bases

0 ———— 15 mls
0 ———— 24 kms

TURKEY

Cyprus

LEBANON

ISRAEL

GREECE

0 ———— 100 mls
0 ———— 100 kms

and nothing much would change. He even emphasized that the intercommunal talks would continue. Turkish-Cypriots and the government in Ankara under the socialist Bulent Ecevit saw matters differently and believed that the coup was an attempt to bring about *Enosis* by force. Ecevit flew to London for talks in the context of the Treaty of Guarantee (he saw no point in discussing the issue with Greece, despite this provision in the treaty), but the British government refused to act jointly with Turkey.[1] Ankara decided to go it alone. On July 20 a Turkish expeditionary force landed on the northern coast of Cyprus close to Kyrenia, supported by paratroop drops into the main Turkish enclave in Nicosia. In Ankara, Premier Ecevit said that Turkey was not bringing war but peace to Cyprus, "to Greek as well as to Turkish-Cypriots." Makarios told the UN that the case of Cyprus was a test, not just of nonalignment but of the UN itself. If the world body failed to make Turkey respect the UN Charter and its resolutions,[2] the faith of small countries in the organization would be seriously shaken. Turkey fell back on its rights under the Treaty of Guarantee to intervene in Cyprus to restore the status quo, although subsequent events were to demonstrate clearly that the status quo was not restored but that the effective partitioning of the island occurred.

The one gain for democracy and constitutional order from the whole sorry Cyprus mess came in Greece itself. Three days after Turkish troops had landed on Cyprus, the regime of the colonels in Athens collapsed, and the former prime minister, Constantine Karamanlis, was called back from his self-imposed exile in Paris and asked to form a government. On the same day, Nicos Sampson resigned after only eight days as president of Cyprus, and he was replaced by Glafcos Clerides, who surrendered the office to Makarios when the archbishop returned to Nicosia the following December. EOKA B, in a ten-point manifesto issued two days before Makarios's return, demanded that he resign the presidency and restrict himself to church affairs. Ecevit in Ankara and Denktash in the Turkish-Cypriot enclave of Nicosia concurred that they no longer accepted him as president of Cyprus. Yet, the archbishop's ambitions may even have grown by the whole affair; he told cheering Greeks in Athens, when he stopped on his way back to Cyprus from exile, that they could thank him for the restoration of democracy in their country.

A tripartite conference in Geneva in furtherance of UN Resolution 353 and chaired with little distinction by the British foreign secretary, James Callaghan, failed to reach agreement, and Turkey

embarked on a new military exercise in Cyprus to extend its initial
stronghold to cover almost 40 percent of the island's land area. This
is not the place to recount in detail the violence, the agony, and the
sheer brutality in the immediate aftermath of the abortive coup
against Makarios and, much more seriously, resulting from the
Turkish invasion. It has been "documented" selectively, and with
extraordinary passion and partisanship, by both island communities. The present writer was in Cyprus at the time, and terrible deeds of violence and massacre were committed in the name of
nationalism on both sides. The scares, the human tragedies of the
refugees, Greek and Turk, left by the events are real, deep, and of
a kind that will last not just through one generation, and they could
provide the stuff of inspiration and reaction for generations to
come. If events since the Zurich and London agreements demonstrated that Greek and Turkish Cypriots found it next to impossible
to live together side by side in peace and harmony, the tragedy of
1974 made it certain in the foreseeable future. The partition line
was ragged but complete, and, for all practical purposes, the two
island communities were separated totally.

The Turkish invasion brought a peace of sorts to the island, but
any agreed settlement, whether on federal lines or any other, will
not remove the resentment of Greek-Cypriots. Makarios has
gone,[3] but the problem remains, a problem brought on largely by
the political violence of a minority faced with the political intransigence of a majority. Neither side appears to have learned very
much, or at least at the level of their respective leaders, and that
qualification might in time offer some hope. The Turkish-Cypriot
leadership, with Turkey's military machine at its back, relates that
the Cyprus problem has been solved; all that remains to be agreed
on is a new political framework. The Greek Cypriots are, un-
characteristically, less expansive, merely telling outsiders that they
should wait and see what happens. Greek dominance has given
way, for the present at least, to Turkish dominance in a large slice
of Cyprus, as the Byzantine Empire gave way to the Ottomans, but
it is naive to suggest that the Cyprus problem has been solved. As
with the determined climber and the highest mountain, the partition line may be attacked in the future simply because it is there.

The qualifications entered here about the attitudes and the rigidity of the leaders on both sides is prompted by two considerations.
The first can be recounted briefly but should not be ignored. It was
a remark by a young Greek-Cypriot university student studying in
Greece beside whom I happened to sit on a flight from Athens to

Larnaca. On discovering that I was interested in the Cyprus problem, she observed that, with a small college concert, she and some Greek friends had raised money to send to Turkish-Cypriot refugees. She added, hopefully, that people of her generation on both sides of the community divide in Cyprus might in time resolve the problem; she was sure that the present committed leaders would not.

The second observation is quoted at some length here because it makes some important and generally correct points that can often be forgotten when there is sharp cleavage between two communities. It comes from a social anthropologist who knows Cyprus well, and whose father was born there.

> As soon as one writes about an ethnic group as if it was a single thing with one mind ("the Greeks maintain" or "the Turks believe") a step in the wrong direction has been taken, but one no author can completely avoid. Both Cypriot communities have complex class structures, and a range of political opinion, from communist and revolutionary socialists through *laissez-faire* pro-capitalist liberals, to traditionist conservatives and extreme rightists of fascist persuasion. These groups tend to have different views and policies on relations with the other ethnic community. While the ethnic communities tend to express unified "Greek" or "Turkish" opinions in times of *intense* conflict with each other, when such conflict subsides they are shown to have sharp differences with their own more extreme co-religionists. Briefly the right-wingers tend to dislike the other ethnic community most sharply, and to pay great attention to what its extremists say. The socialists and communists, while sometimes following a "national" line of ethnic solidarity, are usually more ready to compromise on relations with the other ethnic group, and are able to form alliances and have dialogue (unless stopped by force) with fellow-socialists on the "other side". This is one striking asymmetry in relations between the two communities. The rightists hate and fear opposed rightists, the leftists are more prepared to cooperate with other leftists.[4]

This author will add only two points here. Since independence, and indeed before 1960, leaders in both communities have been of the conservative class, and to the right of the political center. Secondly, the Loizos caveat has applications in Ireland, too, and is not irrelevant in Italy, either, where not even the Communists today are a complete monolith.

NOTES

1. A British Parliamentary Select Committee of Cyprus was subsequently to say that Britain had a legal right, a moral obligation, and the military capacity to intervene in Cyprus during July and August 1974. "She did not intervene for reasons which the Government refuses to give." (introduction to the Report, Session 1975–76, London, HMSO, par. 22). Some British ministers suggested privately later that the government had no wish to get involved "in another Ulster."

2. Resolution 353 of the UN Security Council adopted on the day of the Turkish invasion called, in part, on all states to respect the sovereignty, independence, and territorial integrity of Cyprus and an immediate end to foreign military intervention, "and the "withdrawal without delay . . . of foreign military personnel present otherwise than under the authority of International Agreements." The resolution also called on Britain, Greece, and Turkey "to enter into negotiations without delay for the restoration of peace in the area and constitutional government in Cyprus."

3. He died of a heart attack on August 3, 1977, and is buried at Kykko Monastery. He was replaced as president by his one-time foreign minister, Spyros Kyprianou, who soon proved himself incapable of holding a number of disparate Greek-Cypriot elements together, including, increasingly, the Communists of AKEL.

4. Peter Loizos, *An Alternative Analysis in Cyprus* (London: Minority Rights Group, report no. 30, rev. ed., 1978).

PART IV

Conclusion

1   Is There Another Way?

A great democracy must either sacrifice self-government to unity or preserve it by federalism. . . . The co-existence of several nations under the same State is a test, as well as the best security of its freedom. It is also one of the chief instruments of civilisation. . . . The combination of different nations in one State is as necessary a condition of civilised life as the combination of men in society. Where political and national boundaries coincide, society ceases to advance, and nations relapse into a condition corresponding to that of a man who renounces intercourse with his fellow-men. . . . A State which is incompetent to satisfy different races condemns itself; a State which labours to neutralise, to absorb, or to expel them is destitute of the chief basis of self-government. The theory of nationality, then, is a retrograde step in history.

Lord John Emerich Acton,
Essays on Freedom and Power

In this concluding section I would like, cautiously, to sound some encouraging notes and to explore, tentatively, what might usefully be done to erode over time some of the community divisions, to help in bridging cleavages, or in any event to start the governing process moving in that direction, and with broad community support. In the search for new institutional arrangements or beneficial modifications to existing structures, it would be best to forget, but not wholly to ignore or to refuse to be influenced by, the lessons of the past. In all three countries under review, there has now developed, to varying degrees, a near-total impasse. The Italian case has been described accurately and succinctly, as "surviving without governing".[1] Northern Ireland at this writing has no government of its own, the administration of the substate continuing since 1974 under the direct rule of the British government in London. In Cyprus the writ of the weakened, post-Makarios central government, which is under the exclusive control of the Greek-Cypriot majority, does not touch in any way on the Turkish-Cypriot minority community and, in a sense, it has itself been unconstitutional since the start of 1964. In all three cases there remain major cleavages as between differing traditions, between Catholic and Social-

ist (widely defined) in Italy, Protestant-Unionist and Catholic-
Nationalist in Ireland, and Christian and Moslem in Cyprus. Such
cleavage is not unique to these three countries, however. Barnes,
in his Italian study,[2] has noted that "several countries exhibit
[similar] patterns of the interplay of history, ideology, subcultures
and organisations, and in these countries the institutionalisation of
traditions has [likewise] made great headway. . . . The politics
which reflect these patterns in their purest form are said to be The
Netherlands, Austria, Switzerland and Belgium; Lebanon before
1975 and Canada are also sometimes viewed as approximating
them." A host of capsule descriptions exist for the forms of governing consensus present in these countries, among them "consociational democracy," "segmented pluralism," and "amicable agreement."[3] That such consensus does largely exist should bring some
encouragement to the protagonists in the cases with which we are
involved here, for it demonstrates that unconventional mechanisms have been made to work and, in considerable measure,
effectively, which can help to diffuse the extremes of traditional
cleavage. Of course, there is a need for elements of compromise to
bring agreement on such mechanisms and to win support for them,
but at the same time such compromises need not necessarily involve the undermining of differing traditions or fundamental aspirations, although they will ordinarily entail some modifications to
them, and also to how they are publicly represented and advanced.
At the same time, I would argue that in any event the very concept
of the nation-state, and the exclusive commitment to it, is itself
being eroded gradually as regional structures take root based on
loose federal or confederal principles—including the European
Economic Community (EEC), or Common Market, with which all
the countries involved in the problems under review here are
linked, whether by direct membership or through economic association.

A common feature of the three studies is that conventional majority rule is, at least for the present, not politically practical or
administratively possible, either because a clear electoral majority
does not now exist (in the case of the Christian Democrats in Italy)
or because a significant minority of the electorate has demonstrated that it is no longer prepared to accept the continued hegemonic control of the numerical majority (as in Ulster and Cyprus)
representing a different, and seen widely to be a confronting, tradition. Equally, there has not yet emerged, or at least not on a

significantly wide scale, a positive acceptance of the need to find, and to agree on in detail, alternative patterns of government. These, says Barnes,[4] evolve only when "partisan elites acknowledge that no single tradition can dominate and that all must thus come to terms in order to avoid chaos and stalemate." Impartial observers would, I believe, conclude reasonably that events over the past decade and more demonstrate amply that such chaos and stalemate already exist in the countries with which this study is concerned.

The deadlock is not altogether complete, however, and, when not clouded over by intercommunal confrontation, terrorist violence and traditional hostility, there are a few encouraging signs that within the ranks of the actual or potential hegemonic powers some elements are surfacing in support of—in any event conceptually—attempts to explore at least whether accommodations can be reached away from the rigidities of conventional majority rule. Such accommodations could, of course, take many forms, and this tentative conversion on the part of some is not necessarily the result of a new commitment to, for instance, forms of segmented pluralism. Other factors[5] have also been at work, as they continue to be, to change some minds from their old molds. Yet, whatever the persuading influences, there is in Italy, for example, a developing if reluctant acceptance, and also among some Christian Democrats, that the exclusion permanently of the Italian Communist party from a direct share in the governing process is incompatible with the winning of a broad, national consensus for the legislative and administrative (and perhaps also constitutional) changes that are clearly necessary for the country effectively to tackle its deep-seated economic and social problems. Such a consensus, too, is needed for concerted, sustained, and unambiguous measures to combat violence and, as importantly, to try to remove, if not wholly its causes, at least some of the confrontational tensions that persuade many Italians often to seem indifferent to its use, or to show tolerance toward its perpetrators. In Ireland, too, and also in Cyprus there are some small signs of emerging agreement, although as in Italy it is still nowhere near being universal, on the *principle* of associating the respective minorities with the governing process, even if the divide remains vast on how such a principle could be translated into practice.

For instance, specifically in the case of Northern Ireland, there has been general all-party agreement:[6]

1. That a committee system should be devised to give real and substantial influence to an Opposition [i.e., Catholics] and to make [any devolved] parliament more effective;
2. That covering each department [or ministry] of government, there should be a departmental committee drawn *equally* from Government and Opposition supporters with normal parliamentary voting rights;
3. That each committee would be involved in the legislative process and [the] scrutiny of government action relating to its department.

Significantly, however, there remains at this time outright disagreement between most Protestant-Unionists and Catholic-Nationalists on two central issues—namely, imposed (by the British government) power sharing and some form of institutional link between Northern Ireland and the neighboring Irish Republic, a move that many Ulster Protestants believe could have dangerous political and constitutional implications for them in the long term.

In the case of Cyprus, the then president, the late Archbishop Makarios, met the Turkish-Cypriot leader, Mr. Denktash, in February 1977 in the presence of Kurt Waldheim, the United Nations secretary-general—the first meeting between the two community leaders in fourteen years. A joint public statement recorded their agreement on the following guidelines:

1. We are seeking an independent, non-aligned, bi-communal federal republic;
2. The territory under the administration of each community should be discussed in the light of economic viability or productivity, and land ownership;
3. Questions of principles like freedom of movement, freedom of settlement, the right of property and other specific matters are open for discussion, taking into consideration the fundamental basis of a bi-communal federal system and certain practical difficulties which may arise for the Turkish-Cypriot community;
4. The powers and functions of the central federal government will be such as to safeguard the unity of the country, having regard to the bi-communal character of the State.[7]

These were agreements on broad principles, but as yet with no substantive agreement on detail, and sight should not be lost of the fact that elites often wish, for international as well as domestic reasons, to appear reasonable and accommodating, especially when no fundamental concessions are immediately involved. It is often a pattern of verbal jockeying in order to make the other side appear intransigent. Yet, inherent, however marginally, in the Northern Ireland Convention report and in the bilateral Nicosia declaration, was an acceptance, however qualified, of some erosion of the principle of unfettered majority rule, although still short of Steiner's definition[5] of "proportionality," in essence a delicate process whereby representatives of differing traditions or special interest groups are able to influence decision making roughly in proportion to their size, and with adequate protection for their basic rights. It can, incidentally, be argued, as it has been by a number of observers, that governments in Italy have survived for more than three decades, or in any event throughout the 1970s, neither on the basis of majority rule nor the rule of proportionality but in some curious Italian variation with elements of both and the advantages of neither. Aldo Moro before his kidnapping and assassination by the Red Brigades was among those few DC politicians who saw a clear need for some accommodation with the Communists. However, as the case study of Italy in this work has demonstrated, accommodation in Italian political terms is seldom if ever a clear-cut choice between defined alternatives, between, for instance, the PCI being wholly of the Opposition or wholly of the government. The permutations in between have been many, yet inevitably there are few remaining choices. At issue now and in the years immediately ahead, as in Ulster and Cyprus also, would appear to be the nature and the timing of more radical compromises.

The Italian case is, arguably, the most crucial, for a compromise there could mean, in essence, for the Christian Democrats to lie down with the Communists, for the DC to agree to a coalition administration not with ideological neighbors, but with ideological foes, and one in which, as noted earlier, the PCI could be expected quickly to dominate. Furthermore, I do not think that it can reasonably be argued that such an eventuality in Italy would leave untouched domestic politics in Spain and Portugal, and it could easily bring a sharp reaction—to the right—in West Germany. In addition, and whatever the merits of Eurocommunism, indeed whether myth or reality or something in between, and whatever the existing and earlier differences between the PCI and Moscow on specific policy issues, such an outcome in Italy could not be seen as a setback for the Soviet Union, but quite the reverse.

It has been argued that being Italian, the ranks of PCI support-

ers represent a rather special brand of Communists far removed
from the hard-core variety, and that their *Via Italiana al socialismo*
is little more than the aspirations of progressive but non-Marxist
socialist forces in other democracies. To accept this now would, I
believe, be to take too much on trust. True, PCI leaders insist
continually on their commitment to democracy and to political
pluralism, but they do not yet demonstrate it very convincingly
within their own rigidly structured party organization, and they
have shown in the past a considerable ability to reverse policies
abruptly without unleashing significant internal dissent. Hence,
there can be no *certain* guarantee that today's protestations in
support of democratic principles might not turn out to be the
promises of yesterday in the real world of tomorrow.

This does not represent any felt bias or a refusal to acknowledge
what the PCI says today, but simply a cautionary note about what
the party might do, and how precisely it might use its power, if it
had a dominant role in the governing of Italy. Unfortunately, there
are no precedents on which to build, no cases in which a Communist party has participated from a position of strength (an important
qualification, for it excludes earlier European experiments with
"popular front" administrations) in "bourgeois" governments. True,
the PCI did participate in a number of Italian administrations immediately after the collapse of fascism, but it was a much smaller
party then, and, in any event, under De Gasperi's leadership the
power and authority in cabinet[9] of PCI ministers were quite limited and were quickly ended (February, 1947). More recent cases
in the past decade or so of Communist participation in democratic
governments tell us very little by way of guidance as to what might
happen in Italy, either because the experiments were soon reversed (Chile, Portugal, and Iceland) or owing to special factors
(Finland[10]), and in no case (including France in 1981) did the
electoral strength of the Communists come close to that enjoyed
currently by the PCI in Italy.

A formal coalition in Italy with the Communists would, therefore, be unique and constitute a significant risk which cannot now
be measured, although some do argue that something akin to
Steiner's proportionality does operate informally there, albeit in a
curious Italian form of compromise. It has been, however, more
negative in outcome than positive, and for the most part it has been
of more benefit to the PCI than to the country. We have already
reviewed in some detail the party's "evolution"[11] through various
stages since the fall of Fascism, at opposite extremes being the

period of outright opposition during the cold war (1948-56) and the PCI's participation in the "governing majority" between March 1978 and the end of January of the following year.[12] This evolution, however, whether cosmetic or real in terms of fundamental ideology and ultimate objectives, has, at least in part, been a quite deliberate search by the PCI for legitimacy, internationally as well as within Italy. It represented for the party the sole alternative to armed revolution that realistic PCI leaders from Togliatti onward knew to be no alternative at all. The PCI's strategy has been to broaden its base into the middle ground while trying to ensure that it was not outflanked on its own Left. The widespread acceptance in the West that the concept of Eurocommunism does represent a break with traditional Marxist-Leninist doctrine has helped the PCI's image abroad, as has its belated acceptance of Italy's membership in NATO, its qualified support for the EEC, and its participation in the European Parliament.

Berlinguer's *Reflections after Events in Chile*[13] deserves careful reading:

> We have always thought—and today the Chilean experience strengthens our conviction— that unity among the workers' parties and left-wing forces is not enough to guarantee the defence and progress of democracy in situations where this unity finds itself confronted with a bloc of parties extending from the center to the right. The central political problem of Italy has been, and more than ever remains, the problem of how to avoid the welding of a solid and organic bond between the center and the right, the formation of a broad front of clerico-fascist stamp, and instead succeed in drawing the social and political forces in the center onto consistently democratic positions. Obviously, the unity, the political and electoral strength of the left-wing forces, and an increasingly solid understanding among their various and autonomous expressions, are an indispensable condition for maintaining a growing pressure for change in the country and for bringing such change about. But it would be illusory to think that even if the left-wing parties and forces succeeded in gaining 51 percent of the vote and seats in Parliament (something which would in itself mark a big step forward in the relationship of forces among the parties in Italy), this fact would guarantee the survival of a government representing this 51 percent. This is why we talk not about a "left-wing alternative," but a "democratic alternative," that is a political prospect of collaboration and agreement among the popular forces of Communist and Socialist inspiration and the popular forces of Catholic inspiration, to-

gether with formations of other democratic orientations. Our
stubborn insistence on this prospect is the object of polemics and
criticism of various origin. But the truth is that none of our critics
has succeeded in pointing to another valid prospect capable of
getting Italy out of the crisis in which the policy of division of the
democratic and popular forces has thrown it, of finding a solution
to the immense economic, social and civil problems now open,
of guaranteeing the democratic future of our Republic.

Berlinguer was not merely updating Togliatti's alliance strategy
into the *compromesso storico;* he was acknowledging that for a
Communist party operating in a Western democracy there was no
alternative road to power, although PCI critics noted that in the
same "reflections" he gave unstinted praise to Lenin's "genial capacity" for compromising with opposing forces along the road of
advancing his revolution and guaranteeing its future. Yet, such
compromises, wrote Berlinguer, were

> made under historical circumstances that can not be repeated,
> but this in no way lessens their value as lessons in farsightedness
> and tactical skill. The goal of a revolutionary force is to con-
> cretely transform the existing facts of a given historical and social
> reality. Such a goal can not be reached on the basis of sheer
> willpower and the spontaneous class drives of the most comba-
> tive sectors of the working masses. It can only be reached on the
> basis of a clear vision of what is possible, uniting combativeness
> and determination with prudence and a capacity for maneuver-
> ing. The point of departure for the strategy and tactics of the
> revolutionary movement is an exact assessment of the state of
> existing forces relationships at any given moment and, more in
> general, an understanding of the overall framework of the inter-
> national and internal situation in all its aspects, never unilater-
> ally isolating this or that element.

I have quoted at some length and directly from Berlinguer's
writings, for here surely are some basic answers but also a few
important and unanswered questions that underlie the concern of
many people, both in Italy and outside it, regarding the Communist party and its possible participation in some new governing
order for Italy. His emphasis was on moderate policies and revolutionary principles, a careful attempt to persuade those in doubt
about the party's commitment to democracy and an assurance to
those in PCI ranks that revolutionary aims had not been changed,
but only the means necessary to accommodate changing times and

circumstances. The only road to power was with the DC and others, but excluding the right-wing forces; any other way would risk internal upheaval or international opposition, or quite possibly both. Had not, he charged earlier, the Americans brought down Allende? In addition, there was a scarcely concealed acceptance that an already fragile Italian economy, which is so open in its structure and needs investment from, and understanding by, the international financial community, might not survive the emergence of a left-wing government. Implied, too, in all of this, and indeed in the constant refrain of most PCI leaders in the last couple of years, is the notion that somehow a Communist share directly in government would of itself transform the economy, cure Italy's social ills, and end the terrorist violence. It is at best a doubtful argument that begs a lot of questions and raises quite a few, too. Is the PCI's support being withheld deliberately for policies that could tackle these major problems until the DC and other moderate forces agree to the PCI's political price? Does it suggest to the cynics that somehow the Communist can control the turning on or off of politically motivated violence, or suggest to the less cynical that the party would endorse an iron fist against terrorism, which might also erode some fundamental civil rights? Clearly, Berlinguer raised other nagging questions, or at very least queries. Are the strategy and tactics of the PCI, in his own words, intended to deal with the present and the immediate future in an interim compromise along a revolutionary road? At issue, of course, is not whether the PCI is seeking to maneuver itself into a share in power now, for that is self-evident, but what it would do with this power in the future. Also, in a word, would the process be reversible?

I cannot claim to know the answers to these vital questions, but that is no reason not to raise them. It is even possible that they cannot be answered for certain by the present leaders of the party, nor can there be certainty that repeated and seemingly unambiguous declarations by PCI leaders in outright opposition to political violence and terrorism represent the party's true instincts or, more so, that of its leading activists, and there certainly have been occasions[14] when mob violence showed convincing signs of being orchestrated directly or indirectly by the PCI. However unkindly, there remains in the public mind in Italy a notion that the party does share some responsibility for political violence.[15]

Yet the absence of certain answers to these and other related questions concerning the long-term intentions of the PCI need not necessarily rule out totally the application of some element of structured proportionality to government in Italy. Any such pattern might well require substantial modifications, at least initially, to that applicable elsewhere in situations of opposing traditions. Such a pattern would benefit, too, from some changes in the PCI's own approach or, more explicitly, some more concrete demonstrations that would give greater credence to what the party professes now to believe in and to represent. An Italian pattern of proportionality does not necessarily, or at least immediately, have to go so far as to be reflected formally in, for example, the cabinet or Council of Ministers. A start by all the participating parties might be made with agreed policies and a fixed legislative program and timetable, but also with some institutional and constitutional changes. This process would oblige the Communists to give tangible expression to their commitment to democracy and require them to join in the implementation of intelligent economic and social programs that are not ideologically extreme.

NOTES

1. Giuseppe di Palma, *Surviving without Governing: The Italian Parties in Parliament* (Berkeley and Los Angeles, Calif.: University of California Press, 1977).

2. Samuel H. Barnes, *Representation in Italy: Institutionalised Tradition and Electoral Choice* (Chicago: University of Chicago Press, 1977), p. 19.

3 .There is a vast array of literature, and much ongoing research, on the underlying problem, including (selectively): Arend Lijphart, *The Politics of Accommodating Pluralism and Democracy in the Netherlands* (Berkeley, Calif.: University of California Press, 1968); Jurg Steiner, *Amicable Agreement versus Majority Rule: Conflict Resolution in Switzerland* (Chapel Hill, N.C.: University of North Carolina Press, 1974); Kenneth MacRea, ed., *Consociational Democracy: Political Accommodation in Segmented Societies* (Toronto: McClelland and Stewart, 1974); C. Bingham Powell, Jr., *Social Fragmentation and Political Hostility: An Austrian Case Study* (Stanford, Calif.: Stanford University Press, 1970).

4. *Representation in Italy*, p. 19.

5. Successive British governments, in many reports, have indicated that associating the Catholic minority with the administrative process is a necessary precondition for devolved power in Northern Ireland. Again, both Greece and Turkey would like to see a settlement in Cyprus, but they each have a different asking price, and both adopt in public the rather unrealistic position that a resolution of the Cyprus question is an internal matter for the Cypriots.

6. *Report of the Northern Ireland Constitution Convention*, HMSO, London, 1975, p. 27.

7. Agreed text as released to the local media through the offices of the United Nations.

8. Jurg Steiner, "The Principles of Majority and Proportionality," *British Journal of Political Science*, 1971 (No. 1), pp. 63–70.

9. The author has had accounts from many senior and some now retired civil servants of how sensitive documents, touching on defense, foreign policy, and internal security, were

by agreed convention not available to Communist administrators during those earlier coalitions involving the PCI.

10. Finland's proximity to and special relations with the USSR have been the major factors for including the Communists in government, but it has not helped the growth of the party or saved it from considerable internal dissent.

11. The implied qualification here is deliberate because to do otherwise would be to suggest that changes have, in every single instance, been real and genuine and without regard to any other considerations. There is no way I can be sure of this, or indeed certain of the contrary.

12. Beringuer charged then that the DC "portrayed our party as ideologically and politically responsible for terrorism" and with "a revival (not only on the part of the DC) of the old polemic on the PCI's democratic legitimacy" showed sensitivity to two crucial areas where the party is seen as being suspect by many Italians.

13. Translation here from the original Italian is verbatim as published by the PCI.

14. Including mass demonstrations following an attempt on the life of Togliatti in 1948 and street and factory violence designed to bring down the Tambroni government in 1960, although this violence was represented as a PCI challenge against the neo-Fascist MSI.

15. Opinion poll, showing at that time that more than 58 percent of the sample expressed the view that the PCI was involved in political violence. The author has no reason to believe that the figure would be as high today.

2 Living with the Communists

The 1979 general election in Italy demonstrated that the electoral advance of the Communists was not irreversible, and the outcome of important regional elections there in the middle of 1980 showed that the setback for the PCI was no aberration. The parties making up the then coalition (Christian Democrats, Socialists, and Republicans) took some satisfaction from the fact that the legitimacy of their uneasy governing alliance had actually been advanced, given their combined electoral total of 52.5 percent of the popular vote as against the minimum majority of 51 percent when the coalition was patched together following the general election. Such statistical minutiae have long been the stuff of Italian political analysis, but of course more important was the electoral confirmation that there is still a hard core of PCI support in the country of around a solid 30 percent, although the 1980 regional poll did show a setback for the party in the poorer southern part of the country. Nonetheless, the demonstrable fact remains that just as a coalition with little more than 50 percent of the popular vote cannot command a national consensus, or indeed necessarily guarantee for itself a parliamentary majority on all issues (party defections in secret ballots are a feature of Italian politics, although rarely with the Communists), so the continued exclusion of the PCI from all direct participation in the governing process—which, incidentally, also influences the attitude of the country's largest trade union, CGIL—tends to deny any such consensus. This remains the nub of the Italian problem, and it is what gives the political process there its continuing instability despite, or perhaps largely because of, the underlying stability in Italian voting patterns.

How can this political instability be overcome, or, at very least, how can the process be made somewhat more stable? The answer, it seems to me, must lie in both institutional and constitutional change and, as with France and de Gaulle's Fifth Republic after the governmental crises of the 1950s, there may well now be a need to update the Italian Republic after three and a half decades. This period has brought immense economic and social change throughout Italy, which has transformed the country from an essentially agricultural economy into the top league of world industrial nations. It is hardly surprising that the constitutional mix, given the circumstances prevailing when it was written, no longer adequately fits the altered model.

Sartori[1] has noted the three functions of legislatures as representation, legislation, and control of the administration, and I doubt that he would dissent from the view, which this writer holds, that the Italian Parliament in Rome serves none of these purposes, or at very best serves them badly. Given the party structures, the way in which candidates are selected for overlarge constituencies in general elections and the preference pattern in the electoral system itself, which all the big parties manipulate—none more so than the Communists—parliamentary representation is largely a party matter. In effect, it is (admittedly not totally) party nomination that determines success, not the subsequent election, which for a majority of candidates is a mere routine. Parliament is a place where the parties meet rather than a true forum for representatives of the people.[2] It is a nice cozy club, even offering free haircuts. The electorate commits a party preference, and the parties provide the representatives in proportion to the vote. The party lists are published in advance, but the ballot papers contain no names, leaving the party machines to determine, where considered necessary, personal preferences through instructions to the party faithful. Top party names, such as Berlinguer for the PCI, may appear on up to three constituency lists for the Chamber of Deputies and be elected in all three before surrendering the two unwanted seats to a party colleague in line. In a sense, the Italian system is more one of party democracy than representative democracy.

The government parties determine legislation, with the political horse-trading taking place among coalition partners and in party caucuses; outside pressure groups, such as the main national employers organization and the trade unions, are sometimes consulted, but not the Communists until relatively recently. Parliament is reduced substantially to a rubber-stamp role with, in practice, no real scope for individual legislative initiative, and no encouragement for it from the party managers. Despite some recent improvement in the parliamentary committee system, control by the legislature over the administration is marginal. Collective cabinet responsibility exists notionally, but in Italy the head of the government is, in constitutional title, not prime minister as such but President of a Council of Ministers. In operational practice it is much the same, the nominal leader being first among equals but, with rare exceptions in recent history, having a vote generally no better or more influential than that of his ministerial colleagues. Some powerful politicians—that is, powerful in party terms—run their ministries as personal fiefs, rewarding friends and discriminating against foes at will.

In addition, there are too many parties. In the 1979 general election only four parties (DC, PCI, PSI, and MSI) out of the twelve that won some representation to the chamber crossed the five percent mark of the electorate necessary in West Germany to secure any representation in the Bundestag in Bonn. A similar provision in Italy would not only reduce political fragmentation and eliminate some of the extensive horse-trading necessary before any new government can be formed, but it could also led progressively to a useful realignment in Italian politics and oblige the electorate to make more clear-cut choices between fewer political philosophies. Arguably, the British electoral system of first-past-the-post in single-member constituencies would also benefit Italy by again eliminating the very small parties and reducing, at least theoretically, the influence of the parties in determining who gets elected. There would be the added advantage of encouraging successful candidates to be constituency representatives at least as much as party members.

The realignment in Italian politics and the electoral polarization that could reasonably be expected to result from such changes would, nevertheless, in all probability leave the PCI with its hard core of support and electoral representation and indeed might even increase it. If the normal alternating process of parliamentary democracy functioned in Italy, this would be no real problem, but, for the present anyway, it does not. In Italy to a considerable extent, and in the West as a whole, Communists in opposition within the parliamentary system are acceptable, but not so in government, whether alone or in coalition. The party itself knows this, hence the *compromesso storico*. Yet in the real sense this is a negative policy because in reality it can not be realized by tactics and strategy or even by moderate electoral advance, but can only be conceded to the PCI by the DC, and possibly with others, including the PSI, which for decades has been divided on its attitude to the PCI. I personally hold the view, although it is by no means universal among Italian politicians and observers of the political scene, that faced with no alternative between accepting in full the *compromesso*—namely, the formal participation of the PCI fully in government—and going into parliamentary opposition, the Christian Democrats—or at least very many in the party—would opt reluctantly for the latter. If I am correct in this assumption, and given no change in Berlinguer's attitude to a "left alternative" administration (to say nothing of the attitude within Socialist ranks under the leadership of Bettino Craxi) then we do really have a stalemated situation.

Is there then any acceptable alternative for Italy? Here one inevitably enters the arena of the possible, which may not always be practical in current political terms. Sight should not be lost of the extraordinary ability of Italians, in Sartori's terms, of "floating and remaining afloat, their inventiveness in patching up, and their resourcefulness in making the provisional endure, in buying time."[3] In the same context, he observed that Italians "distinguish between (1), my problem, (2), your problem, and (3), their problem. Maybe the Communist Party can not afford to wait, but an Italian would say, or might say, that this is their problem." Another perceptive Italian noted: "During the First World War we used to say that the situation in Germany was serious but not desperate, in Austria desperate but not serious, and in Italy desperate, but normal. The Italian situation is always desperate, but normal."[4]

It is a fair commentary, but it does not give any guarantees for the future or hold out real prospects for eliminating political instability and providing the country with governments that can both endure and tackle realistically, and with broad community support, the many grave problems facing Italy. A necessary prerequisite remains a wider national consensus. Electoral reforms as suggested could help and might concentrate the minds of the electorate. A realignment on the left is not impossible, particularly if the PCI loses further electoral ground. The party is already moving tentatively toward bridge building with Socialist parties in the European Parliament,[5] and developments elsewhere (for example, if the leftwing of the British Labour party gains full party control) could encourage the Italian Communists to dilute further their links with Moscow and seek to plot instead, and to campaign for, "a third road to socialism," one that is neither Marxist nor social democratic. It would be much more than the German party did after its electoral reversals and the 1959 Bad Godesberg conference, when the SPD ceased to be a Marxist party. The parallel is by no means exact, but politics—even Communist politics—are about securing power, or at the very least sharing in it.

The PCI does, of course, share a measure of power in a number of Italian regions, and in some of the largest cities, but the party has complained of having little real authority, in part owing to the rigidities of Italy's regional structure and also the limitations and the bureaucracy of political and fiscal devolution. A central government controlled effectively by the Christian Democrats could hardly be expected to make life easier for regional PCI-dominated administrations, but could the DC not yet be obliged to agree on a real power-sharing formula at that level if they insist on denying it to the PCI at the national level? Might a formula not be found to help bridge the existing cleavage, and in the process to advance consensus nationally, through a restructuring of the Senate along the lines of the West German Bundesrat to make it directly representative of the regions? The present Italian bicameral system serves little real purpose (senators and, no doubt, constitutional experts hooked on the need for checks and balances would, presumably, dissent from this view, although their case is not immediately apparent in the Italian situation) and is essentially an exercise in duplication. Although differing somewhat in mechanism, the process of electing deputies and senators is broadly the same; the present higher age requirement for candidates for the Senate, and of those who elect them, does not result in any material difference in party composition in the two chambers. In party political balance and in legislative competence, one is almost a mirror image of the other.

The PCI is known to be interested in constitutional reform, and some of its leading members are on record as being opposed to the Senate while, for the moment anyway, being less specific in advocating what might replace it. Might there not be a basis here for a compromise different from that envisaged in the *compromesso storico*, with a restructured second chamber of the Italian Parliament reflecting the existing strong Communist influence in many of the regions, coupled with a considerable increase in the powers devolved to these regions by the central government? That would be a halfway solution along vaguely federal lines, to be sure, but there are many who assert that Italy is more a loose federation of regions than a unitary state, whatever the fine constitutional assertions. The Communists might even be persuaded to drop, in fact if not in appearance, their demand for full participation in the central government in return for a share in real power in some regions and, conceivably, either alone or in an alliance with others, a majority in a second parliamentary chamber with defined authority to delay, and to help in the revision of, proposed legislation, although not with an absolute and permanent veto.

Any such reordered parliamentary and administrative skeleton would, of course, require a great deal more flesh than it is appropriate to fill in in this study, but it could be a framework for tackling the core of the Italian political problem and for doing so in a manner that could in time create a better consensus nationally while also ensuring that the composition of government in Italy was broadly acceptable in the context of the country's continued participation in the Western Alliance. Needless to say, given present-day political realities, such changes, whether singularly or in combination, could in practice be made only with the agreement of the Communists. That is the PCI's real power, its capacity to prevent change if it cannot dictate it. If, however, the PCI is persuaded to look for an alternative to the *compromesso*, whether under the present leadership or another (and there are Communists among those in Italy today who believe it to be dead anyway), then democratic centralism may not indefinitely cloak moves to find such an alternative. Italy being Italy, the alternative could take time to surface, whatever its ultimate form toward power sharing. This, of course, excludes a return to hard-line Marxist doctrine, but in Italy there are no more PCI votes in that direction, and the party today knows it.

NOTES

1. Giovanni Sartori, "Introductory Report," Roundtable Meeting on Parliamentary Government, Bellagio, 1963.

2. Samuel H. Barnes, in his *Representation in Italy: Institutionalised Tradition and Electoral Choice* (Chicago: University of Chicago Press, 1977), argues correctly, I believe, that in Italy, even by European standards, a sizable independence exists between electoral inputs and policy outputs.

3. Paolo Filo della Torre et al., *Eurocommunism: Myth or Reality* (London: Penguin, 1979), p. 181.

4. Gaetano Salvemini, *Lettere dall'America*, vol. 2, Bari, 1967–68, p. 148.

5. Berlinguer had a meeting during 1980 with the French Socialist leader, François Mitterrand, much to the annoyance of the French Communist leader, Georges Marchais.

3   The Divided Islands

What of the Irish imbroglio and the framework of a possible solution there? On paper at least, the problem is not insoluble, nor need it be so in practice, provided those in authority act with a little vision and a lot of political courage and resolution. Both traditions in Ulster, and even more so the extremists in the two factions, must be made to realize that their primary objectives cannot now be achieved, whatever the longer term prospects. The united Ireland demanded by the IRA and secretly wished by a lot of Dublin politicians is not a present prospect because it is plainly unacceptable to Northern Protestants. A return to unfettered Protestant majority rule in Belfast is also not possible because it is unacceptable to the Catholic minority, and the British government must make this crystal clear because it alone has ultimate authority over, and constitutional responsibility for, the substate. "Crystal clear" should mean just that, not hints and private understandings, but a firm, unambiguous declaration openly made of the position and resolve of the British government and, hopefully, with the full endorsement of that clear position by all other parties at Westminster. Ulster's Protestant extremists in the past successfully challenged the resolve of the British government, when they wrecked the Sunningdale peace formula that carried virtually unanimous bipartisan support in the British House of Commons. Such an occurrence should not be allowed to happen again. James Callaghan, who was British home secretary and later prime minister, and thus was very much involved in the Ulster crisis, backed Sunningdale on paper but was less resolute in government. He wrote: "If, at any time, the Assembly and the Executive should be made unworkable through a deliberate refusal by the [Northern Ireland] majority to play their part, then in my judgment the United Kingdom would be entitled to reconsider her position and her pledges on all matters."[1] But his own government did not act accordingly.

214

There have been other Protestant challenges in the past, indeed over the very creation of the provincial entity, and British governments have been seen to be paper tigers. Having been seen to have lost credibility over Sunningdale, the UK government must, if anything, now overemphasize its resolution and accept the political (and military, if necessary) implications of enforcing its writ should circumstances arise. There should be no more successful political strikes in Ulster; otherwise no political initiative will succeed, despite the best efforts of Britain's latest secretary of state for Northern Ireland, Mr. Jim Prior, to try yet again in the spring of 1982.

In Dublin, too, there is a need for political honesty and also for resolution. The declaration of the Irish Republic at Sunningdale to the effect that Irish unity could come about only with the consent of a majority of the people of Northern Ireland was little more than an exercise in political doublethink. In practical terms, at least given present realities, this was the apparent acceptance that unity would *not* come about because the community balance in the province is such that no such spontaneous majority seems likely to exist in any foreseeable future relevant to current political judgment and effective decision making. The size of Catholic families in Ulster is, admittedly, larger than that of the average Protestant family, but there can be no guarantee that it will remain so, and, in any event, it is a doubtful proposition on which to assemble public policy. Extrapolating birth patterns well into the next century on the basis of unchanged assumptions is, at best, a dubious exercise, and already emigration patterns are emerging (because of the violence) that seem to cancel out any higher birth rate on the Catholic side. Sunningdale declaration or not, the fact remains that the declared policy of the three main political parties represented in Dail Eireann supports Irish unity, whatever the qualifications, and the present Dublin constitution lays claim to the whole island territory. In that sense, Dublin's declaration at Sunningdale hardly squared with the constitutional facts, and Ulster Protestants knew it. The government's majority in the Dail vote on the peace package was, as noted earlier, exactly five.

Problem solving at any level, including that of politics, is best tackled, it seems to me, by first acknowledging whatever facts exist or can be reasonably deduced. In the case of a Northern Ireland settlement, the main facts appear rather clear-cut as follows. Firstly, Northern Ireland is constitutionally part of the United Kingdom and, hence, the ultimate responsible authority is the

government in London answerable to the whole of the UK electorate,[2] including (but not only, an important qualification) voters in
Northern Ireland. Secondly, the unilateral guarantee affirmed in
the 1949 Ireland Act[3] on the constitutional status of Northern Ireland, and confirmed by successive British governments, was a decision by Westminster, a British commitment, not an Ulster right.
Like any other such commitment, it could, of course, be withdrawn by the British Parliament, or indeed varied just as the level
of the British financial subsidy to Ulster—currently running at an
estimated $6 billion plus annually—can and is altered.

   This point is fairly crucial in the whole Irish debate, although I
appreciate fully that the very suggestion of such a withdrawal can
send shock waves through Ulster Protestants and, further, that its
actual withdrawal could well result in a full-scale civil war in the
province, although this can not be certain. However, the risk at
this time may well be too great to take, although it is demanded by
the IRA, by the Catholic SDLP, and by the Fianna Fail party in
Dublin. The argument in favor of withdrawal, however hedged
about with qualifications, rests largely on the notion that nothing
short of this will concentrate the minds of Ulster Protestants and
persuade them to sit down with their fellow Irish in the republic
and endeavor to thrash out an acceptable solution. It may well be
so, but the immediate price could be very high in terms of
bloodshed, and a dirty little religious war is an obscene way of
attempting to resolve political problems in the twentieth century.

   Thirdly, any form of devolved local government in Northern
Ireland will require some element of proportionality if it is to
survive and command the support of the Catholic minority there.
There can be arguments and debate over mechanisms but, after a
decade and more of bloody violence, little realistically over the
principle. The fourth evident fact is that Ireland as a whole is a
small island country, a geographical unit if not a political one, and
that it must be desirable at the very least to have harmonious
relations, to say nothing of economic links, between its component
parts. Further, it is naive to believe that any solution in Ulster that
is not acceptable generally in the Irish Republic is likely to survive
in the long term. Some generation of Irish nationalists will seek to
undermine any settlement that is seen to be one-sided in favor of
another tradition, and no government in Dublin will always act
resolutely to defeat the terrorism of the IRA if, deep down, the
politicians there reflect nationalist aspirations, but not the gunmen's determination and methods. Finally, there is the fact that

Ireland and Britain, near neighbors and members of the same European Community, must coexist in reasonable harmony, and they will not always do so as long as Ulster remains an issue between them.

Is it possible, then, to assemble even a theoretical framework for a solution around these basic facts? I would have thought so, although I have no wish to play down the very real difficulties. The pattern that evolved at Sunningdale was impressive, but it was an attempt to build too much too quickly and to do so without having sufficient regard for the reasonable fears of even moderate Ulster Protestants. There was evidence, as noted earlier, to suggest that there existed, however reluctantly, a majority in Ulster in support of the *principle* of power sharing,[3] but not for the proposed Council of Ireland, which easily evoked Protestant fears of an eventual slide into Irish unity. The whole package was an attempt to impose cooperation, both within Northern Ireland and between the two parts of Ireland, from the top. A wiser but slower course—as the evolution of Scandinavian cooperation, including the Nordic Council, has demonstrated[4]—might be to plan less ambitiously, to encourage cooperation by building from the bottom up, preparing the peoples' minds and embracing initially mainly those areas in the economic domain where early and mutual benefits might reasonably ensue.

The intended Council of Ireland (1973 variety) was designed to reflect an "Irish dimension" to the Ulster problem, a dimension that the Dublin government and the Ulster minority insisted on, one that London now acknowledges, but one that is still rejected fiercely by Northern Ireland Protestants. They had been asked, simultaneously, to share power with those of a different tradition, people perceived as being suspect in their loyalty to the British connection, and also with a government in Dublin that they saw as having designs on the whole of Ireland and one that, they professed to believe, was turning a blind eye to those of violent intent out to bomb Ulster into an all-Ireland state. It was asking too much of them, and too quickly, and, in fact, the Protestant politicians who accepted the package on their behalf at Sunningdale no longer had a clear mandate. Further, as a total package, it confused unnecessarily two separate, if related, issues—that of internal government in Ulster and that of relations between the two parts of Ireland and with Britain.

On any objective analysis, the first issue was and still remains the more important, and the final arbiter there must be London.

Yet there does remain an "Irish dimension." If for the present it is
not widely acceptable in Ulster to afford this some cross-border
expression, then why not have it reflected in an Anglo-Irish context
linking the two sovereign governments, preferably (if possible)
within the broad framework of the European Common Market, or
at least under EEC aegis. After all, both countries are members,
and each professes to have an interest in the economic and social
welfare of Northern Ireland. There are already very close ties between the two countries, including unrestricted freedom of movement. For most practical purposes, citizens of each enjoy reciprocal rights in the other country. Irish citizens have the right to
vote in British elections, and the existing provision that prevents
British citizens from voting in Irish general elections is being reviewed. The Irish Republic has, in consequence of EEC membership, diversified considerably its external trading pattern away
from Britain and toward Europe, but close trade and general economic relations between the two countries remain. Each, needless
to say, has a vested interest in an early and peaceful settlement in
Ulster.

Here, surely, are some established contacts and some new seeds
that might take root in time, perhaps also laying a groundwork for
some loose North/South federal linkup within Ireland itself or,
even at a lesser level, some moves toward a confederal structure.
As with East-West disarmament, what are wanted urgently in Ireland are some confidence-building mechanisms designed to erode
progressively some real fears and mutual misunderstandings. Mar-
rying the fears to the underlying facts is the only effective alternative, and certainly the best starting point; failing to appreciate the
former, or misrepresenting the latter, whether deliberately or
otherwise, is a recipe for more bloodshed and for exacerbated
community and traditional cleavage. Clearly, Britain should act
wisely and with resolution over devolved government in Northern
Ireland. The two sovereign governments should work together to
encourage over time the evolution of a spirit of real cooperation
between them—not least on the question of security along the
border zone. A unilateral and *open-ended* British political and constitutional guarantee that encourages intransigence and the rejection of reasonable mechanisms toward overcoming traditional conflicts must be a dangerous anachronism today. This, to repeat, is
not an argument for immediately undermining such a guarantee,
but it is for Britain to make clear that such a guarantee has a price
and cannot, in *all* circumstances, be considered sacrosanct.

Parnell, when leading the Irish party at Westminster in the last century, declared that "he did not know how this great question [concerning Ireland and its relations with Britain] will be eventually settled." In the same address in Cork in 1885 he asserted that "no man has the right to fix the boundary to the march of a nation," an assertion to which militant Irish nationalists have had recourse in order to try to justify a murderous campaign to extend Ireland's political boundaries to the whole of Ireland. Like Parnell, I claim no prescience on the age-old Irish question, but history has demonstrated only too tragically, and not only in Ireland, that one individual's absolute rights can be won and maintained at the expense of tyranny for another, and a reasonable and impartial examination of the Irish story does not suggest that a monopoly of right has been on any one side. Most of those who now talk of a "New Ireland," including many politicians in Dublin, are still inclined to work from old memories and old molds. Within Ireland, and between Ireland and Britain, an element of federalism, or even a loose confederal structure, could in time help chart a new way forward, but at a measured pace.[5]

In many ways, a resolution of the Cyprus problem should be much easier. In Ireland the idea of an evolving federal or confederal structure linked perhaps in a very loose Anglo-Irish condominium framework has not yet taken root. In Cyprus, however, as noted above, the Makarios-Denktash summit agreement of 1977 resulted in a general consensus on an independent, nonaligned, bicommunal federal republic, although admittedly the Greek-Cypriot side following the death of the archbishop showed some signs of wanting to water down this outline agreement. The reason for this apparent shift is not difficult to determine, and of itself it may not be important in the longer term. The successor to Makarios as president, Spyros Kyprianou, also has had meetings with Denktash, but he lacks the popularity and the political muscle of the archbishop with the Greek-Cypriot community—both elements could yet be necessary to sell any final agreement to the island's majority—and some of his advisers believe that Makarios gave away too much at the 1977 summit. In addition, there have been arguments, largely semantical when viewed against the reality in Cyprus, over interpretations of "bi-zonal" and "bi-communal" concepts. Nevertheless, there is a general acceptance of the principle of a federal solution for Cyprus; the debate is about mechanics, the size of the federal units, the question of the refugees, the powers of the central government, and the like. This is not to say that Greek-Cypriots like the notion of a federation, for in truth they do not, but most of them are prepared to acknowledge that the Turkish invasion of 1974 did, from their viewpoint, change everything, and, given that change a federal solution would appear to be the best available, and better than an unsatisfactory status quo—a not wholly unsatisfactory situation for some hard-liners in majority ranks. The Turkish-Cypriot leadership, backed by Turkey's military power,[6] has adopted a tough negotiating stance based primarily on its professed or actual belief that a physical separation of the two communities is the only immediate guarantee of the safety of the minority.

There is, then, a clear need to take stock of the present reality in approaching a possible solution, but, I would argue, it is just as important, perhaps indeed even more so in the longer term, to try to find a solution that, as in the case of Ireland, provides specifically for evolution when, hopefully, the current community cleavage has been eroded somewhat over time. Thus, no solution should be considered permanent or be framed in an inflexible mold, for in truth Cyprus surely is too small an island to be denied at least the possibility of a coming together of its two communities. Nor can it be in the long-term interests of either Greece or Turkey to have reflected there their own historical enmities. After all, Greece started its transition period as a full member of the European Common Market in 1981, and Turkey has already indicated to Brussels that it, too, aspires to full membership by the end of the century. Membership for both countries could bring new economic opportunities, but also new obligations, including freedom of movement of populations, and the EEC has no wish to inherit the thorny Cyprus problem.

The Cyprus issue, essentially, is one in which the island's minority has a generally held mistrust of the majority, and this is exploited by a Turkish-Cypriot leadership currently reinforced in its inflexibility by the muscle of the Turkish army and influenced deep down by an almost paranoid reaction to all things Greek. However, is it unreasonable to assume that another generation may change, if permitted? Hence it is important to avoid in any Cyprus settlement a rigid formula that does not encourage positively an opening over time to intercommunal harmony but seeks instead to confirm a dangerous status quo because too many of those now involved in leadership are set in their confrontational ways.

Turkey and Greece have never been agreeable partners, yet farsighted statesmen like Atatürk and Venizelos hoped for a better tomorrow, even to the point post-Lausanne of agreeing that Greek and Turkish textbooks should be rewritten to help in promoting rapprochement rather than confirming conflict. The fact that this did not happen widely is no argument against making another attempt, and in Cyprus in a much wider context. Constitutional formulas being explored on the Turkish-Cypriot side are based on the possibility of an immediately rigid separation of peoples and functions being subject to a review after a period of trial—perhaps seven years. Yet, surely a more hopeful course is to include confidence-building mechanisms from the start, even if it takes a while before they can be implemented. The alternative approach, it seems to me, risks the possibility that separatist mechanisms will become frozen and that any review will be iced over.

In capsule, the best practical remedy for Cyprus is a new constitutional arrangement that would encourage positively the emergence of intercommunal harmony while taking note of existing realities, and any reasonable solution must reflect a fair degree of equity. It is, for instance, self-evident that the Turkish minority must surrender some territory in any settlement; the argument can be over how much, but there are some practical criteria, and some precedents, to work on.[7] It is equally true that some outside and potentially effective authority should be available to guarantee the preservation undisturbed of new constitutional arrangements, and preferably not the great powers, whose interests are often to exploit pawns rather than to protect them. Ideally, neither Greece nor Turkey should be involved directly in such guarantees and certainly not be involved alone, but the present realities dictate otherwise because the Cyprus minority demands a role for Turkey. A bilateral pact between Greece and Turkey to avoid recourse to arms or to armed invasion, specifically over Cyprus, would be a help, as would a recourse to external arbitration on a number of sensitive issues within Cyprus, including the protection of human rights and the impartiality of justice. Is there not a potential role here for both the European Court of Human Rights and the International Court of Justice? Whatever the seen inequity, and it is very real, might there not be an equality of representation on some at least of the new federal institutions—just as in Ireland a case could be made for equal North-South representation in a federal assembly whenever and if a consensus emerges in support of such an institution. Those still arguing for a rigid relationship between population and representation are, fundamentally, interested only in majority hegemony, whatever their protestations to the contrary. However, is there not an acceptable and largely workable precedent in the Senate of the United States, where tiny New Jersey, for example, ranks equal with two senators to the vastness of Texas or California.

Accommodating cleavage between conflicting traditions and the establishment of intercommunal trust require today some unconventional mechanisms. Pierre Trudeau has argued well that "the first law of politics is to start from the facts rather than from historic might-have-beens."[8] He went on to recognize, in the context of French Canada, that "federal compromize thus becomes imperative." The facts now and in the foreseeable future are likely to be little different in Cyprus or in Ireland, and a Second Republic in Italy might well reflect better the social, political, and economic facts of the 1980s, and also the deep instincts of the Italian people and their traditional mistrust of central authority.

Moreover, albeit very slowly, Western Europe is moving in vaguely federalist directions. It is surely both salutary and encouraging to remember, in the face of seemingly intractable problems, that, more than forty years after the capitulation of France to Nazi Germany, Franco-German rapprochement is both a reality and a sheet anchor in Europe. Adenauer, de Gasperi, Schuman, Monnet, and the other founding fathers of today's Europe also faced intractable problems. There is certainly no need to exaggerate their achievements or to minimize them, and their vision and their efforts have produced some lessons in how to erode, if not wholly to overcome, cleavages between nations. Lessons have no relevance unless we learn from them.

NOTES

1. James Callaghan, *A House Divided: The Dilemma of Northern Ireland* (London: Collins, 1973).

2. In December 1980, the Reverend Paisley suggested a referendum in Britain to determine the relationship between Northern Ireland and the mainland. The London *Sunday Times* followed up with an opinion poll and, excluding the undecided and those who said that they would not vote, the newspaper reported that 63 percent indicated that they would vote to end the union. A latter poll, conducted on behalf of the *Sun* newspaper of London, put the majority in favor of a united Ireland at 61 percent, while 57 percent said that the British army should be pulled out of Northern Ireland. Both opinion polls were of a limited sample taken from Britain only.

3. "It is hereby declared that Northern Ireland remains part of His Majesty's Dominions and of the United Kingdom, and it is hereby affirmed that in no event will Northern Ireland

or any part thereof cease to be part of His Majesty's Dominions and of the United Kingdom without the consent of the parliament of Northern Ireland."

3. Brian Faulkner, chief minister in the brief power-sharing executive, thought otherwise, believing that the outcry against the Council of Ireland "was only a useful red herring—the real opposition was to the sharing of power." See *Memoirs of a Statesman: Brian Faulkner*, ed. John Houston (London: Weidenfeld and Nicolson, 1978), p. 287.

4. For a useful account, see Frantz Wendt, *The Nordic Council and Co-operation in Scandinavia*, pub. by the Council, 1959.

5. A series of bilateral studies, set in progress following an Anglo-Irish "summit" between Britain's Margaret Thatcher and the then Irish Taoiseach, Charles Haughey, in December 1980, were concerned with "possible new institutional structures, economic cooperation, security matters, citizenship rights and measures to improve mutual understanding." An embyro Anglo-Irish intergovernmental Council was agreed upon in Dublin-London talks in November, 1981, but its scope was not immediately defined and its very existence could give Ulster's militant Protestants yet another target to aim at—unless London stands firm after the post-Sunningdale debacle.

6. The military seized power in Turkey in a bloodless coup on September 12, 1980.

7. The Turkish-Cypriot leadership marked the seventh anniversary of the Turkish invasion by tabling an outline settlement package in August 1981 through the United Nations. This provided for some conditional territorial concessions.

8. Speaking to the Canadian Political Science Association and the Association of Canadian Law Teachers, June 1964, and pub. subsequently in *The Future of Canadian Federation*, eds. P. A. Crepeau and C. B. Macpherson, Toronto: University of Toronto Press, 1965.

APPENDIX A
Sunningdale Communiqué

NORTHERN IRELAND

Agreed Communiqué issued following the Conference between the Irish and British Governments and the parties involved in the Northern Ireland Executive (designate) on 6th, 7th, 8th, and 9th December, 1973.

1. The Conference between the British and Irish Governments and the parties involved in the Northern Ireland Executive (designate) met at Sunningdale on 6, 7, 8 and 9 December 1973.

2. During the Conference, each delegation stated their position on the status of Northern Ireland.

3. The Taoiseach said that the basic principle of the Conference was that the participants had tried to see what measure of agreement of benefit to all the people concerned could be secured. In doing so, all had reached accommodation with one another on practical arrangements. But none had compromised, and none had asked others to compromise, in relation to basic aspirations. The people of the Republic, together with a minority in Northern Ireland as represented by the SDLP delegation, continued to uphold the aspiration towards a united Ireland. The only unity they wanted to see was a unity established by consent.

4. Mr. Brian Faulkner said that delegates from Northern Ireland came to the Conference as representatives of apparently incompatible sets of political aspirations who had found it possible to reach agreement to join together in government because each accepted that in doing so they were not sacrificing principles or aspirations. The desire of the majority of the people of Northern Ireland to remain part of the United Kingdom, as represented by the Unionist and Alliance delegations, remained firm.

5. The Irish Government fully accepted and solemnly declared that there could be no change in the status of Northern Ireland until a majority of the people of Northern Ireland desired a change in that status.

The British Government solemnly declared that it was, and would

225

226   MINORITIES IN REVOLT/

remain, their policy to support the wishes of the majority of the people of Northern Ireland. The present status of Northern Ireland is that it is part of the United Kingdom. If in the future the majority of the people of Northern Ireland should indicate a wish to become part of a united Ireland, the British Government would support that wish.

6. The Conference agreed that a formal agreement incorporating the declarations of the British and Irish Governments would be signed at the formal stage of the Conference and registered at the United Nations.

7. The Conference agreed that a Council of Ireland would be set up. It would be confined to representatives of the two parts of Ireland, with appropriate safeguards for the British Government's financial and other interests. It would comprise a Council of Ministers with executive and harmonising functions and a consultative role, and a Consultative Assembly with advisory and review functions. The Council of Ministers would act by unanimity, and would comprise a core of seven members of the Irish Government and an equal number of members of the Northern Ireland Executive with provision for the participation of other non-voting members of the Irish Government and the Northern Ireland Executive or Administration when matters within their departmental competence were discussed. The Council of Ministers would control the functions of the Council. The Chairmanship would rotate on an agreed basis betwen representatives of the Irish Government and of the Northern Ireland Executive. Arrangements would be made for the location of the first meeting, and the location of subsequent meetings would be determined by the Council of Ministers. The Consultative Assembly would consist of 60 members, 30 members from Dáil Éireann chosen by the Dáil on the basis of proportional representation by the single transferable vote, and 30 members from the Northern Ireland Assembly chosen by that Assembly and also on that basis. The members of the Consultative Assembly would be paid allowances. There would be a Secretariat to the Council, which would be kept as small as might be commensurate with efficiency in the operation of the Council. The Secretariat would service the institutions of the Council and would, under the Council of Ministers, supervise the carrying out of the executive and harmonising functions and the consultative role of the Council. The Secretariat would be headed by a Secretary-General. Following the appointment of a Northern Ireland Executive, the Irish Government and the Northern Ireland Executive would nominate their representatives to a Council of Ministers. The Council of Ministers would then appoint a Secretary-General and decide upon the location of its permanent headquarters. The Secretary-General would be directed to proceed with the drawing up of plans for such headquarters. The Council of Ministers would also make arrangements for the recruitment of the staff of the Secretariat in a manner and on conditions which would, as far as is practicable, be consistent with those applying to public servants in the two administrations.

8. In the context of its harmonising functions and consultative role, the Council of Ireland would undertake important work relating, for instance, to the impact of EEC membership. As for executive functions, the first step would be to define and agree these in detail. The Conference therefore decided that, in view of the administrative complexities involved, studies would at once be set in hand to identify and, prior to the formal stage of the conference, report on areas of common interest in relation to which a Council of Ireland would take executive decisions, and, in appropriate cases, be responsible for carrying those decisions into effect. In carrying out these studies, and also in determining what should be done by the Council in terms of harmonisation, the objectives to be borne in mind would include the following:

(1) to achieve the best utilisation of scarce skills, expertise and resources;
(2) to avoid, in the interests of economy and efficiency, unnecessary duplication of effort; and
(3) to ensure complementary rather than competitive effort where this is to the advantage of agriculture, commerce and industry.

In particular, these studies would be directed to identifying, for the purposes of executive action by the Council of Ireland, suitable aspects of activities in the following broad fields:

(a) exploitation, conservation and development of natural resources and the environment;
(b) agricultural matters (including agricultural research, animal health and operational aspects of the Common Agriculture Policy), forestry and fisheries;
(c) co-operative ventures in the fields of trade and industry;
(d) electricity generation;
(e) tourism;
(f) roads and transport;
(g) advisory services in the field of public health;
(h) sport, culture and the arts.

It would be for the Oireachtas and the Northern Ireland Assembly to legislate from time to time as to the extent of functions to be devolved to the Council of Ireland. Where necessary, the British Government will cooperate in this devolution of functions. Initially, the functions to be vested would be those identified in accordance with the procedures set out above and decided, at the formal stage of the conference, to be transferred.

9. (i) During the initial period following the establishment of the Council, the revenue of the Council would be provided by means of

grants from the two administrations in Ireland towards agreed projects and budgets, according to the nature of the service involved.

(ii) It was also agreed that further studies would be put in hand forthwith and completed as soon as possible of methods of financing the Council after the initial period which would be consonant with the responsibilities and functions assigned to it.

(iii) It was agreed that the cost of the Secretariat of the Council of Ireland would be shared equally, and other services would be financed broadly in proportion to where expenditure or benefit accrues.

(iv) The amount of money required to finance the Council's activities will depend upon the functions assigned to it from time to time.

(v) While Britain continues to pay subsidies to Northern Ireland, such payments would not involve Britain participating in the Council, it being accepted nevertheless that it would be legitimate for Britain to safeguard in an appropriate way her financial involvement in Northern Ireland.

10. It was agreed by all parties that persons committing crimes of violence, however motivated, in any part of Ireland should be brought to trial irrespective of the part of Ireland in which they are located. The concern which large sections of the people of Northern Ireland felt about this problem was in particular forcefully expressed by the representatives of the Unionist and Alliance parties. The representatives of the Irish Government stated that they understood and fully shared this concern. Different ways of solving this problem were discussed; among them were the amendment of legislation operating in the two jurisdictions on extradition, the creation of a common law enforcement area in which an all-Ireland court would have jurisdiction, and the extension of the jurisdiction of domestic courts so as to enable them to try offences committed outside the jurisdiction. It was agreed that problems of considerable legal complexity were involved, and that the British and Irish Governments would jointly set up a commission to consider all the proposals put forward at the Conference and to recommend as a matter of extreme urgency the most effective means of dealing with those who commit these crimes. The Irish Government undertook to take immediate and effective legal steps so that persons coming within their jurisdiction and accused of murder, however motivated, committed in Northern Ireland will be brought to trial, and it was agreed that any similar reciprocal action that may be needed in Northern Ireland be taken by the appropriate authorities.

11. It was agreed that the Council would be invited to consider in what way the principles of the European Convention on Human Rights and Fundamental Freedoms would be expressed in domestic legislation in each part of Ireland. It would recommend whether further legislation or the creation of other institutions, administrative or judicial, is required in either part or embracing the whole island to provide additional protection in the field of human rights. Such recommendations could include the

functions of an Ombudsman or Commissioner for Complaints, or other arrangements of a similar nature which the Council of Ireland might think appropriate.

12. The Conference also discussed the question of policing and the need to ensure public support for and identification with the police service throughout the whole community. It was agreed that no single set of proposals would achieve these aims overnight, and that time would be necessary. The Conference expressed the hope that the wide range of agreement that had been reached, and the consequent formation of a power-sharing Executive, would make a major contribution to the creation of an atmosphere throughout the community where there would be widespread support for and identification with all the institutions of Northern Ireland.

13. It was broadly accepted that the two parts of Ireland are to a considerable extent inter-dependent in the whole field of law and order, and that the problems of political violence and identification with the police service cannot be solved without taking account of that fact.

14. Accordingly, the British Government stated that, as soon as the security problems were resolved and the new institutions were seen to be working effectively, they would wish to discuss the devolution of responsibility for normal policing and how this might be achieved with the Northern Ireland Executive and the Police.

15. With a view to improving policing throughout the island and developing community identification with and support for the police services, the governments concerned will cooperate under the auspices of a Council of Ireland through their respective police authorities. To this end, the Irish Government would set up a Police Authority, appointments to which would be made after consultation with the Council of Ministers of the Council of Ireland. In the case of the Northern Ireland Police Authority, appointments would be made after consultation with the Northern Ireland Executive, which would consult with the Council of Ministers of the Council of Ireland. When the two Police Authorities are constituted, they will make their own arrangements to achieve the objectives set out above.

16. An independent complaints procedure for dealing with complaints against the police will be set up.

17. The Secretary of State for Northern Ireland will set up an all-party committee from the Assembly to examine how best to introduce effective policing throughout Northern Ireland with particular reference to the need to achieve public identification with the police.

18. The Conference took note of a reaffirmation by the British Government of their firm commitment to bring detention to an end in Northern Ireland for all sections of the community as soon as the security situation permits, and noted also that the Secretary of State for Northern Ireland hopes to be able to bring into use his statutory powers of selective release in time for a number of detainees to be released before Christmas.

19. The British Government stated that, in the light of the decisions reached at the Conference, they would now seek the authority of Parliament to devolve full powers to the Northern Ireland Executive and Northern Ireland Assembly as soon as possible. The formal appointment of the Northern Ireland Executive would then be made.

20. The Conference agreed that a formal conference would be held early in the New Year at which the British and Irish Governments and the Northern Ireland Executive would meet together to consider reports on the studies which have been commissioned and to sign the agreement reached.

EOKA's First Revolutionary Leaflet
Distributed on April 1, 1955

PROCLAMATION

With the help of God, with faith in our honourable struggle, with the backing of all Hellenism and the help of the Cypriots, we have taken up the struggle to throw off the English yoke, our banners high, bearing the slogan which our ancestors have handed down to us as a holy trust—*Death or Victory*.

Brother Cypriots, from the depths of past centuries all those who glorified Greek history while preserving their freedom are looking to us; the warriors of Marathon, the warriors of Salamis; the 300 of Leonidas and those who, in more recent times, fought in the epic Albanian war. The fighters of 1821 are looking to us—those fighters who showed us that liberation from the yoke of ruler is always won by bloodshed. All Hellenism is looking to us, and following us anxiously, but with national pride.

Let us reply with deeds. Let us be worthy of them. It is we [who] showed the world that international diplomacy is *unjust* and in many ways *cowardly*, and that the Cypriot soul is brave. If our rulers refuse to give us back our freedom, we shall claim it with our own *hands* and with our own *blood*. Let us show the world once more that the neck of the contemporary Greek refuses to accept the yoke. Our struggle will be hard. The ruler has the means and he is strong in numbers. We have the heart, and we have *right* on our side and that is why we *will win*.

Diplomats of the World

Look to your duty. It is shameful that, in the twentieth century, people should have to shed blood for freedom, that divine gift for which we too fought at your side and for which you, at least, claim that you fought against Nazism.

Greeks

Wherever you may be, hear our call: *Forward all together for the freedom of our Cyprus.*

EOKA,
The Leader,
Dighenis.

APPENDIX C
Makarios Proposals

[On November 30, 1963, President Makarios submitted the following thirteen points for the consideration of his Turkish-Cypriot Vice-President. Copies of the proposals were also submitted to Greece, Turkey and Britain—whose High Commissioner in Nicosia, Sir Arthur Clarke, was thought to have inspired at least some of them, either personally or on the direct behalf of the British Government in London.]

1. The right of veto of the President and Vice-President of the Republic to be abandoned.
2. The Vice-President of the Republic to deputise for the President in case of his temporary absence or incapacity to perform his duties.
3. The Greek President of the House of Representatives and the Turkish-Cypriot Vice-President to be elected by the House as a whole and not as under the Constitution, the President by the Greek-Cypriot Members of the House and the Vice-President by the Turkish-Cypriot Members of the House.
4. The Vice-President of the House of Representatives to deputise for the President of the House in case of his temporary absence or incapacity to perform his duties.
5. The constitutional provisions regarding separate majorities for [the] enactment of certain laws by the House of Representatives to be abolished.
6. Unified Municipalities to be established.
7. The administration of Justice to be unified.
8. The division of the Security Forces into Police and Gendarmerie to be abolished.
9. The numerical strength of the Security Forces and the Defence Forces to be determined by a Law.
10. The proportion of the participation of Greek-Cyprios and Turkish-

Cypriots in the composition of the Public Service and the Forces of the Republic to be modified in proportion to the ratio of the population of Greek and Turkish-Cypriots.

11. The number of the Members of the Public Service Commission to be reduced from ten to five.

12. All decisions by the Public Service Commission to be taken by simple majority.

13. The Constitution provides that there shall be two Communal Chambers, one Greek and one Turkish, each having jurisdiction in matters of religion, education, cultural affairs and personal status over members of its respective community, as well as control over communal co-operative societies. These Communal Chambers should be abolished and a new system should be devised.

APPENDIX D

Letter from President Lyndon B. Johnson to Ismet Inonu

June 5, 1964

Dear Mr. Prime Minister,

I am gravely concerned by the information which I have had through [U.S.] Ambassador Hare from you and your Foreign Minister that the Turkish Government is contemplating a decision to intervene by military force to occupy a portion of Cyprus. I wish to emphasize in the fullest friendship and frankness that I do not consider that such a course of action by Turkey, fraught with such far reaching consequences, is consistent with the commitment of your Government to consult fully in advance with the United States. Ambassador Hare has indicated that you postponed your decision for a few hours in order to obtain my views. I put to you personally whether you really believe that it is appropriate for your Government, in effect, to present an ultimatum to an ally who has demonstrated such staunch support over the years for Turkey. I must, therefore, first urge you to accept responsibility for complete consultation with the United States before any such action is taken.

It is my impression that you believe that such intervention by Turkey is permissible under the provisions of the Treaty of Guarantee of 1960. I must call your attention, however, to our understanding that the proposed intervention by Turkey would be for the purpose of supporting an attempt by Turkish-Cypriot leaders to partition the island, a solution which is specifically excluded by the Treaty of Guarantee. Further, that Treaty requires consultation among the guarantor powers. It is the view of the United States that the possibilities of such consultation have by no means

235

been exhausted in this situation and that, therefore, the reservation of the right to take unilateral action is not yet applicable.

I must call your attention also, Mr. Prime Minister, to the obligations of NATO. There can be no question in your mind that a Turkish intervention in Cyprus would lead to a military engagement between Turkish and Greek forces. Secretary of State [Dean] Rusk declared at the recent meeting of the ministerial council of NATO in the Hague that war between Turkey and Greece must be considered as "literally unthinkable." Adhesion to NATO in its very essence means that NATO countries will not wage war on each other. Germany and France have buried centuries of animosity in becoming NATO allies; nothing less can be expected from Greece and Turkey. Furthermore, a military intervention in Cyprus by Turkey could lead to direct involvement by the Soviet Union. I hope you will understand that your NATO allies have not had a chance to consider whether they have an obligation to protect Turkey against the Soviet Union if Turkey takes a step which results in Soviet intervention without the full consent and understanding of its NATO allies.

Further, Mr. Prime Minister, I am concerned about the obligations of Turkey as a member of the United Nations. The United Nations has provided forces on the island to keep the peace. Their task has been difficult but, during the past several weeks, they have been progressively successful in reducing the incidents of violence of that island. The United Nations Mediator has not yet completed his work. I have no doubt that the general membership of the United Nations would react in the strongest terms to unilateral action by Turkey which would defy the efforts of the United Nations and destroy any prospect that the United Nations could assist in obtaining a reasonable and peaceful settlement of this difficult problem.

I wish also, Mr. Prime Minister, to call your attention to the bilateral agreement between the United States and Turkey in the field of military assistance. Under Article IV of the agreement with Turkey of July, 1947, your Government is required to obtain United States consent for the use of military assistance for purposes other than those for which such assistance was furnished. Your Government has on several occasions acknowledged to the United Sttes that you fully understand this condition. I must tell you in all candor that the United States cannot agree to the use of any United States supplied military equipment for a Turkish intervention in Cyprus in present circumstances.

Moving to the practical results of the contemplated Turkish move, I feel obligated to call to your attention in the most friendly fashion that such a Turkish move could lead to the slaughter of tens of thousands of Turkish-Cypriots on the island of Cyprus. Such an action on your part would unleash the furies and there is no way by which military action on your part could be sufficiently effective to prevent wholesale destruction of many of those whom you are trying to protect. The presence of United Nations forces could not prevent such a catastrophe.

You may consider that what I have said is much too severe and that we are disregardful of Turkish interests in the Cyprus situation. I should like to assure you that this is not the case. We have exerted ourselves both publicly and privately to assure the safety of Turkish-Cypriots and to insist that a final solution of the Cyprus problem should rest upon the consent of the parties most directly concerned. It is possible that you feel in Ankara that the United States has not been sufficiently active in your behalf. But surely you know that our policy has caused the liveliest resentments in Athens (where demonstrations have been aimed against us) and has led to a basic alienation between the United States and Archbishop Makarios. As I said to your Foreign Minister in our conversation just a few weeks ago, we value very highly our relations with Turkey. We have considered you as a great ally with fundamental common interests. Your security and prosperity have been a deep concern of the American people and we have expressed that concern in the most practical terms. You and we have fought together to resist the ambitions of the communist world revolution. This solidarity has meant a great deal to us and I would hope that it means a great deal to your Government, and to your people. We have no intention of lending any support to any solution of Cyprus which endangers the Turkish-Cypriot community. We have not been able to find a solution because this is, admittedly, one of the most complex problems on earth. But I wish to assure you that we have been deeply concerned about the interests of Turkey and of the Turkish-Cypriots, and will remain so.

Finally, Mr. Prime Minister, I must tell you that you have posed the gravest issues of war and peace. These are issues which go beyond the bilateral relations between Turkey and the United States. They not only will certainly involve war between Turkey and Greece, but could involve wider hostilities because of the unpredictable consequences which a unilateral intervention in Cyprus could produce. You have your responsibilities as Chief of the Government of Turkey; I also have mine as President of the United States. I must, therefore, inform you in the deepest friendship that unless I can have your assurance that you will not take such action without further and fullest consultations, I cannot accept your injunction to Ambassador Hare of secrecy and must immediately ask for emergency meetings of the NATO Council and of the United Nations Security Council.

I wish it were possible for us to have a personal discussion of this situation. Unfortunately, because of the special circumstances of our present constitutional position, I am not able to leave the United States. If you could come here for a full discussion, I would welcome it. I do feel that you and I carry a very heavy responsibility for the general peace and for the possibilities of a sane and peaceful resolution of the Cyprus problem. I ask you, therefore, to delay any decisions which you and your colleagues might have in mind until you and I have had the fullest and frankest consultation.

Sincerely,
Lyndon B. Johnson

Bibliography

GENERAL WORKS

Lijphart, Arend. *The Politics of Accommodating Pluralism and Democracy in the Netherlands*. Berkeley, Calif.: University of California Press, 1968.

MacRea, Kenneth, ed. *Consociational Democracy: Political Accommodation in Segmented Societies*. Toronto: McClelland and Stewart, 1974.

Powell, C. Bingham, Jr. *Social Fragmentation and Political Hostility: An Austrian Case Study*. Stanford, Calif.; Stanford University Press, 1970.

Smelser, N. J. *Theory of Collective Behaviour*. London: Routledge and Kegan Paul, 1962.

Steiner, Jurg. *Amicable Agreement versus Majority Rule: Conflict Resolution in Switzerland*. Chapel Hill, N.C.: University of North Carolina Press, 1974.

Wendt, Frantz. *The Nordic Council and Co-operation in Scandinavia*. Copenhagen: The Nordic Council, 1959.

IRELAND

Official Documents

The Cameron Report: Disturbances in Northern Ireland, Her Majesty's Stationery Office (HMSO), Belfast, Cmnd 534, 1969.

The Compton Report: Allegations against the Security Forces of Physical Brutality in Northern Ireland. HMSO, London, Cmnd 4823, 1971.

The Diplock Report: Legal Procedure to Deal with Terrorist Activities in Northern Ireland. HMSO, London, Cmnd 5185, 1972.

239

The Future of Northern Ireland: A Paper for Discussion. HMSO, London, 1972.

The Hunt Report: Report of the Advisory Committee on Police in Northern Ireland. HMSO, Belfast, Cmnd 535, 1969.

The MacRory Report: Local Government in Northern Ireland. HMSO, Belfast, Cmnd 546, 1970.

Northern Ireland Constitutional Proposals. HMSO, London, Cmnd 5259, 1973.

Report of the Widgery Tribunal. HMSO, London, H.C.220, 1972.

The Scarman Report: Violence and Civil Disturbances in Northern Ireland in 1969. HMSO, Belfast, Cmnd 566, 1972.

General Studies

Barzilay, David. *The British Army in Ulster*. Belfast: Century Services, 1973.

Beckett, J. C. *The Making of Modern Ireland 1603–1921*. London: Faber and Faber, 1966.

Bell, J. Bowyer. *The Secret Army*. London: Anthony Blond, 1970.

Bleakley, David. *Peace in Ulster*. London: Mowbrays, 1972.

Boyd, Andrew. *The UVF*. Dublin: Torc Books, 1973.

Buckland, P. *The Origins of Northern Ireland: Ulster Unionism 1885–1923*. Dublin: Gill and Macmillan, 1973.

Callaghan, James. *A House Divided: The Dilemma of Northern Ireland*. London: Collins, 1973.

Campbell, J. J. *Catholic Schools: A Survey of a Northern Ireland Problem*. Dublin: Fallons, 1964.

Churchill, Winston. *Lord Randolph Churchill*. London: Odhams, 1951.

Coogan, T. P. *The IRA*. London: Pall Mall, 1970.

de Paor, Liam. *Divided Ulster*. London: Penguin Books, 1970.

de Tocqueville, Alexis. *Journeys to England and Ireland*. Edited by J. Mayer. London: Faber and Faber, 1958.

Deutsch, Richard, and Magowan, Vivien. *Northern Ireland: A Chronology of Events*. 3 vols. Belfast: Blackstaff Press, 1968–74.

Dolley, M. *Anglo-Norman Ireland:* Dublin: Gill and Macmillan, 1972.

Edwards, Owen Dudley. *The Sins of Our Fathers*. Dublin: Gill and Macmillan, 1970.

FitzGerald, Garret. *Towards a New Ireland*. London: Charles Knight, 1972.

Fitzgibbon, C. *Red Hand: The Ulster Colony*. London: Michael Joseph, 1972.

Gray, T. *The Orange Order*. London: The Bodley Head, 1972.

Heslinga, M. W. *The Irish Border as a Cultural Divide*. Assen, Netherlands: Van Gorcum, 1962.

Houston, John, ed. *Memoirs of a Statesman*. London: Weidenfeld and Nicolson, 1978.

Kee, Robert. *The Green Flag: A History of Irish Nationalism*. London: Weidenfeld and Nicolson, 1972.

MacNiocail, G. *Ireland before the Vikings*. Dublin: Gill and Macmillan, 1972.

Magee, John. *Northern Ireland: Crisis and Conflict*. London: Routledge and Kegan Paul, 1974.

Mansergh, Nicholas. *The Irish Question 1840–1921*. London: Allen and Unwin, 1965.

Moneypenny M. *The Two Irish Nations*. London: Murray, 1913.

Moody, T. W. *The Ulster Question, 1603–1973*. Cork: Mercier Press, 1974.

O Corrain, D. *Ireland before the Normans*. Dublin: Gill and Macmillan, 1972.

O'Neill, Terence. *Autobiography*. London: Hart-Davis, 1972.

Rose, Richard. *Governing without Consensus*. London: Faber and Faber, 1971.

Sweetman, Rosita. *On Our Knees*. London: Pan Books, 1972.

Tone, W. T. Wolfe, *Life of Theobald Wolfe Tone*. 2 vols. Washington: Gales and Seaton, 1826.

Ward, A. J. *Ireland and Anglo-American Relations 1899–1921*. London: Weidenfeld and Nicolson, 1969.

ITALY

General Studies

Acquaviva, Sabino. *Guerriglia e guerra revoluzionaria in Italia*. Milan: Rizzoli, 1979.

Allum, P. A. *The Italian Communist Party since 1945*. Reading, Eng.: University of Reading Press, 1970.

Barnes, Samuel H. *Representation in Italy: Institutionalised Tradition and Electoral Choice*. Chicago: University of Chicago Press, 1977.

Barzini, Luigi. *The Italians*. New York: Atheneum, 1964.

Blackmer, Donald L. M., and Tarrow, Sidney, eds. *Communism in Italy and France*. Princeton, N.J.: Princeton University Press, 1975.

Bocca, Giorgio. *Il terrorismo Italiano*. Milan: Rizzoli, 1978.

Bufalini, Paolo. *Terrorismo e Democrazia*. Rome: Editori Riuniti, 1978.

Calamandrei, Piero, et al. *Dieci anni dopo, 1945–55*. La Costituzione e La leggi per attuarla. Bari: Laterza, 1955.

Cammett, John. *Antonio Gramsci and the Origins of Italian Communism*. Stanford, Calif.: Stanford University Press, 1979.

Crick, Bernard, ed. *Machiavelli: The Discourses*, London: Penguin Books, 1970.

della Torre, Paolo Filo; Mortimer, Edward; and Story, Jonathan, eds. *Eurocommunism: Myth or Reality*. London: Penguin Books, 1979.

Di Palma, Giuseppe. *Surviving without Governing:* The Italian Parties in Parliament. Berkeley and Los Angeles, Calif.: University of California Press, 1977.

Eurocommunism: The Italian Case, Ed. Austin Ranney and Giovanni Sartori. Washington: The American Institute for Public Policy Research, 1978.

Galli, Giorgio. *Il difficile governo*. Bologna: Il Mulino, 1972.

Gramsci, Antonio. *Quaderni del carcere*. Edited by Felice Platone. 6 vols. Turin: Einaudi, 1948–51.

Greyson, Cecil, ed. *Guicciardini: Selected Writings*. Oxford: Oxford University Press, 1965.

Guiducci, Roberto. *New Deal Socialista*. Florence: Vallecchi, 1965.

Mammarella, Giuseppe. *L'Italia dopo il Fascismo, 1943–1968*. Bologna: Il Mulino, 1970.

Nenni, Pietro. *Storia di quattro anni*. Rome: Einaudi, 1946.

Reale, Eugenio. *Nascita del Cominform*. Verona: Mondadori Editore, 1958.

Rosso, Soccorso, ed. *Brigate Rosso*. Milan: Feltrinelli, 1977.

Silj, A. *Mai piu senza fucile*. Florence: Vallecchi, 1977.

Somogyi, S., et al. *Il Parlamento Italiano, 1946–63*. Naples: Edizioni Scientifiche Italiane, 1963.

Tamburrano, Giuseppe. *Storia del Centro-Sinistra*. Milan: Feltrinelli, 1972.

Tassandori, V. *BR imputazione banda armata*. Milan: Garzanti, 1977.

Woolf, S. J., ed. *The Rebirth of Italy, 1943–50*. London: Longman, 1972.

CYPRUS

Official Documents

Constitutional Proposals for Cyprus (Radcliffe Report). HMSO, London, Cmnd 42, 1956.

Cyprus: A Handbook on the Island's Past and Present. Nicosia: Greek Communal Chamber, 1964.

Cyprus: The London and Zurich Agreements and Report on the Implementation. HMSO, London, Cmnd 1093, 1960.

Terrorism in Cyprus: The Captured Documents of George Grivas. UK Foreign Office paper, London, 1956.

Treaty of Lausanne. Treaty Series no. 16, HMSO, London, Cmnd 1929, 1923.

Tripartite Conference on the Eastern Mediterranean and Cyprus. HMSO, London, Cmnd 9594, 1955.

The Turkish Case, 70-30, and the Greek Tactics. Nicosia: Turkish Communal Chamber, 1963.

United Nations. *Proceedings of the Security Council and the General Assembly*. 1954–81.

United Nations. *Reports on Cyprus by the Secretary-General and/or his Special Representative*. 1964–81.

General Studies

Bitsios, D. *Cyprus: The Vulnerable Republic*. Thessaloniki: Institute for Balkan Studies, 1975.

Byford-Jones, W. *Grivas and the Story of EOKA*. London: Robert Hale, 1959.

Eden, Anthony. *Full Circle: The Memoirs of Sir Anthony Eden*. London: Cassell, 1960.

Foley, Charles. *Island in Revolt*. London: Longman, 1962.

———. *Legacy of Strife: Cyprus from Rebellion to Civil War*. London: Penguin Books, 1964.

Foot, Hugh. *A Start to Freedom*. London: Hodder and Stoughton, 1964.

Gibbons, H. A. *The Foundations of the Ottoman Empire*. Oxford: Oxford University Press, 1916.

Grivas, George. *Memoirs*. Edited by Charles Foley. London: Longman, 1964.

Hackett, J. *A History of the Orthodox Church of Cyprus*. London: Methuen, 1901.

Hill, George. *History of Cyprus*. 4 vols. Cambridge, Eng.: Cambridge University Press, 1940–52.

Kinross, Lord. *Atatürk*. London: Weidenfeld and Nicolson, 1964.

Lee, D. E. *Great Britain and the Cyprus Convention Policy of 1878*. Cambridge, Mass.: Harvard University Press, 1934.

Lewis, Geoffrey. *Modern Turkey*. London: Ernest Benn, 1974.

Loizos, Peter. *An Alternative analysis in Cyprus*. London: Minority Rights Group, report no. 30, rev. ed., 1978.

Modinos, Peter. *The Events in Cyprus*. Paris: American Hellenic Institute, 1974.

Papandreou, Andreas. *Democracy at Gunpoint*. London: Deutsch, 1971.

Polyviou, P. Cyprus: *The Tragedy and the Challenge*. London: John Swain, 1975.

Stephens, Robert. *Cyprus: A Place of Arms*. London: Pall Mall, 1966.

Vanezis, P. N. *Cyprus: The Unfinished Agony*. London: Abelard Schuman, 1977.

Windsor, P. *NATO and the Cyprus Crisis*. London: Institute of Strategic Studies, Adelphi Papers, no. 14, 1964.

Index

Brookeborough, Lord, 47, 48
Bufalini, Paolo, 100, 135, 140
Bulgaria, 15
Burke, Edmund, 83
Burntollet Bridge, 54
Byzantine Empire, 192

Cagol, Margherita, 114, 126, 132
Cagol, Milena, 126
Calamandrei, Piero, 108
Caledon, 51
Callaghan, James, 191, 214
Cameron Commission, 50, 51, 53–54
Cammett, John, 100–101
Campaign for Social Justice, 51
Canada, 198, 222
Capuzzo, General Umberto, 142
Carson, Sir Edward, 46
Casabona, Vincenzo, 133–34
Castro, Fidel, 134
Catholic Church (Italy): and division of
  Italy, 89; and the Italian Popular
  party, 99; and the PCI's alliance
  strategy, 107
Catholics (Irish), 60; "Bloody Sunday,"
  69; civil rights campaign, 50–55; and
  the creation of Ulster, 33; cultural
  and religious division in Ireland, 84–
  86; discrimination against, 34, 47; in-
  ternment, 20, 70–71; and Irish his-
  tory, 39–41; "no-go" areas, 68, 73,
  75; outbreak of violence, 62; power
  sharing, 72; Protestant attitudes toward, 15, 17, 35; relationship with
  IRA, 63–64; rise of Irish nationalism,
  40–41, 43–48; size of Ulster population, 215; and the Sunningdale Conference, 79
Cavan, 45
Cavour, Camillo di, 18, 83, 90
Celts, 36, 38
CGIL (Italian Confederation of Labor),
  110, 117, 208
Chiavari, 118
Chichester-Clark, James, 61, 62, 68
Chile, 127, 202, 203
China, 115
Christian Democrats (Italy), 11, 99; al-
  liance with Socialists, 111; attitude to
  Communists, 15, 17; and the com-

promesso storico, 127–28, 137, 144,
  199, 201–2; and the Moro kidnap-
  ping, 138–39, 140–41; 1948 elec-
  tions, 108; and the PCI's alliance
  strategy, 107; and the Red Brigades,
  133, 135; relations with PCI, 111;
  student opposition to, 116
Christianity, introduction to Ireland,
  38
Churchill, Sir Winston, 83
Citizen Army (Ireland), 58
Clan na Gael, 58
Clarke, Sir Arthur, 2233
Clerides, Glafcos, 191
Coalisland-to-Dungannon march
  (1968), 51–53
Coco, Francesco, 131, 134, 135, 141
Cold war, 108–9, 177
Columbanus (saint), 38
Columcille (saint), 38
Cominform, 108–9, 111
Comintern, 98, 101, 103, 111
Committee of National Liberation
  (CLN), 103–4, 107
Commonwealth, 182
Communism, and democracy, 15–16.
  See also AKEL (Cypriot Communist
  Party); Italian Communist Party
Communist International, 101
Connolly, James, 53, 58
Conservative party (Britain), 81; and
  Cyprus, 168, 170, 171; and Irish
  home rule, 44, 58
Cosgrave, Liam, 76, 80, 82
Cosgrave, W. T., 76
Cossiga, Francesco, 135
Council of Europe, 14, 182
Council of Ireland (proposed), 75–76,
  79–80, 81–82, 217, 227–29
Craig, William, 34, 61, 71, 75, 81
Craxi, Bettino, 140, 211
Crispi, Francesco, 97
Croce, Fulvio, 134
Cromwell, Oliver, 39
Cuba, 115, 134
Curcio, Renato, 114–15, 117–18, 122,
  125–27, 131–32, 135, 139, 143
Curcio, Yolanda, 126
Cypriot National Guard, 187, 189
Cyprus: attitudes to violence, 13–14,